Coaching Understood

Praise for *Coaching Understood*

'In *Coaching Understood*, Elaine Cox offers a most extensive, most accessible, holistic examination of theories from across disciplines, to explore and discuss every nuance and aspect of the coaching relationship and task. *Coaching Understood* is full of applications to practice, with examples and coaching excerpts to illustrate, and thus a most comprehensive evidence-based text becomes practical and pragmatic through its easily readable presentation. Refreshingly, concepts such as mindfulness, flow and presence are given attention. This book will leave researchers, coaches and clients wanting to know more, do more and think more about how the coaching process really works.'

Jan Robertson, Senior Researcher, University of Waikato, New Zealand.
Senior Associate, New Zealand Coaching and Mentoring Centre

'In *Coaching Understood*, Dr. Elaine Cox masterfully blends theory, research and pragmatism in the development of her Experiential Coaching Cycle which is a universally applicable coaching framework. Her book is a necessary foundational resource for those with a passion for coaching. It is especially relevant for those who wish to become more effective coaches, and for those who engage in research about coaching. Readers will come to understand coaching as a "communicative learning process" that is uniquely distinct from counselling and mentoring.'

Andrea D. Ellinger, Ph.D., PHR, Professor of Human Resource Development, The University of Texas at Tyler

'If you are looking to truly understand the coaching process, this book is for you. Novices, advanced beginners and experts alike will find evidence-based insights into the philosophical and scientific foundations underpinning contemporary coaching practice. Highly recommended.'

Anthony Grant PhD, Director, Coaching Psychology Unit, University of Sydney

Coaching Understood

A pragmatic inquiry into the coaching process

Elaine Cox

Los Angeles | London | New Delhi
Singapore | Washington DC

Los Angeles | London | New Delhi
Singapore | Washington DC

SAGE Publications Ltd
1 Oliver's Yard
55 City Road
London EC1Y 1SP

SAGE Publications Inc.
2455 Teller Road
Thousand Oaks, California 91320

SAGE Publications India Pvt Ltd
B 1/I 1 Mohan Cooperative Industrial Area
Mathura Road
New Delhi 110 044

SAGE Publications Asia-Pacific Pte Ltd
3 Church Street
#10-04 Samsung Hub
Singapore 049483

Editor: Kirsty Smy
Editorial assistant: Ruth Stitt
Production editor: Rachel Eley
Copyeditor: Rosemary Campbell
Proofreader: Jill Birch
Indexer: Elizabeth Ball
Marketing manager: Alison Borg
Cover design: Wendy Scott
Typeset by: C&M Digitals (P) Ltd, Chennai, India
Printed and bound by CPI Group (UK) Ltd,
Croydon, CR0 4YY

Library of Congress Control Number: 2012937872

British Library Cataloguing in Publication data

A catalogue record for this book is available from
the British Library

ISBN 978-0-85702-825-9
ISBN 978-0-85702-826-6 (pbk)

Contents

List of Tables

List of Figures

About the Author

Dr Elaine Cox is a principal lecturer and the director of Masters and Doctoral level coaching and mentoring programmes in the Business School at Oxford Brookes University. She holds a Masters degree (with distinction) from the University of Warwick and a PhD from Lancaster University. Elaine is an experienced researcher who has authored many academic papers and book chapters on coaching-related issues. She co-edited *The Complete Handbook of Coaching* and is the co-author of *Goal-focused Coaching* with Yossi Ives. Elaine is also the founding editor of *The International Journal of Evidence Based Coaching and Mentoring*, an online open access, peer reviewed journal aimed at sharing coaching and mentoring research with a broad, international audience.

Acknowledgements

I would like to thank the following people for their helpful feedback on early drafts of chapters of this book: David Drake, Peter Jackson, Ian Wycherley and Linda Neal.

1

Introduction

Chapter Aims:

- To introduce a cyclical coaching model that explains the coaching process
- To explain the functions of the different parts of the model, together with the important transition points
- To introduce the chapters of the book

In this book I explain how coaching works. Coaching is a facilitated, dialogic, reflective learning process, and its popularity reflects a need arising in society driven by complex situations and the individual nature of problems affecting people. But, there is a problem with coaching in that, although anecdotally we know it works, it is not clearly defined, and the research underpinning it is notably sparse. Furthermore, it is supported by a collection of loosely aligned interventions and activities, all necessarily adopted from other disciplines, but often without clear justification. Fortunately many of the components of coaching have been researched in their own right, within their own disciplines. Therefore, in this book I work from a pragmatic perspective, drawing extensively on this research in order to provide a comprehensive evidence-based understanding of coaching that will begin to explain its unique power and appeal.

I believe that as coaches we should each adopt a pragmatic approach to our work and our research. We need to recognise theories as important, but also see them as socially constructed 'truths' that are open to challenge. Pragmatism is derived from the Greek word *pragma*, meaning action. Pragmatist coaches therefore, take the theories, tools and techniques that they deem useful, employ them in their practice, and then report on their effectiveness, mapping them back to their respective theoretical origins. The pragmatic method insists that truths be 'tested' against practice or action. As I have explained elsewhere, I see the pragmatic approach to coaching practice as overcoming many of the flaws in current thinking about coaching:

It justifies an initial eclectic approach, appeases calls for integration, overrides a top-down, single school approach and gets us away from an emphasis on the individual coaches' values and beliefs. A pragmatic, empirical position expands the meaning perspectives of the practitioner, takes the emphasis away from the individual as having some core of inner 'truth' and extends human knowledge beyond the personal knowledge of the individual, or the orthodoxy of particular theories, and outwards towards a more comprehensive, socially constructed, theoretical commons that can become a basis for a profession and a professional philosophy that all can build and share. (Cox, 2011: 61)

This then is the philosophy underpinning this book. The model of coaching presented in the book is necessarily pragmatic – it uses cognitive and behavioural science wherever they can best be useful. However, it is also essentially phenomenological and constructivist: it begins with attempts to understand the client's experience, moves through clarification, reflection and critical thinking, which are highly cognitive, and then looks at ways of facilitating the transfer of understanding back into experience. So it goes beyond cognitive change, suggesting that the cycle is not complete until there is actual embodied, physical change as well.

In the book I also present coaching as synonymous with facilitated reflective practice. I describe how coaching begins and ends with the client's experience, whether that is specifically workplace experience or whole life experience, and in between is a complex process of phenomenological reflection augmented by critical thinking. Beginning with clients' attempts to articulate their experiential dilemmas, I particularly want to explain the coaching process through a lens of phenomenological reflection, beginning with how clients' experiences lead to dilemmas that provide grounds for coaching, and ending with the resolution of those particular dilemmas via integration of new learning back into experience.

Although many books mention the importance of reflection, few really place reflective practice at the centre of their coaching universe. One text that does attempt to give a fuller account is Brockbank, McGill and Beech (2002). These authors define reflection as 'an intentional process, where social context and experience are acknowledged, in which learners are active individuals, wholly present, engaging with another, open to challenge, and the outcome involves transformation as well as improvement for both individuals and their organisation' (Brockbank et al., 2002: 6). Later, Brockbank and McGill (2006) focus on reflective dialogue and point out that the idea of reflection as solely an individual activity belongs to the 'rational model of learning that suggests that the cognitive mind alone can solve any problem, sort out any confusion ...' (2006: 53). They further suggest that 'while intrapersonal reflection can be effective and may offer opportunities for deep learning, which may or may not be shared with another, it is ultimately not enough to promote transformative learning' (2006:53). Thus they suggest that for transformation to occur, reflection work must be undertaken with help from other people. The argument here is that, without dialogue, assumptions and unhelpful beliefs are not challenged, and so reflection is limited to the insights of the individual. Thus these authors identify the special role that 'intentional dialogue', such as that initiated by coaching, has in promoting reflection.

About this Book

In order to structure the book, I introduce a practical and holistic model of the coaching process that shows a progression, beginning with unarticulated experience and moving through various stages of cognitive exploration towards the integration of reformulated understanding that informs future experience. In order to make the structure of this process clearer, I introduce here a new cyclical coaching model (Figure 1.1). The model has spaces and spokes, like a wheel, which are all key stages necessary to help clients transition through the coaching assignment.

Skiffington and Zeus argue that coaching demands 'a conceptual framework that will provide a common language and a basis for research and create a blueprint for coaching practice and education' (2003: 29). This book is an answer to that demand. It is also an answer to Jackson's lament that coaching is not being based on theory: 'The fast growth of the coaching industry has created structural weaknesses', he argues, adding that 'it is never too early to attend to foundations' (Jackson, 2008: 74). This book then, heeds Jackson's call and is part of that constructive investigation into the foundations of coaching that is so badly needed. I hope that the book will provide a strong underpinning for coaching so that others may build confidently on its ideas and proposals.

Underneath the frequent calls in the profession for dialogue about the future of coaching lies an inherent lack of understanding about what coaching is and what it can do. Sometimes we have been starting our investigations in the wrong place. I have watched coaching researchers focus on exploring sites of application through numerous case studies and have watched them grasp at attractive theories and models from a range of disciplines, particularly psychotherapy. What I have not seen yet is an explanation of how coaching works or why it works – the fundamental process that underpins all coaching. Furthermore, in a struggle to find an identity, coaching has tried to identify boundaries between itself and counselling or mentoring or training (Bachkirova and Cox, 2005; Lawton-Smith and Cox, 2007). But its identity has also been blurred by adoption of techniques from other fields. By explaining in this book how coaching really works, I uncover fundamental differences that will enable coaching researchers to focus more explicitly on the process of coaching as a distinct area of study.

Coaching is multidisciplinary and there are many established and effective approaches that enable coaches to work in a number of different contrasting or overlapping ways (see Cox et al., 2010, for examples). However, I would argue that a fundamental process underpins all coaching, and it is this process that informs how it differs from other helping approaches such as mentoring and counselling. Thus the book provides a new, holistic and very practical model that gives clients an understanding of the process, and provides coaches with a framework to guide their practice – and indeed to underpin their own learning and development.

There are lots of books about coaching. They mainly talk about the psychology of coaching, how to do coaching, the coaching process, or the role and benefits of coaching in a variety of different contexts. But an unambiguous extended definition of coaching remains elusive, and the workings of the coaching interaction itself are still a mystery. This book plugs that gap. It makes clear what happens and why it works. It uses theory and examples of coaching dialogue to build an understanding of how all the basic elements present in the coaching interaction (questioning, listening, challenging, reflecting, etc.) work and interact, and thereby exposes the inscrutability that underlies coaching's success as a personal and professional development intervention.

About Coaching

When clients first come to coaching it is often because their recent experience has driven them there. Something needs to change or improve, or something within their pre-reflective, experiential 'soup' has bubbled through to become conscious. It might be that they have a hunch, a feeling or an intuition that is troubling them. In Mezirow's (1991) terms they may have a disorienting dilemma. The dilemma may have arisen from a sudden feeling that something is not right, or it may be something that has built up in importance over time and one further event has tipped the balance. Either way, they feel that something needs to change and that is what brings them to coaching.

The issues a client may bring to a coach may be feelings of being stuck, feeling as if no progress is being made, frustration that the same thing keeps happening, or a feeling of going back and forth with no apparent resolution. Intuitively, people in these situations feel that they need to make changes or they need support at work to overcome an impasse. They may come to coaching feeling that they are at a point of transition. They often feel they are on the cusp of something, or that something needs to alter, but they are not clear what. The coach then needs to help the client identify the nature of the experience in order ultimately to inform necessary change. Other clients may be clearer about where they want to be in their life, but they still want help getting there.

The Coaching Cycle

Very many coaches want to work holistically, but do not have access to an evidence base to enable them to do that. The cyclical model described in this book explains an holistic approach that satisfies that need, and, I would argue, actually underpins all coaching. The model has client experience at its core and takes account of a comprehensive range of theories, including experiential learning, intuition, focusing, phenomenology, critical reflection, rationality and tacit understanding, and also draws on current thinking in neuroscience in order to consider how our thinking and reflective faculties are linked to emotions and brain function.

The Experiential Coaching Cycle (shown in Figure 1.1) has three substantive constituent spaces: Pre-reflective Experience, Reflection on Experience and Post-reflective Thinking. Each space is a hiatus where events occur or reflection happens. The cycle also has three major 'spokes', or transition phases: Touching Experience, Becoming Critical and Integrating. Spokes invariably involve more emotional, cognitive or physical effort than spaces, and are particularly challenging for both coach and client because of the emotional struggle and uncertainty inherent in them. These spaces and transitions are described further below.

In developing this cycle I owe an intellectual debt to Kolb (1984; Kolb and Kolb, 2005). Kolb explained in detail how knowledge results from 'the combination of grasping and transforming experience' (Kolb, 1984: 41). What drives clients to come to coaching are events in their everyday experience, and what they need then at the end of the coaching is to take the enhanced, often transformed, understanding back into their everyday life. In his experiential learning cycle Kolb (1984) identifies an active experimentation phase as well as three other learning phases: concrete experience, reflective observation and abstract conceptualisation. During active experimentation, Kolb suggested, the new understanding, gleaned through earlier phases equips learners to do things differently.

Figure 1.1   The Experiential Coaching Cycle

However, although the Experiential Coaching Cycle owes a debt to Kolb, it differs from that earlier model in its emphasis on the transitions. What is missing from Kolb's learning cycle is a discussion of the transition from one state of being to another. Between his 'bases' of concrete experience and reflective observation, for example, I would argue that there is much uncertainty for the individual; there is transitory activity which necessitates dialogue and support from a coach. The Experiential Coaching Cycle foregrounds those transitory points, or edges, where much learning occurs. Interestingly, Brockbank and McGill (2006: 57) also identify reflective dialogue as engaging clients 'at the edge of their knowledge, sense of self and the world', and other authors that I draw upon in this book, such as Gendlin, Claxton and Fitzgerald talk about 'edges'. In describing the cyclical model, I refer to these edges as spokes because, although they feel edgy, they also have a driving effect, motivating clients and moving them towards understanding, and ultimately transformation. The spaces in between the spokes differ in that they provide the freedom to explore, often involving silence or contemplation.

The three spaces and the three spokes are introduced below, and their nature and their challenges are discussed in more detail in the chapters that follow.

The Three Constituent Spaces

The primary constituent space is Pre-reflective Experience, which informs everything the client eventually reflects on and talks about in the coaching. Boyd and Fales (1983: 100) define reflecting as 'the process of internally examining and exploring an issue of concern, *triggered by an experience*, which creates and clarifies meaning in terms of self, and which results in and changes conceptual perspective' (my emphasis). Thus, we cannot reflect without an experience to reflect on. However, the fissure between the nature of experience and the language available to describe it are a challenge for coaching.

The second constituent space is Reflection on Experience, which involves deliberation and detailed descriptive articulations of experiences and their associated perceptions and emotions. A variety of theories and models of reflective practice are commonly used for deconstructing and these are discussed in Chapter 6.

The third constituent space, I have called Post-reflective Thinking. As well as thinking which involves logical, cognitive processing, such as metacognitive activity and post-rationalisation, this also encompasses the effectiveness of mindfulness and other embodied practices.

The Three Spokes

The first transition or spoke is the edge between Pre-reflective Experience and the more conscious Reflection on Experience. I call the dynamic movement between the two 'Touching Experience' since there is an inarticulate attempt to grasp feelings or intuitions which appear to be buried or submerged. This transition point is a vital stage in the reflection process.

The second spoke comes at the point of 'Becoming Critical' and is the transition from Reflection on Experience to Post-reflective Thinking, encouraged by critical, rational thought that aims to move the client towards a more critical stance. This cusp may be characterised by the transformative awakening that can arise here, particularly through expanding and enhancing the client's perspectives.

The third spoke I call 'Integrating'. It is the final crossing point that heralds the shift of learning from its created cognitive position in the Post-reflective Thinking space to eventual assimilation within ongoing Pre-reflective Experience. It is characterised by testing ideas and making changes. Literature on the transfer of learning informs an understanding of this transition and is discussed in Chapter 10.

The Chapters in this Book

The chapters follow the process implied in the Experiential Coaching Cycle and examine elements of coaching as they inform progression through the cycle. Each chapter includes a comprehensive overview of its subject, drawing on a range of theories, including experiential learning, intuition, focusing, reflective practice, critical reflection, rationality and tacit understanding. The aim is firstly to help with an understanding of how coaching really works, and secondly to provide substance for the cycle as described above, which will give coaches an explanatory framework for their practice where none existed before. The cycle itself may be pertinent to other fields, not only coaching, and has a particular application for practitioners wishing to articulate and develop their own practice. Into it all other models can be poured!

The book also draws on wider theories of education and workplace learning where much has been written about reflective practice, and on current thinking in neuroscience, in order to consider how our thinking and reflective faculties are linked to emotions and brain function.

In order to explain how coaching works in concert with the cycle, each of the chapters examines an element of the coaching interaction, such as Articulating Experience or Reflecting, Listening or Questioning, exploring in depth the specific role of each element in the coaching process and how each works in service of the client at different points in the coaching cycle. The chapters and how they relate to the cycle are set out in Table 1.1.

Nine chapters describe the fundamental elements of the coaching process as informed by the Experiential Coaching Cycle. Each describes a particular coaching activity and how it transports the coaching through a constructivist trajectory, from the purely phenomenological, through the critical and back again to the phenomenological.

Table 1.1   Relationship of chapters to the Experiential Coaching Cycle

Chapter title	Relationship to the Experiential Coaching Cycle
1. Introduction	
2. Touching Experience	Pre-reflective Experience and difficulties of touching
3. Articulating Experience	and articulating experience
4. Listening	
5. Clarifying	Reflection on Experience and the shift from reflection
6. Reflecting	to becoming critical
7. Becoming Critical	
8. Questioning	Post-reflective Thinking and the need to integrate
9. Being Present	learning
10. Integrating Experience	

Chapter 2. Touching Experience

The problems clients present are rooted in their experience. This chapter describes the first transition in the cycle set out in Figure 1.1. It explains the nature of experience and how difficult it can be for clients to articulate their experiences. Concepts such as focusing are discussed as ways of getting closer to experience.

Chapter 3. Articulating Experience

This chapter discusses how clients need to construct stories that are congruent with their current conceptions of themselves. These stories are a form of autobiography. The chapter uses theories of narrative meaning making to consider what it is that the coach listens to, and highlights the importance of narrative deconstruction to the coach and the client in achieving a coaching outcome. Clients position themselves in order to narrate a story and this is a natural process, but it is one that the coach also needs to be cautious of.

Chapter 4. Listening

Chapter 4 focuses on listening, which, since it is what coaches do for a major portion of their time with the client, is one of the most vital elements of coaching to understand. The chapter draws on theories of listening, together with client-centred theories, to look at why listening is important. Theories of levels of listening and types of listening and their implications for the client are examined.

Chapter 5. Clarifying

This chapter examines clarification techniques as they apply to coaching, and differentiates between the techniques of mirroring and reflecting back. Drawing on translation theory and literary criticism, this chapter also unpacks the role of clean language in helping the client think, but also looks at the 'dirty language' functions of paraphrasing and summarising as aspects of clarifying.

Chapter 6. Reflecting

This chapter draws on relevant theories and models of reflective practice and introduces two distinct types of reflection – phenomenological reflecting and critical thinking. It examines the concept of phenomenological reflecting in some detail and explores its use in coaching. Reflective practice models that may be useful for promoting phenomenological description are also discussed.

Chapter 7. Becoming Critical

The challenges created by our beliefs and assumptions, and how critical thinking can be encouraged are the topics of this chapter. The chapter focuses initially on how critical thinking is treated in the literature, and then looks at strategies for encouraging criticality and how the coach can begin to challenge the client to think differently.

Chapter 8. Questioning

This chapter examines why questioning is the most powerful element for coaching. Drawing on theories from the learning sciences it looks at the purposes and functions of questioning for the coach and the client. It explores where questions come from and the different types of questioning, including the effectiveness of Socratic questioning and the significance of the 'why' question, which is often held to be out of bounds for the coach.

Chapter 9. Being Present

In this chapter the nature of mindfulness and presence and their role within coaching is examined. Then a model is presented that illuminates the interplay between these two important concepts and their role in the more ecological state of 'Being Present'.

Chapter 10. Integrating Experience

In Chapter 10 the theory of transfer of learning is examined, and the nature of what is being transferred back into the workplace following a coaching intervention is discussed. It is assumed that coaching will result in a new and enhanced understanding of situations – a type of expertise. Therefore, integration of that understanding involves encouraging the application of increased cognitive awareness and skill to future experiential use. The chapter looks at ways of effecting this transfer through extrapolation techniques, such as role play and scenario planning.

How to Read this Book

Logic would suggest that there are more clients than coaches. However, there are very few books written with the client in mind. Certainly there are no books that explain how and why coaching works so that both the coach and the client can understand just why it can become such a powerful force for change. But, adult learning theory tells us that people put learning to use much better when they know why something works and why it is important. That is why this book is addressed not only to coaches, but also to their clients and potential clients.

Because of the linear process implied by the Experiential Coaching Cycle, it is suggested that readers read the book from start to finish. Chapter 2 is particularly important to read and take note of, since understanding the nature of the client's dilemma is important for defining the coaching task and generating reflective practice. In fact, Chapters 2, 5 and 6 form the core theoretical chapters, the spokes of the cyclical model that move clients from attempting to grasp or touch experience, and attempting to describe that experience to then looking at ways of analysing experience. Chapter 10 completes the cycle by explaining the transfer process. It is also possible for experienced coaches to dip into the book to read specific chapters. For example the chapters on listening and questioning can stand alone. Chapters 4 and 5 in particular could be read in isolation.

Definitions and Lexicon

From a reading of the many books and articles on coaching that have been published in recent years it could be concluded that coaching is the victim of an identity crisis, and that 'creating a unique identity of coaching is still an unresolved problem' (Bachkirova et al., 2010: 3). A further aim of this book, therefore, is to underscore differences between coaching and other helping strategies such as mentoring or counselling. This is done by highlighting clear theories for coaching, and creating explanations of the elements of the coaching process in a way that develops a theory of coaching. In addition, a new lexicon for coaching emerges through the introduction of consistent terminology. For example:

- 'Client' is used to refer to the individual recipient of the coaching;
- 'Coaching task' (or just task) is used to refer to the goal or subject of the coaching;
- 'Coaching alliance' is used to refer to the relationship between the coach and the client;
- 'Session' is used to refer to the coaching meeting;
- 'Coaching assignment' is used to describe a complete set of coaching sessions with one client.

2
Touching Experience

Chapter Aims:

- To explore how normally pre-reflective experience can begin to emerge into conscious awareness
- To examine how becoming aware involves struggle and consider the implication this has for the coaching alliance
- To highlight ways in which the coach can facilitate clients in coming closer to their experience in readiness for reflective and critical exploration during coaching

This chapter explores the importance of helping clients to understand their experience. Getting in touch with experience can usually reveal the issues at the heart of what brings clients to coaching, and is therefore crucial in facilitating an understanding of the nature of the coaching task. Such understanding is the first part of the shift of pre-conscious experience into consciousness, leading ultimately to what Damasio calls awareness in higher consciousness (2000).

The importance of facilitating the client in making experiences explicit has not been discussed in the coaching literature, despite its fundamental consequence. It has however been a focus of some studies in psychotherapy. Pos, Greenberg and Elliott for example, explain how experience is the domain of the whole and embodied person and that to experience means to 'live through': 'to have firsthand knowledge of states, situations, emotions or sensations' (2008: 80). Their perspective is that experience is in-the-moment and phenomenal. It is fundamental data that is valid and 'an important source of information about the self and the world in which that self is situated' (2008: 80). For our purposes here then, it is important to note how experience is foundational. The coaching alliance exists, as I shall explain further throughout this book, in order to assist clients in being aware of and articulating their experience, and so tap vital information that can then be used to guide coaching goals or tasks, and ultimately transform future experience.

Not only does articulating experience help clients begin to understand themselves, it also provides an opportunity for the coach to understand the situation. It is important that the coach and the client do not take things at face value: what the client says is the problem upon his/her arrival in the coaching room, might on further exploration of lived experience be only a part of what the coaching task needs to focus on. An embodied phenomenological exploration at the outset can reveal other features that the coach and client may miss if they jump to conclusions.

Experience has been described by Throop (2003) as either granular, fragmented and lacking in coherence and continuity, what Mattingly (1998: 32) calls a 'paralinguistic bombardment of the senses'; or as coherent, where it is seen as ordered by memory and anticipation. Before getting further into the discussion of the nature of what is essentially a pre-reflective phenomenon, we can assume that despite whether it is defined as fragmented or ordered in some way, some experiences are very easy to talk about, while others are decidedly difficult to articulate and to comprehend. In this chapter, I want to focus on those times when experience is difficult to talk about, since it is those experiences, I would suggest, that ultimately inform clients' goals and so become the basis of their coaching tasks.

In this chapter, I draw on a number of texts including those from psychotherapy, philosophy and neuroscience. In the first section of the chapter the nature of pre-reflective, lived experience is examined. Section II looks at the ways in which normally pre-reflective experiences become conscious and Section III explores strategies the coach might use to help the client surface experiences ready for exploration during subsequent coaching sessions.

I. The Nature of Lived Experience

This section looks at the nature of lived experience, and several theories are introduced. The main focus is on pragmatic explanations of how experience is a continuous transaction between people and their worlds (Elkjaer, 2009). Elkjaer explains how Dewey's concept of experience differs from the traditional understanding of it. For Dewey (1910, 1916, 1934), knowledge is seen as an ordered subset of experience rather than the totality of it: experience is both subjective and objective and is inherently future oriented. The subject–worlds relation that he identifies makes the experience possible. This explanation of experience is interesting because Dewey stresses the importance of sensory and affective sense-making. Experience includes bodily sensations, emotions and intuitions, and these are ways of knowing that inform our reflecting and thinking. Dewey's notion of experience is, therefore, different from the concept of experience underpinning humanistic and other individually-oriented psychologies, where it is seen as a private mental process. For Dewey experience is non-dualist and encompasses the individual and the world: it is culturally mediated. Dewey (1916) also explains how there is a continuous interaction, or transaction, between our worlds and us as subjects in those worlds.

Dewey also talks about the unity of experience, and contrasts it with the way we invariably 'fractionise' it through thought when we are working. Experience cannot be captured in its entirety, he argues, since 'thought withdraws us from the world' (1934: 24). However, Elkjaer contends that if experience is to become a learning experience at all, in the sense that it is able to inform future experience, then it has to 'get out of the bodily and non-discursive field and into the cognitive and conscious field of experience' (2009: 82). In effect, she argues, experience has to become 'reflective and communicated (with self and other) in order to later be used in an anticipatory way' (2009: 82). But before that can happen, the fragmented nature of pre-reflective experience has to be grasped in some way by consciousness.

Pre-reflective experience has been described as 'an experience ... which is lived without being fully aware of itself or self-aware' (Petitmengin, 2009: 7). The term 'pre-reflective' describes experience before it is recognised by any form of cognitive self. Another way of describing it is as tacit or unarticulated. The example that Schooler and Mauss (2010: 244) use is that it is possible to experience emotions, such as pleasure, without being aware of them. These authors distinguish between two types of consciousness: experiential consciousness (i.e. the contents of ongoing experience) and meta-awareness (i.e. one's explicit awareness of the contents of consciousness). They claim that we have experiences, such as pleasure, that are in our 'experiential consciousness', but that we are not necessarily contemporaneously aware of the nature of those experiences. They report how neuroscientific evidence suggests that the brain does in fact 'register valenced responses to events (e.g. subliminally presented stimuli) but that a reaction need not be consciously experienced' (Schooler and Mauss, 2010: 244).

Despite experience being pre-reflective, it is not possible really to use the term experience without assuming there is something or someone doing the experiencing. The neuroscientific study referred to above (Schooler and Mauss, 2010) points to this, suggesting there is some kind of 'register' in the brain. Damasio refers to this subliminal pre-reflective activity as the 'proto-self', which is unconscious and comprises 'a collection of brain devices whose main job is the automated management of the organism's life' (2000: 23). Thus the proto-self is a biological 'being in the world' (to use Heidegger's terminology).

A second kind of self, which arises when the proto-self is modified by events or experiences, Damasio refers to as the core self. This is our more familiar conception of consciousness, which, as Damasio explains, is frequently seen as fairly stable throughout a lifetime: we are conscious of it, and it is used to match events to perceptions and values. The third self is the autobiographical self, which is based on our memories and thoughts about the future. This develops gradually over our lifetime and allows us to make meaning from our experiences. The autobiographical self leads to a much richer form of consciousness, which Damasio calls extended consciousness. The three main constituents of the Experiential Coaching Cycle introduced in Chapter 1 could be seen to correspond to these three selves: Proto (Pre-reflective Experience); Core (Reflecting on Experience); Autobiographical (Post-reflective Thinking).

Emotions

Damasio also suggests that emotions are pre-reflective, arguing that they are part of our 'biological machinery' and are not dependent on consciousness. He further explains how 'we do not need to be conscious of the inducer of an emotion and often are not, and we cannot control emotions wilfully' (2000: 48). He gives the example of a spontaneous smile 'that comes from genuine delight or the spontaneous sobbing that is caused by grief' as being executed by structures that are located deep in the brain. In addition, Damasio points out that 'we have no means of exerting direct voluntary control over the neural processes in those regions', suggesting that this is why 'causal voluntary mimicking of expressions of emotion is easily detected as fake' (2000: 49).

It could also be argued that, since emotions arise from our valuing of certain experiences, the operation of values as emotion influencers must also belong in the pre-reflective realm. Dilemmas, problems and uncertainties invariably arise when our emotions are aroused and when our values, in this pre-reflective state.

Thus, the emotions can be seen as an example of the bubbling up of pre-reflective experience towards consciousness. Clients come to coaching with a feeling caused by the impact of experience on their regulatory processes and emotions (see Figure 2.1). Any client dilemma identified as a result of such feelings is still very much a pre-reflective dilemma. It is semi-visceral, belonging to the first stage in the movement from pre-reflective experience to fully cognitive thinking activity, shown in Figure 2.1. The dilemma is very much still tied to

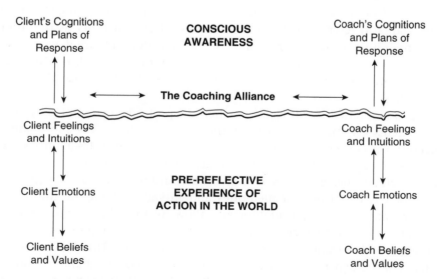

Figure 2.1   The place of coaching in the shift from Pre-reflective Experience to Conscious Awareness

the action, but has revealed itself because it has some importance to the client's basic survival regulation, to his/her values and beliefs. In Figure 2.1, which is based on Damasio's work, we see how basic regulation and emotions inform our feelings and subsequently our conscious awareness, and how this is the same process for client and the coach. In between, at the point where we become conscious of experience, is the space where coaching occurs, or in the case of the coach, it is where supervision occurs.

So the proto-self is the first part of the process of being conscious. With a proto-self present, it could be argued that pre-reflective experience, although not conscious, can never be inert. It always has the potential to be interpreted on some level whether in conscious awareness or out of conscious awareness – somatically, for example. Sometimes it appears then that pre-reflective experience bubbles, almost like a hot spring, giving glimpses of the 'heat' of the experience itself, before being interpreted by the core self as information. Such bubbling gives rise to pre-reflective activity such as intuition or hunches, which are often considered to be forms of knowledge or understanding (Atkinson and Claxton, 2000) providing us with the material to create knowledge and understanding.

Three Types of Disturbance

Dreyfus (1991) commenting on Heidegger's work, has delineated three kinds of disturbance or surprise that may occur in pre-reflective experience when events do not match our expectations. The first is 'malfunction', where, as Yanow and Tsoukas state, 'the practitioner is momentarily startled but almost immediately shifts to a new form of action that enables him [sic] to cope with the surprise, and he resumes what he was doing' (2009: 13). They liken this to being on 'automatic pilot' and refer to it as 'absorbed coping'.

The next kind of disturbance, termed 'temporary breakdown' by Dreyfus (1991: 72), is when what was previously transparent or subsidiary in awareness begins to become more explicit. As Dreyfus observes, 'deprived of access to what we normally count on, we act deliberately, paying attention to what we are doing' in order to resolve the 'breakdown' (1991: 72). This notion of improvisation has also been discussed by Yanow and Tsoukas (2009) who suggest that Schön's (1983) account of the concept as a way of responding to surprise is under-theorised. Yanow and Tsoukas support the notion of 'developing interpretations in rapidly moving situations or flows of interaction and acting on them in the moment' (2009: 3) in order to create new insight and enhance learning. Schön referred to this ability as 'Reflection in Action', which, if we take a phenomenological approach to reflection, as suggested here, makes sense; although it makes less sense in purely cognitive models of reflection.

Yanow and Tsoukas further explain how the phenomenological view of reflection in action emphasises its embedded (social), engaged (practice), and embodied (material) aspects:

Within such social practices, reflection in action is triggered by 'backtalk' – surprise – from the 'materials' of the practice, leading the practitioner to improvise a reaction or response. There are different kinds of surprise, ranging from 'malfunction' through 'temporary breakdown' to 'total breakdown'. Each one elicits a different type of improvisational response, ranging from 'non-deliberate' (spontaneous readjustments) through 'deliberate' to 'thematic' (explicitly intentional). (2009: 4)

Once pre-reflective experience has been fractured by the element of surprise then the client's uncertainties and hunches need to be uncovered and ultimately described in order to enable further reflective work to proceed.

The third kind of disturbance is when there is a total breakdown between experience and expectation, so that tacit processing is completely interrupted. The absorbed coping or the involved deliberation that enabled us to cope *in situ* with a 'malfunction' or a 'temporary breakdown' is no longer possible, and a more focused approach to events is needed in order to try to comprehend and articulate the problem. Such a total breakdown can also lead someone to seek coaching.

For Dewey there is also a developmental agenda linked to breakdown. He sees emotion and feelings as a 'conscious sign of a break, actual or impending' but argues that:

> ... in a growing life, the recovery is never a mere return to a prior state, for it is enriched by the state of disparity and resistance through which it has successfully passed. If its activity is not enhanced by the temporary alienation, it merely subsists. Life grows when a temporary falling out is a transition to a more extensive balance of the energies of the organism with those of the conditions under which it lives. (1934: 12–13)

By this view it could be argued that there is always a developmental agenda in coaching. If the coach is addressing issues of importance to the client because they are in some ways out of step 'with the march of surrounding things' (Dewey, 1934: 19), then there is inevitable growth or development in the way Dewey suggests.

II. From Pre-reflective to Conscious Awareness

In the next part of this chapter I discuss the variety of ways in which pre-reflective material can emerge into consciousness to become reflective. I highlight further the mechanisms through which normally unconscious experiences can suddenly come into consciousness, and discuss the role of the coach in supporting clients in articulating their experiences as the first stage in the reflection process. As mentioned, feelings, intuitions and hunches can be seen as involuntary 'spillages' of our experience. These will be examined in more detail before going further.

(1) Feelings

Damasio (2000) distinguishes between emotions and feelings. The basic functions of emotions are preset: they are 'bioregulatory devices which are instinctive and autonomic' (Damasio, 2000: 15). He argues that, 'consciousness allows feelings to be known and thus promotes the impact of emotion internally, allows emotion to permeate the thought process through the agency of feeling' (2000: 56). Feelings are therefore, sensory signals that interact with consciousness, bringing emotions to our attention. A combination of input and assessment reaches a level of consciousness and the emotion then becomes a feeling, or what Damasio calls the feeling of emotion. Thus one of the ways in which experience emerges into consciousness is through feelings.

Traditionally, coaches may have steered away from addressing feelings in the coaching session (Bachkirova and Cox, 2007), but this aversion should be seen as misplaced since feelings are the initial mechanism through which understanding is ultimately achieved.

(2) Intuition

Another common bubbling over of experience into consciousness is experienced as intuition. Intuition has been described as an 'immediate apprehension, without the intervention of any reasoning process' (Atkinson and Claxton, 2000: 34). Its root meaning is to guard or protect, and so intuition should serve as an invaluable tool.

Hodgkinson, Langan-Fox and Sadler-Smith (2008) also explore a number of descriptions of intuition, eventually championing Dane and Pratt's definition that intuitions are 'affectively-charged judgments that arise through rapid, non-conscious and holistic associations' (2007: 40). Hodgkinson et al. further deduce that intuition does not involve conscious and deliberative rational processing, since there is no conscious awareness of the knowledge source; rather intuition occurs instantaneously and is emotionally charged. As such, they suggest, intuition is a bridging construct that is accompanied by a 'somatic awareness which influences decision choices' (Hodgkinson et al., 2008: 3).

My understanding of intuition is more in tune with Miller and Ireland who say that intuition can be conceptualised in two distinct ways: 'as holistic hunch and as automated expertise' (2005: 21). Intuition as holistic hunch, they suggest, 'corresponds to judgment or choice made through a subconscious synthesis of information drawn from diverse experiences' (2005: 21), and is often described as a 'gut feeling'. Intuition as automated expertise, they describe as 'less mystical, corresponding to recognition of a familiar situation and the straightforward but partially subconscious application of previous learning related to that situation' (2005: 21). Miller and Ireland argue that this form of intuition develops over time as relevant experience is accumulated in a particular domain. This second explanation will be discussed further in Chapter 10.

Claxton identifies a number of other 'voices of intuition', which include physical feelings, insights, images and dreams, guesses, inklings, hunches and the aesthetic sense. Intuition, he claims, is based on 'deep intellectual knowledge of the subject [that] makes use of expert knowledge and manifests as intuitive, elegant and beautiful responses' (Claxton, 1999: 159). It often comes with a kind of 'built-in confidence rating, a subjective feeling of 'rightness', that may vary in its strength from 'complete guess' to absolute certainty' (Atkinson and Claxton, 2000: 40). This observation is interesting, as the 'rightness' could be seen to arise from a direct link between the emotion (as defined by Damasio), which is linked to our values, the feeling generated in the body as a result, and the accompanying brain signal that we subsequently call intuition.

(3) Hunches

Intuition is also implicated in hunches, and indeed Hodgkinson et al. (2008) see intuition as a process, where hunches are included as an outcome of that process. They cite Bowers et al., who suggest that we recognise intuition as a 'perception of coherence at first not consciously represented but which comes to guide our thoughts toward a "hunch" or hypothesis' (1990: 74).

Feigl defines a hunch as a product of learning from past experience, which is not made 'explicit at the moment of the use of judgment' (1958: 6). By this account, if we have a hunch then we are following an empirical rule of which we have no awareness. Our knowledge is tacit. Hunches can be differentiated from what Feigl calls 'trans-empirical intuitions' because 'unlike the target of a hunch, the target of a trans-empirical intuition cannot be tested empirically' (Feigl, 1958: 6f.). Simply put, hunches can be explained; reasons come easily, whereas intuitions seem beyond rationalisation.

III. Phenomenological Reflection Strategies for Articulating Experience

So far I have explored feelings, intuitions and hunches as the main wordless ways in which experience can make a more explicit presence in conscious awareness. I now turn to look at strategies that the coach might use to help the client heed and explore these in order to understand the dilemma more readily. In this part of the chapter, having explained what pre-reflective experience is, I want to move from the nature of tacit experiencing to our conscious attempts to make it more overtly reflective, thus ultimately facilitating better and more learning. As well as artefacts such as drawing, other strategies may be used to try to grasp experience and make it palpable. Another way of trying to touch experience is through what I will call embodied reflection strategies that help symbolise the experience. These involve recreating the event without evalua-tion or interpretation in order to limit the use of language. Artistic tropes may be used in conjunction with this technique since they reduce the use of lan-guage. Emotions are also included in these re-creations because they are inher-ent in our pre-reflective experience, as identified in Figure 2.1. The three methods of embodied reflection that I have singled out as having particular relevance for coaching are: using art as a holistic embodiment of experience, memory-enhancing visualisation and experiential focusing.

(1) Art as Holistic Embodiment of Experience

For Dewey there is an artistic and aesthetic quality implicit in every normal experience, one which generally fails to become explicit. In his early work Dewey describes experience as the 'fulfilment of an organism in its struggles and achievements in a world of things, it is art in germ' (1934: 25). Taylor has also suggested that creative techniques, such as drawing, encourage a non-discursive representation of a tacit, 'gut-felt knowing', and that the resulting object can be reflected upon and worked with in ways that are impossible until the felt knowing becomes an 'object in the world' (2003: 274). Through working with the created object, the knowing it embodies can then be intellectualised into cognitive knowing, and this knowing, according to Taylor, is now much richer, more nuanced and more complete than it would otherwise be.

Many coaches make use of creative media, although sometimes they use it because they believe the client to have a different learning style, rather than using it to overcome any impasse between pre-reflective experience and con-scious knowing. In my experience, most clients like to use drawing or other materials in a coaching session, even though in their everyday working lives this may be alien to them. In coaching sessions I often suggest that clients draw a picture of where they see themselves, either now or in the future, to represent on paper the path their life has taken and will take. They may draw a river or a road, or a tree or an image that encompasses their situation more holistically and immanently than words can. Sometimes coaches use creative activities that involve materials, such as building blocks or fabrics for similar purposes.

Taylor and Ladkin suggest that by making art about our own experience we make that experience exist as an object in the world. However, they go on to suggest that it is:

> an object that can contain contradictions (logical and/or moral) as well as unrealized possibilities that are not constrained by logic or the limitations of our current lives. In this way, art making enables us to draw upon, and subsequently reflect on, a deep well of 'unconscious stuff'. (2009: 58)

The use of art as an overt psychological projective method, as suggested by Taylor and Ladkin, is not, I would suggest, totally congruent with a pragmatic coaching approach. It belongs to classical (i.e. rational) cognitive therapy, designed to activate unconscious processes, which are then projected onto appropriate material (such as pictures). Used carefully as talking points, art created by clients in coaching sessions may be useful, but as Storch confirms, they should not be used as diagnostics, because 'the problem-centred visual materials of typical projective methods appeal to the client's deficits, not his/her resources' (2004: 32).

(2) Episodic Memory Recall

Mace (2010) claims that although autobiographical memories are personal memories of past experiences, and combine to form our life history, they only represent the reconstruction of fragments of experience combined with our knowledge of such experiences and the historical knowledge of our self. He reminds us that memory is not linguistically based and explains that it is: 'a highly dynamic system in which information is represented at multiple levels, including sensory experience, emotional experience, semantic information and conceptual knowledge' (2010: 267).

Coaches sometimes use the technique of Episodic Memory Recall (EMR), although they may not call it that, in order to help clients bring memories of experiences immanently into the coaching session. Often coaches refer to this process as visualisation or memory-enhancing visualisation (Parkin, 2001). An example of EMR is where I ask my client, Jasmine, to close her eyes, to reduce the impact of current surroundings, and try to imagine or visualise having a certain experience once more. I may ask her what she can see, hear, smell or feel within the recalled setting in order to enhance sensory awareness.

According to Hassabis and Maguire, scene construction such as this must include 'the retrieval of relevant semantic and sensory information' (2007: 301) and its integration into a coherent spatial context. They suggest that this is necessary for 'online maintenance for later manipulation and visualization including possible viewpoint transformation' (2007: 301).

Thus scene construction is a key process in the brain for supporting recollective experiences: it provides the 'stage on which the remembered event is played' (Hassabis and Maguire, 2007: 304). Such recall of real episodic memories accordingly produces a phenomenological feeling of re-experience. EMR produces vivid recollections of personal past events.

Hassabis and Maguire also note how:

> If scene construction is a key underlying component process of episodic memory, this would accord well with theories of memory that propose the recollection of complex episodic memories is actually a (re)constructive process as opposed to the all-or-nothing retrieval of a perfect 'holistic' record often implicitly assumed. (2007: 300)

Indeed, they confirm that 'well-known memory errors and inconsistencies, such as misattribution provide further tacit evidence for constructivist views of episodic memory' (2007: 300). So, the very act of the re-creation of an event implies, as Mace also suggests, a 'revisioning', and so invites a tacit evaluation of the way in which the client has already experienced the event. In the re-visions the event does not come back to the client as it was experienced, it comes to the client afresh, with new insights. As Newman (2007: 10) explains, lifting it artificially out of the continuous flow of being results in added reflexivity: 'We add to ourselves in the process of experiencing; and in the process of recalling and reconstructing our experience, we add further to ourselves and further to the experience'.

Newman's quite poetic account of experience and how it may be recalled is particularly helpful:

> Experience is complex, made up of sight, sound, the feeling of someone's arm against yours, the other senses, emotions, thoughts, events and other people. Experience is true in the moment but immediately falsified as it banks away into the past and becomes a recollection. In recalling experience we construct it, giving it a beginning and an end, making it *an* experience, an episode, and so lifting it artificially out of the continuous flow of our being. (2007: 10)

As long as the coach and client are aware of and celebrate the augmentation inherent in the recollective visioning, and do not look for veracity in the account, this should not impede the process. It can be a powerful way of embodying past experience and bringing it into the session, thus enabling any obvious bias or internal inconsistency to be articulated and challenged.

(3) Experiential Focusing

Gendlin's theory of experience (1962) is consistent with Merleau-Ponty's (1962) theory of tacit knowing. Both claim that our bodies present perceptions of events that are felt implicitly, but that these cannot be explicit because they are pre-verbal, or as Damasio (2000) describes them they are pre-reflective. Polanyi similarly argued that 'we know more than we can tell' (1967: 108). He called this pre-logical phase of knowing 'tacit knowledge', and described it as consisting of *a range* of conceptual and sensory information and images that could in fact be used to make sense of a situation or event, despite being inarticulate.

Gendlin further argued that we can sense our living body directly under our thoughts and memories and under our familiar feelings, but explains that focusing happens at a deeper level than feelings: 'Under them you can discover a physically sensed "murky zone" which you can enter and open. This is the source from which new steps emerge' (2003: ix).

However, Gendlin also explained how bodily experiences are not just 'sitting there' waiting for words to describe them; they are deeply buried and need to be surfaced. Experiential focusing is the act of directly attending to the bodily felt sense of an issue, memory, or experience and allowing new meanings to emerge

(Gendlin, 1962, 2009). He also talks about having 'focusing partners' who give no advice, judgements or comments, although they may clarify what is said in order to help understand the experience. This is a role that coaches could easily take.

McGuire-Bouwman (2010) has suggested that when the client is doing Experiential Focusing, the most appropriate interventions are:

a Experiential Focusing Suggestions that encourage the client to stop talking and just to sit quietly with the bodily felt sense.
b Experiential Listening Responses, where the helper reflects the clients' words back to them, particularly in relation to feelings (Gendlin, 1962, 2009). Clients can then check the words against the felt sense and continue to find more words or images until there is an exact fit with the felt sense.

In Experiential Focusing, after choosing an issue or dilemma to work on, clients close their eyes and attend to the bodily feel of the issue, looking for words or images which resonate with the bodily felt sense. The coach in this scenario will facilitate the development of a 'full felt sense' that includes an image or symbol, the emotional quality, a body sensation, and the life connection or story related to the felt sense (Cornell, 1993). When images are located that seem to capture the 'feel of it all', clients experience a 'felt shift', described as 'a tension-release accompanied by the unfolding of the previously blocked material into the creation of new meanings' (McGuire-Bouwman, 2010: 5). McGuire-Bouwman's protocol for Experiential Focusing (2010) involves seven steps, which are adapted here for reference.

> **Step One: Clearing a Space**. The client is helped to take an 'inventory' of the various issues being carried in the body that day.
> **Step Two: Getting a Felt Sense**. The client is helped to choose one issue to work on and to get a 'body-feel' for the whole of it.
> **Step Three: Getting a handle**. The client is helped to find some words or an image that are just right in capturing the 'feel of it all'.
> **Step Four: Checking or resonating**. The client is helped to take any words or images which have come and to check them against the body-feel of it all, refining the words or images until they are 'just right'.
> **Step Five: Asking an open-ended question**. The client is helped to ask questions of their body-feel, such as 'What would it take for this to be all okay?' or 'What does this stuckness need?' or 'What's so hard about this issue for you?', and, instead of answering immediately from the head, to wait quietly and pay attention to the body-feel which comes in the centre of the body in response to the question.
> **Step Six: Receiving and nurturing whatever has come**. The client is encouraged to sit for a moment with whatever new information has emerged, thanking the body for its cooperation, and gently being with whatever has come, but without judging it.
> **Step Seven: Another round**. Client and helper decide whether they want to begin another cycle of Experiential Focusing.

Gendlin's ideas about focusing are built on Dewey's notion of the felt experience. Rodgers (2002) explains how in Dewey's view interpretation is involuntary in the beginning phases of reflective thought, and things just leap to mind. However, meanings then begin to emerge from the 'feltness' of the experience. Dewey refers to these as 'suggestions' and explains how they arise from our previous experience. He further argues that if we stop the thought processes it can be irresponsible, leading to hasty interpretation. Reflection is required, and this requires patience: 'one can think reflectively only when one is willing to endure suspense and to undergo the trouble of searching' (Dewey, 1910: 16). So, if clients have a disorienting dilemma or total breakdown, either at the outset of the coaching or during coaching as the exploration and challenge proceeds, it is important for them to stay with it and reflect on it fully.

Ixer (1999) identifies how in our attempts to consider how a problem appears to us with all its 'felt difficulty' (to use Dewey's term) we use definitions, assumptions and explanations. In the literature, for example, the felt difficulty is referred to in a variety of ways. For Mezirow (1991) it is a 'disorienting dilemma', that is, something that does not match the habits of mind already formed. Brookfield describes it as 'an unanticipated event [that] comes tearing through the fabric of our well-ordered lives' (Brookfield, 1987: 24–25). Earlier Dewey had noted that 'life itself consists of phases in which the organism falls out of step with the march of surrounding things and then recovers unison with it – either through effort or by some happy chance' (1934: 19). Thus, the felt difficulty is the point at which a client recognises there is problem, so the felt difficulty becomes cognisable. This is why in Mezirow's theory the dilemma seems quite cognitive in nature, as the shift from feeling to thinking has already been made by the learner or client (or is created in session in dialogue with them).

Jordi (2011) also refers to Gendlin's 'philosophy of the implicit' which underpins a focusing methodology, where the ability to focus on vague, yet distinctly felt bodily experiencing (the 'felt-sense'), creates an evocative catalyst for the insightful reflection that follows. It could be argued that the space of coaching is the most appropriate place to explore this felt-sense. Focusing is a conscious strategy for gaining more information about pre-reflective experience in preparation for reflection. It could be seen as forming a 'semi-conscious' bridge between the pre-reflective experience and more orchestrated reflective processes.

'Staying with'

Dewey similarly argued that we think reflectively only when we are 'willing to endure suspense and to undergo the trouble of searching' (1910: 16). Thus he advocated 'enduring suspense'. Gendlin advocated 'staying with'. The difference is that Dewey's suspense involved perception, rather than feeling, and so, as Jordi points out, it left behind the 'complex, rich, and subtle implicit, embodied dimensions of experiencing, aspects that lie between the "incompleteness" and the "suggestion" and that probably get suppressed in the process of pursu-ing rational analysis' (Jordi, 2011: 192). Gendlin's practice of focusing then, taps this normally suppressed dimension, or 'felt-sense'. However, as Jordi explains, such felt-sense ultimately demands action, or what Gendlin himself referred to as 'carrying forward' or a 'felt-shift' from implicit to explicit.

Gendlin's most recent work concentrates on how language mediates what is implicit. He suggests that we can think with the implicit, as well as with fully-formed concepts and describes a procedure for 'fresh thinking'. He suggests that 'when we think freshly into something that is not yet clear to us, fresh phrases come to us' (2009: 149). The process he has devised for fresh thinking involves asking people to think about something they know deeply but have always been unable to say much about. They are then asked to write a few sentences and underline key words. The words are then examined in turn by asking 'If this word could mean just what you want it to mean, what would it mean?' In response, says Gendlin, come 'fresh metaphorical sentences to say what has never been said before' (2009: 149). In its aim to tap such metaphor-ical descriptions, this process resembles the clean language discussed later in Chapter 5.

Metaphor, as Gendlin explains, is a form of 'carrying forward' of the implicit idea, or moving it into the shared world of language:

> When people explicate something implicit they usually say that their words 'match' their experience, as if they were comparing two forms. But an implicit sense does not have the kind of form that could match words or concepts. What people call 'matching' is indeed an important relation between implicit and explicit but the relation is not representation. It is rather the characteristic continuity we experience when new sentences and then new concepts articulate and explain what we had understood only implicitly. (2009: 151)

The implicit is always highly demanding, Gendlin confirms and leads the cli-ent to 'special phrases and concepts' (2009: 151) that retain their link to their origin. For example, Jasmine may report feeling a heavy weight pressing on her. Then, from identification of that feeling comes the word 'oppressed' and the sense for her that that word really 'fits' the situation. It is important then that the coach and client do not suggest other words or create a more acceptable term. Focusing necessitates acknowledging the truth of what emerges, and then staying with it, rather than trying to do things to it.

Afford (2008) explains how, until now, we have felt that body and brain are separate, but that recent neuroscience is explaining that this is because we have more nerve endings from the body that feed into the right brain than the left. He explains how the functional specialisation in the human brain has meant that it is possible for thinking to become dissociated from feeling, and for lan-guage to take us away from a sense of being in the body. Afford sees this as a design problem. He points out how 'the felt sense seems to be a right brain dominant phenomenon: the right brain senses a bodily experience, the left struggles to find words to describe it' (2008: 2). This is why it appears easier to express a felt sense in an image or a metaphor, since these are right brain dominant, whereas words are left brain dominant. The practice of focusing, Afford claims, 'counters dissociation and encourages neural integration', and so practising focusing may fuel improvisation and creativity in response to the felt sense.

Afford (2008) also argues that because the brain is part of the central nervous system extending down through the spinal cord to the lower back, and the brain initiates feelings we receive in the body in response to external and internal triggers, it appears as if our brains are in our bodies as well as in our heads. After all, he says, 'brain and body are fundamentally one thing, it's only the human mind that even dreams of separating them' (2008: 2). Thus Afford explains how while focusing, we should allow our attention to wander freely amongst all the brain areas involved in sensing and mapping the body, 'generating and registering emotion and feeling, consciousness and language, and all our other cognitive processes' (2008: 2).

Focusing may also happen naturally, Afford argues. But it seems that facilitated focusing goes beyond the natural process by actively weaving together feeling and thinking, words and body, image and sensation: 'in re-associating left brain with right brain, and cortex with sub-cortex, it has a special role to play in helping our brains work in more integrated ways' (Afford, 2008: 3). So it is claimed that focusing actually helps in making the shift from pre-reflective to reflective. It is therefore a strategy that the coach can consider to enable clients to get closer to their experience and begin to understand it.

Summary

This chapter has highlighted how the reflective process begins with pre-reflective experience. Problems clients present are rooted in their experience, and the first inklings of a problem or dilemma are manifested through intuitions, hunches and feelings of unease. It is most often a confusing or disturbing experience that brings the client to coaching, and the coaches' role is therefore to help the client describe the experience in order to bring it into consciousness.

In this chapter three strategies for facilitating awareness were discussed: art as a representation of tacit knowing and something that can be worked with in the coaching session; Episodic Memory Recall (EMR), which aids recollection of events through visualisation techniques, and is a non-verbal method of making experience immanent in the session; and focusing, which involves the use of language to accurately name and describe an experience. It is during the focus on the 'felt sense', through these techniques, that feelings of ease are often reported by coaching clients, suggesting that some form of integration is taking place between the experience and the recognition of that experience through naming and knowing.

This chapter also highlights an intrinsic developmental imperative in our experiencing of events: the body knows when it is being threatened or compromised and sends signals. This suggests that all coaching is developmental coaching to some extent in that it helps clients to synthesise new 'threatening' experience with their existing meaning structures. Even in skills coaching, where there is emphasis on performance, there will be ongoing construal of experience by clients. The implications of touching experience for developmental coaches are greater however, since they will want to spend longer helping clients to focus on the nuances of their experience, understand the incongruities, and thus increasing coherence, awareness, agency, creativity and adaptive flexibility. A skills-focused coach will want to explore experience, but maybe only in so far as it informs the subsequent clarity of the coaching task.

One important point to make here is that the symbolisation of experience through processes such as focusing, are not processes of representation, but of *construction*, and constructions cannot ever be complete because they do not include all available tacit information (Pos et al., 2008): they are creations rather than representations. In fact it could be argued that there is no such thing as representation. All attempts at description are constructions. This problem is explored in different ways in Chapter 3, where the focus is on how the client's newly acquired conscious awareness of experience is remembered and presented in the coaching session, giving rise to narrative accounts and positioning by the client.

3
Articulating Experience

Chapter Aims:

- To explore how clients begin to articulate their experience
- To examine the usefulness of positioning and narrative theories for coaching

---

As discussed in Chapter 2, it is not possible to recount experience exactly. Malouf explains how this is because we have already changed, and the body experience, the lived experience, is out of reach:

> It isn't simply a matter of its being forgotten in us – of a failure of memory or imagination to summon it up, but of a change in perceiving itself. What moving back into it would demand is an act of un-remembering, a dismantling of the body's experience that would be a kind of dying, a casting off, one by one, of all the tissues of perception, conscious and not, through which our very notion of body has been remade. (Malouf, 1986: 64)

In this chapter I focus on how attempts to articulate experience in the coaching session are made in spite of this fissure between actual experience and the possibility of recollection of experience. I explain how this leads to shifting interpretations and explanations of events and explore theories of how people communicate their experiences. This sheds light on how the coach gradually comes to know the nature of the coaching task. The chapter begins with a further brief exploration of memory, since recollection sits at the boundary between experience and understanding. It then identifies two expressive processes evident when the client comes to the coaching session; the first is positioning and the second is narrative redescription. The usefulness of these processes is considered and some of the dangers inherent in them are also discussed.

Memory

In the schematic Figure 3.1 it can be seen that memories are generated in a complex mental system, which Conway (2001) terms the self-memory-system. In

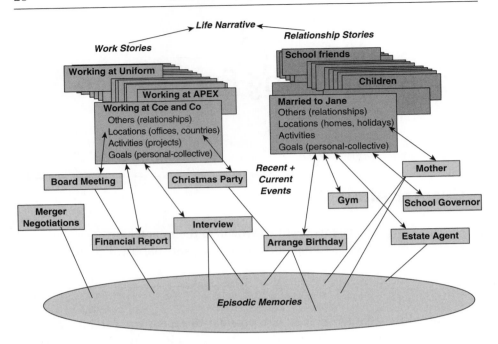

Figure 3.1 How stories and narratives are formed

this system there is a knowledge base of sensory-perceptual episodic memories (long-term memory), shown as a large bubble at the base of the figure. Plus there are sets of control processes (the working self). From this evolve two forms of memory – correspondence and coherence – that are activated by different parts of the brain. In Figure 3.1 it can also be seen how the sensory-perceptual episodic memories do not endure in memory unless they become linked to more permanent autobiographical memory knowledge structures, such as recent or current events or life course events, where they induce recollective experience in autobiographical remembering. Conway (2001) confirms that episodic memories degrade and are mostly lost within 24 hours of formation. He explains that only those episodic memories integrated at the time or consolidated later, possibly during the sleep period following formation, or through the use of Episodic Memory Recall (EMR) as described in Chapter 2, remain accessible, and can enter into the subsequent formation of autobiographical memories.

Bruner has further explained how ' … a story's components, insofar as they become its "functions" or captives, lose their status as singular and definite referring expressions' (1991: 13). This is also illustrated in Figure 3.1. There seems to be a process whereby recent or current events are linked with sensory-perceptual episodic memories, and then laid down as schema or script. As Schank also argues, we have difficulty remembering abstractions (generalisations or principles), and more easily remember stories: 'Stories make the events in memory memorable to others and to ourselves' (1995: 10). Scripts then are a form of memory structure from which longer stories and ultimately life narratives are built.

Schank explains that a script is 'a set of expectations about what will happen next in a well-understood situation. Life experience means quite often knowing how to act and how others will act in given stereotypical situations. That knowledge is called a script' (1995: 7). Scripts can be helpful because they provide a map of what is supposed to happen in given situations: they make mental processing easier by 'allowing us to think less'. Blenkinsopp further explains how both narratives and scripts serve as heuristics, which means that as a consequence we are inclined to attend 'less to information which conflicts with the narrative, whereby progressively reducing the likelihood that new information will be noticed and a better narrative developed' (Blenkinsopp, 2009: 6). Thus clients' narratives and scripts act as patterns that guide their lives.

In transformative learning theory, Mezirow (1991, 2000) referred to such collections of script phenomena as 'meaning perspectives' or, later, as 'frames of reference'. Such frames of reference encompass theories and beliefs, as well as values and goal orientations. When something happens we have to be able to assimilate the new information into a script or frame of reference so that it will be 'scripted' for next time. So scripts change over time and embody what we have learned. In any situation scripts provide a set of rules to follow, and, as Schank suggests (1995: 8), the more scripts we know, the more situations there are in which we feel comfortable and capable of playing our roles effectively.

Two ways in which scripts emerge are now discussed. The first is positioning and the second is narrative redescription.

I. Positioning

When a client is endeavouring to articulate his or her experience, it could be argued that a key factor affecting that articulation is audience expectation. My client, Jasmine, will not answer until she is clear about what I, as her coach, am expecting to hear. From my *demeanour* and the context within which we are meeting, she will decide whether to give an open account or whether to modify her response according to the current context (i.e. maybe she doesn't quite trust me yet, and so she will only tell me part of the story). Thus she will edit her response depending on whether she is talking to me as her trusted coach, or whether she sees me as a stranger or a threat. So as well as providing the information requested, often in the form of a narrative, when clients are articulating their experience they are also positioning themselves.

In their discussion of positioning theory, Harré and van Langenhove (1999) present positioning as a conceptual and methodological framework based on a Position/Act-Action/Storyline triad, where Position refers to the moral position that speakers might take according to the rights or duties they perceive that they have to say certain things in certain contexts. Act-Action refers to the conversational history that already exists (i.e. what has already been said by the speakers, either in this conversation or previous conversations), and Storyline is the speakers' actual utterances; their responses that convey their position to the world. The dynamics of this positioning process are shown in Figure 3.2.

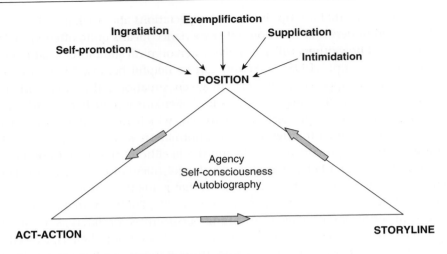

Figure 3.2 The dynamics of the positioning process

In addition, according to the theory proposed by Harré and van Langenhove (1999), a positioning response involves three different activities, each of which can be seen to be linked to the expression (and experiencing) of elements of personal identity: agency; self-consciousness and autobiography. These are shown in Figure 3.2 as integral aspects of the responding process. Following the arrows, once a position has been adopted, an act or action is planned, taking account of the current context and environmental pressures and the storyline presented. The story reinforces the position further and a certain congruence is built by:

1 *stressing agency* – clients present a course of action as one chosen from among various possibilities, suggesting a sense of personal responsibility. Coaches should be aware that as clients position themselves there are other positions that they could (and may well) adopt in other circumstances;
2 *being self-conscious* – clients use self-referential indexing statements that communicate their unique point of view;
3 *drawing on autobiography* – the description of past events makes a contribution to the client's biography during the response.

At the top of the positioning triangle in Figure 3.2, five self-presentational strategies identified by Jones and Pittman (1982) are included: self-promotion, ingratiation, exemplification, supplication and intimidation. These strategies relate to choices that people make when positioning themselves. They reveal their relational intentions. For example:

Self-promotion implies the client wants to be seen as competent. Clients will want to stress their abilities and accomplishments. A client may say: *'I've learnt from every experience since I've been here and now I'm ready for the next stage. I'm definitely better than anyone else who is likely to apply.'* We can note the frequent use of 'I' in this self-promotion strategy.

Ingratiation suggests that the client wants to be liked. Clients presenting this strategy will flatter others and appear to conform to their views: *'I really like my manager and she has excellent ideas. The team is good too and we really get on.'*

Exemplification relates to moral worthiness and integrity. Clients adopting this position will seek to demonstrate their dedication above and beyond the call of duty: *'I've been working all the hours God sends to finish the report on time and on top of this I've been up three nights this week with a sick child.'*

Supplication is in evidence when clients advertise their weaknesses and limitations and present themselves as helpless or needy. For example, a client may explain: *'My manager is really helpful, when I have a problem she spends time explaining things and I feel less of a fool.'* Again, we can note the frequent use of 'I' in this strategy.

Intimidation is the opposite of ingratiation. Clients will speak as if they are in control of others and may even position themselves as threatening: *'Explaining to the Board the way we have to go is difficult. They don't understand. So sometimes you have to shout or railroad them.'* Interestingly there is no use of 'I' in this intimidation strategy.

Such positioning strategies may be useful for the coach to notice and feedback to the client at an appropriate point in the coaching process.

Positions can also be detected through the language used by clients, and coaches may particularly wish to listen for the words the client selects, especially the indexing pronouns, for example, 'I' or 'we' or 'they'. These 'mediating pronouns', discussed by Harré and van Langenhove (1999: 26), are interesting to observe since they may indicate relational intention. Being aware of the tacit self-positioning that reflects the 'self' of the client can be useful. But positioning can also be intentional, and this is where coaches can be helpful, both in making clients aware and in helping them reposition themselves. Noticing and feeding back on the indexicals or pronouns is one way to explore different positions.

Positioning is presented as an interactive process with participants in the conversation positioning both themselves and the other: Harré and van Langenhove confirm that 'deliberate self-positioning occurs in every conversation where one wants to express his/her personal identity' (1999: 24). As suggested by Figure 3.2, clients respond according to the position that they want to present to the coach, and their initial perception of the coach as a trustworthy person.

This theory also suggests that coaches need to be particularly aware and avoid reacting, since having been positioned and invited to reciprocate, coaches could find themselves becoming part of a storyline themselves. Coaches necessarily have to endeavour to remain impartial and non-judgemental in relation to the positions clients take, and to consider carefully how they position themselves. There is an injunction on coaches to try not to position their clients or to use the coaching encounter to position themselves. Coaching is not a typical discursive process; the client's conversation is more like a soliloquy – it is not a mutual positioning each of the other as experienced in everyday conversation.

However, it is interesting to consider whether, in the coaching alliance, the expression of personal identity can indeed remain one sided. From the coach's perspective, there is the attempt to remain non-judgemental in response to positioning responses and to adopt something like Coleridge's suggestion to readers of literature to 'suspend disbelief and stand, as it were, naked before the text' (quoted in Bruner, 1991: 17). Thus coaches stand naked before the client. However there are dangers here, since this could be interpreted as an idealisation of the client which could deny or distort the usual process of understanding. As much as coaches attempt to remain non-judgemental they still do absorb the client's storyline on their own terms and in the light of their own presuppositions: this influences the choices they make throughout the coaching process. If this is the case, perhaps the honest and open sharing by coaches of their reactions and feelings as part of a more conventional, mutual discourse would be more desirable. It could be that the interplay of perspectives between coaches and clients would help them to address the coaching task more directly.

Gergen and Gergen established the concept of 'narratives of the self' in which individuals also position themselves. These narratives are stories that operate as a way in which people make themselves intelligible in the social world. Gergen and Gergen describe the narratives of the self as 'products of social interchange' (1988: xx). However, although coaches facilitate clients' narratives, helping them to reconstruct events and clarify them, they stop short at everyday conversation, which would contaminate the coaching process by introducing the coaches' own cultural and historical baggage. Coaching is not a regular social interchange, so it is interesting to consider whether the development of the client's self narrative is hindered if the coach is not active in the interchange through the desire to be client centred. I would argue that it is not. The focus on clients reworking their narratives without the coaches' interjections and interpretations is what makes coaching different from everyday conversation, and the benefits are far reaching, not least because when coaches are not focused on exchanging their own narratives, they can focus on helping the client to see as many different perspectives and interpretations in their story as possible. In a regular interchange there may be only one supporting or conflicting opinion.

Further research into the impact of forms of coaching conversation would be illuminating.

II. Narrative Redescription

McAdams (1993) explains why listening to the telling of a personal story is so important. He believes that a verbal account shows the outlines of internalised personal myths, and summarises this imperative:

> If you want to know me, then you must know my story, for my story defines who I am. And if I want to know myself, to gain insight into the meaning of my own life, then I, too, must come to know my own story. (1993: 11)

This suggests that clients' stories are important and can give coaches information about clients' ongoing life narratives.

Surprisingly, considering the centrality of language to the coaching enterprise, the coaching literature has said very little about how clients actually articulate their experience and the issues this might present. Some authors do, however, introduce the idea of storytelling as important. Brockbank and McGill, for example, argue that a story is an 'authentic self-disclosure – an attempt to reveal the self as a person and to reach the listener', suggesting that a 'story is a signal of invitation' (2006: 156) through which the client opens a door to his or her self. Brockbank and McGill contrast story with history, which, they say, is more a statement of fact. So, one kind of client response to the coach's opening question could be an account of facts, such as 'the communication amongst the team is failing and we are not meeting targets'. In this statement there is no use of 'I' and so the coach does not yet know the client's position in relation to the situation, and, as Brockbank and McGill further confirm, there is a difference between telling the story where clients are giving an historical account of facts, and where they are expressing feelings and disclosing something about themselves: 'Story is selective in detail – not necessarily complete in communicating fact, but complete in communicating self' (2006: 156). This view of history as being synonymous with facts is contentious, however, and it could be argued that factual history is also a narrative.

Lee talks about how coaches create their own custom version of the client's story in their heads. He includes a chapter on 'story-making', in which he proposes that from a client's responses the coach often 'seeks to construct a meaningful story' (2003: 94). He suggests that coaches need to be very aware of their biases and hypotheses in this process, since any story that they formulate will be influenced by their existing mindsets and value systems. This danger is also highlighted by Corrie and Lane: 'If coaches are not careful they end up serving their own formulations more than those befitting their coachees or what is actually happening in the session' (2010: 242). Thus, if the coach begins the analysing/reflecting process too soon, the relevance of the client's story is lost.

Drake also confirms the importance of the client's story. He suggests people form stories in response to disruptions in their world: 'their goal in telling stories is to resolve the discrepancies between what they expected and what actually happened ... and to integrate the resulting disorder' (2010a: 123). So, Drake suggests, the role of the narrative coach is to help clients 'forge new connections between their stories, their identity and their behaviours in order to generate and embody new options in these three domains' (2010a: 120). He also describes how there is a close connection between how people view themselves, how they describe their daily lives, and how they subsequently behave. He suggests that stories are a good way of exploring these connections, providing material that is indicative of opportunities for inner development.

Thus the idea of narrative as a guiding force within our lives is hugely popular. It manifests in therapy literatures as well as in coaching (for example, Payne, 2006). The claim by advocates of this theory is that we 'dream in narrative, daydream in narrative, remember, anticipate, hope, despair, believe, doubt, plan, revise, criticise, construct, gossip, learn, hate and love by narrative' (Hardy, 1968: 5). The notion of narrative storytelling is also useful in the field of career counselling (Blenkinsopp, 2009).

The distinction between narrative and story is explained by Hyvärinen (2008: 47). A story is a sequence of events, whilst a narrative is how the events are accounted for. If I think of my four-year-old grandson and how the narrative of his life so far may be being formed, I can see that when I ask 'what did you do at playgroup today?' he is searching to name the activities in which he took part, and these then become part of his story. I might say 'you can tell Daddy about that later', which reinforces the story. Without this social construction my grandson would not develop his language skills, and arguably would not develop his memory. As more years go by and he moves into his schooling, the themes embedded in the stories begin to form ongoing narratives. Patterns emerge that are identified as belonging to 'me'.

The Importance of Stories

In Figure 3.2, it can be seen that the client's positioning response includes the development of a 'storyline' too. Stories are important to the client and should therefore be of equal concern to the coach. In what follows, the effectiveness of stories, as a way of articulating experience and building a longer life narrative, is explored in some detail. This is not to say that coaches should necessarily always take a narrative approach in their coaching, but rather to suggest that they understand the narrative metaphor more fully, to see if, as an explanation of the structure of our meaning making, it has usefulness for coaching, especially in relation to helping clients re-write their stories.

According to Bruner (1991) narrative understanding is one of two basic types of cognitive functioning; the other being logico-scientific understanding. The innate tendency to impose a narrative onto events helps us to understand them by ordering them within the whole to which they contribute (Polkinghorne, 1988). Polkinghorne goes on to explain that this ordering process 'operates by linking diverse happenings along a temporal dimension and by identifying the effect one event has on another, and it serves to cohere human actions and the events that affect human life into a temporal gestalt' (1988: 18). Thus stories have temporality: they have a beginning, middle and end (Labov and Waletzky, 1967).

Geertz describes stories as 'hindsight accounts of the connectedness of things that seem to have happened: pieced-together patternings, after the fact' (1995: 2–3). According to Geertz, narrative shows how 'particular events and unique occasions, an encounter here, a development there, can be woven together with a variety of facts and a battery of interpretations to produce a sense of how things go, have been going, and are likely to go' (1995: 2). So the client tells a story at first meeting (which is, by some accounts, part of their bigger narrative), and the coach helps ultimately to construct a new narrative.

Thus as Weick (1995: 129) argues, stories play a critical part in sensemaking. He proposes at least seven ways in which stories function to facilitate understanding:

1 They aid comprehension by integrating that which is known about an event and that which is conjectural.
2 They suggest a causal order for events originally perceived as unrelated.
3 They enable people to talk about absent things and connect them with present things in the interest of meaning.
4 They are mnemonics that enable people to reconstruct earlier complex events.
5 They guide action before routines are formulated and can enrich routines after they are formulated.
6 They enable people to build a database of experience from which they can infer how things work.
7 They can be transmitted and can convey shared values and meaning.

MacIntyre (1985) too has noted the importance of narrative in explaining human behaviour and recounts how our actions only make sense in the light of the history that surrounds them. So, when clients identify a particular action they position their intentions in the causal and temporal order with reference to their perceived history and the setting in which they belong. In so doing, they write a further part of their story. MacIntyre also proposes a 'narrative self' rather than an emotivist self. The self then becomes not something disembodied and abstract but rather it is embedded in and partially constituted by its social setting: 'I am someone's son or daughter, someone else's cousin or uncle; I am a citizen of this or that city, a member of this or that guild or profession; I belong to this clan, that tribe, this nation' (MacIntyre, 1985: 220). Clients' storied responses will, on this account, uncover their embeddedness and the nature of their social setting.

It follows then that, as Polkinghorne (1988) perceives it, narrative responses are affected by culture, which implies that if coaches facilitate the construction of stories, they are indeed helping with the 'writing' of clients' stories and bringing their own culture into play. As discussed earlier in this chapter, a tension may be perceived here in that whatever coaches do or do not do, however much they try not to 'get in the way', they may not be able to help but write, and be part of, those stories. It could further be argued that after telling the developing story, when a client hears the comments and responses of the coach who is in the role of an 'outsider witness' (Payne, 2006: 126), he or she has the newly told and rather fragile sub-plot either confirmed, enlarged or embedded.

Frozen Narratives, Frozen Scripts

Having established that the way in which clients articulate experience appears to be governed by a narrative form, it is important to recognise how such structures may restrict and bind, as well as aid articulation.

In therapy, Spence (1982) suggests that the main goal is an effort to free clients from relatively 'frozen' narratives and enable them to construct new personal stories. This is also true for narrative coaching, albeit that those narratives are frequently work related rather than personal or psychological. Moghaddam (1999), for example, suggests that it is possible that some storylines and specific reflexive positions may sometimes become more salient than others:

> the respective narratives of the 'former alcoholic', 'orphan', 'underdog', 'struggling artist', or 'future lawyer', and the accompanying range of positions these themes make available, may tempt the speaker into compelling narratives that fit so comfortably that they may even conceal possibilities of choice. (1999: 78)

We might consider this scenario: If I ask Jasmine a question she will answer with some facts and maybe tell a story that includes some self-assessment. She does not normally proceed to tell me about her *whole* life or where her current story fits into the various narratives she may have hitherto constructed to give her life meaning – unless prompted by me to do so, as part of a 'life chapters' exercise for instance (Hudson and McLean, 2000). Rather, she is intent on making sure that I understand her current situation. She may give clues, however, during her response of where the explanation fits in her wider life narrative. She might, in recounting something that has gone wrong this week, exclaim 'that's the story of my life', or she may more overtly say that her life has been a succession of disappointments. The key word in Jasmine's claim is 'succession' – this suggests that a series of stories are linked together to form some kind of coherent narrative, and so, rather than the 'truth', which is more chaotic, the narrative becomes a tidy fiction overlayed onto the facts of a number of stories (this overlay is indicated in Figure 3.1). For the coach, oeuvres such as this are not to be missed: understanding how the story being presented is interpreted and fits into a client's wider narrative is important. Identification and challenge of self-limiting stories is a significant part of the work of the coach.

Bruner suggests that what he calls 'genres' might be seen as 'conventionalized representations of human plights' (1991: 14). Put another way they are the different 'spins' we put on our stories. Genres are like scripts and achieve their effects by using language in a particular way. The alert coach can pick up on this language and identify the danger that comes when the client always tells his/her story from a particular genre, like Jasmine in the example above. These genres are, in a sense, faulty scripts that contribute over time to a frozen narrative – they 'predispose us to use our minds and sensibilities in particular ways' (Bruner, 1991: 15). The genre or script begins to dominate, and, as a result, as Bruner explains, the world to which it refers becomes 'the creature of the text' (1991: 16) or, in this case, the frozen narrative. Blenkinsopp (2009: 1) describes how his own career was wrong-footed through a faulty script. He recounts how his narrative about dropping out of university 'was told and retold for years' and hints that it prevented him from re-examining events in a more detached manner. The role of the coach therefore, is to help clients translate their 'way of telling' into another language to escape the genre/script trap and recognise how the various scripts influence their lives. As Harré and van Langenhove (1999) suggests, the more people engage in rhetorical re-descriptions of their 'selves' the more they will become 'round' characters who are taking full responsibility for their lives.

Breaches in the Narrative

As indicated earlier, when a client first comes to coaching it is often because an event 'breaches' the normative narrative script. It is then that the client experiences a dilemma. Several authors suggest that such breaches are a response to the emotion triggered by events. For example, Blenkinsopp explains that such breaches do not have to be novel events in order to trigger an emotional response. However, where they are, the response is prone to be more intense and more prolonged: 'more intense because the disruption is greater, more prolonged because it will take longer to develop a plausible narrative' (Blenkinsopp, 2009: 6). Weick et al. argue that when such efforts are made to construct a plausible sense of what is happening, this 'sense of plausibility normalizes the breach, restores the expectation, and enables projects to continue' (2005: 415).

Bruner supports the notion that to be worth telling, a story needs to be about how an 'implicit canonical script' has been 'breached, violated, or deviated from' in a way that does 'violence to the "legitimacy" of the script' (1991: 8). So, in coaching terms, the client always comes to coaching with something worth telling, something they want to work on – what we may call a 'precipitating event' (Labov and Waletzky, 1967).

In Mezirow's (1991) terms such an event could be called a disorienting dilemma brought about by a challenge to an existing meaning perspective. Mezirow sees this dilemma as a trigger for transformative learning. The transformation can be seen as the translation, or improvisation, of chaotic events into a coherent component of the life narrative. So by this analysis, what Mezirow calls meaning perspectives are scripts that have out-served their purpose, they are the frozen narratives, the 'self' stories we cling to that hold us back. The meaning perspectives also involve our values and beliefs, which are, in effect, just scripts too, based on our cultural background, early experiences and later reinforcement.

The Dangers of Coherent Narrative

Hyvärinen, Hydén, Saarenheimo and Tamboukou (2010) describe how narratives have been frequently conceptualised in terms of coherence and unity: a coherent narrative has to progress linearly and needs some form of closure. In the context of a life, telling stories has principally been perceived as a way to create a coherent identity from seemingly disparate experiences. However, despite the attractiveness of this process, the coach needs to be aware that there is an ever-present tendency to exaggerate our lives when seeking a single coherent biography. There is the danger of creating what might be termed 'blind narratives', where fixed values and beliefs drive the life, like frozen scripts.

In fact there are a number of other objections to the narrative thesis that will now be considered. Strawson (2004) for example, argues that not all people think narratively. He presents a complex argument that makes a distinction between people who have a 'Diachronic' concept of self, that is one where the self is perceived as having continuity over the lifespan, and people who are 'Episodic' and experience the self as momentary. For Episodics, he argues, 'the past can be alive – arguably more genuinely alive – in the present simply in so far as it has helped to shape the way one is in the present ... ' (Strawson, 2004: 432). Strawson's argument hinges on his claim that in his remoter past events did not happen to him, since he feels that metaphysically he is a different 'him' than he was at that earlier time.

Strawson is concerned that narrative self-articulation is natural and helpful for some people, but for others it is 'a gross hindrance'. His concern is that the consequence of the neuropsychological process governing how memories are laid down means that every 'studied conscious recall of past events brings about an alteration' (2004: 447), and that these 'changes, smoothings, enhancements' are shifts away from the facts: 'so the more you recall, retell, narrate yourself the further you risk moving away from accurate self-understanding – from the truth of your being' (2004: 447). Strawson also notes that almost all narratives are compromised by revision, and since we always revise in our own favour, they are always biased. The implication of Strawson's objection for coaches is that some clients may also be averse to an overt focus on stories, narratives or scripts, and so a preoccupation with this by the coach could be a hindrance, as Strawson suggests. Other ways would need to be sought to work with such clients.

Strawson seems to imply that any earlier narrative is at a remove from current concerns. He sees it as only making sense of what happened *then*. So he has identified an important problem for coaches if they accept the client's narrative at face value. If they do that then they pin the client's current predicament or goals to a pre-existing idiosyncratic, culturally bound and potentially option-limiting narrative. If, on the other hand, the construction of the narrative is an ongoing and contingent activity in the way that Hiles (2005) suggests, for example, this might allay some of the concerns that Strawson presents. If, rather than being used as a limiting heuristic by the client, stories are used as indicators by the coach that there is work to be done, the frozen scripts, so feared by Strawson, are continually either forestalled or modernised. Then what we perceive about our self in the moment does differ from 'what we know of our being in the past' (Strawson, 2004: 447). This then is probably one of the most important tasks of the coach.

One of Strawson's main concerns appears to have its origin in the dilemma presented by Dewey and discussed in Chapter 2. Dewey (1934) contrasts the unity of experience with the way we invariably 'fractionise' it when we are thinking. Strawson is also convinced that the past is figured in the present and so does not need narrative exploration to give it meaning. He is one of those philosophers who believe that there are elements of the real that lie beyond language, and that these elements are never captured fully by our fictions. A narrative account would only fractionise, and any technique, such as focusing would similarly rupture the whole. Strawson is thus suggesting that the past is palpable in the now. Many coaches and therapists do work in a gestalt way, claiming that it behoves the coach to stay in the present. Yontef, for example, explains how in therapy a gestalt approach 'focuses more on the immediacy of how the patient functions moment-to-moment and on what is happening in each moment between therapist and patient and less on content (story, history, reinforcement schedules etc.)' (2007: 17).

Part of Strawson's problem with the narrative thesis then, lies in the authenticity of accounts. Jasmine may tell a story in the present about herself in the past, and she may intentionally or non-intentionally falsify part of it, since it is her perception. Strawson says that the more we recall and retell our story the further we move away from an accurate self-understanding. His conclusion is that the best lives 'almost never involve this kind of self-telling' (2004: 437). Conversely, Harré and van Langenhove argue that:

> since there is nothing to which the discourse of selfhood refers except itself, the paradoxical air of internal contradiction vanishes. However, were one's self like one's hat, a real entity existing independently of discourses, a contradictory story told about it could be a cause for concern. (1999: 61)

So essentially, contradictory stories are not a problem – it is awareness of the contradiction in them that is important.

Verisimilitude – Problems of Interpretation

Bruner agrees that narrative constructions can only ever achieve 'verisimilitude'. They are only a version of reality 'whose acceptability is governed by convention and 'narrative necessity' rather than by empirical verification or logical requiredness' (1991: 4). Bruner further suggests that interpretation is unavoidable: 'at the moment a hearer is made suspicious of the "facts" of a story or the ulterior motives of a narrator, he or she immediately becomes hermeneutically alert' (1991: 10). He goes on to highlight two problems of interpretation. The first is 'intention attribution', or why the story is told, how and when it is told and why it is interpreted as it is by the listener. The second is the issue of 'background knowledge' of both the narrator and the listener, and how each of them interprets the background knowledge of the other. However, the client does not need to do the two-way interpersonal interpretive or hermeneutic work required in a normal conversation – because coaching is no ordinary conversation.

Clients are free to examine and interpret only their own stories, unhampered by the response of the coach. When people listen to each others' stories in everyday conversation they are not really listening, only listening well enough to find a link to one of their own stories so that they can have something to say in response.

Not the Whole or Only Story

In the field of narrative therapy, Payne (2006) describes how clients are invited to talk about their concerns and how they often tell stories that embody the present 'dominant story' of their lives. The therapist takes this description seriously, but importantly recognises that it is not the whole, or only, story. Payne explains how narrative therapy also 'embodies an assumption that cultural, social and political factors are enmeshed with the problems people bring to therapy' (2006: 12), and contrasts this with a more humanist tradition. Thus he argues that, unlike person centred therapy, narrative therapy assumes that both human nature and the self are socially constructed (Payne, 2006: 159), so questioning the concept of a 'core self', and suggesting that identity is negotiated (i.e. socially constructed) from moment to moment. From a social constructionist perspective, memories of experiences are not linked; they are more immanent, in the way Strawson argues. They are not imbued with meaning until the autobiographical self (Damasio, 2000) strings memories of experience together in a logical form and a story forms. Story-telling is a way of making experience intelligible to others. Communicating experience in this way helps clients create meaning, helps them position themselves, and provides coaches with information. From what has been discussed here, it seems that people may have a particular imperative to relate stories of experiences that (a) have real meaning to relate in a particular conversational context, or (b) are confusing to them and need to be understood, as in a coaching setting.

Summary

In this chapter I demonstrated how the attempt to articulate experience is a complex process. Clients position themselves in relation to the current conversation with the coach, taking account of all that has transpired between them already, and at the same time explaining how the experience influences the coaching task that will provide the ground for the ongoing coaching alliance. Figure 3.2 showed how any of five self-presentational strategies might be adopted by the client as they attempt to position themselves. These provide the coach with clues to how clients perceive themselves in relation to others. It was also suggested that there is an opportunity to encourage clients to experiment with different strategies in order to broaden their perspectives.

Through the positioning process the coach is able to perceive and feed back on the client's sense of agency or personal responsibility, their self-consciousness which is presented through articulation of points of view, and the narrative ordering of a story as the client continues to explain the experience. An awareness of these elements provides the coach with hints about how to work with the client, maybe by bolstering the sense of agency, or by exploring other viewpoints and perspectives, or by examining how stories might fit a certain narrative, and seeing those narratives as contingent. The chapter also emphasised how clients' articulation of experience includes the development of a storyline, which in turn is linked to a narrative ordering of events that helps them to understand and give meaning to aspects of their lives.

I also suggested here that coaching is not a two-way communication. Because coaches encourage clients to tell their stories without counter-narrative interruption, they have the nature of a soliloquy. I maintain that this client-centred approach allows the coach to facilitate consideration of a variety of alternative perspectives, rather than valorising one response. This is one area where coaching differs from mentoring, since mentors do share their own experiences and perspectives in order to bolster the knowledge of the mentee. In that sense the mentor–mentee interchange is more like everyday conversation.

In the chapter I also identified the danger of the fixed narrative – the reification of the self-story to the exclusion of the development of wider perspectives. The recognition that stories are about me, they are not *me* (Strawson, 2004) is something that coaches of all orientations might want to convey to their clients. There could be something quite liberating about not internalising a narrative and instead letting it remain contingent. Then using narrative techniques and theory becomes a useful heuristic. If coaches do not keep in mind the 'me/not *me*' distinction they may risk never helping their clients to melt the frozen narratives that they find themselves trapped within. The dilemma clients bring to coaching can be viewed as an opportunity to break the ice of the frozen narrative; a chance to explore and thaw.

Whether or not coaches decide to work with a narrative approach in their coaching, they might still agree that it is useful to understand the story and why the client is telling it. The coach then has the option of whether to work with clients on narrative themes and re-storying using a narrative approach as described by Drake (2010a, 2010b), or to adopt another coaching strategy.

4

Listening

Chapter Aims:

- To examine existing theories of listening and their applicability in coaching
- To contrast empathic listening with authentic listening and consider an integrative model of listening for coaches

For all humans there is a yearning for 'witnessed significance' which is satisfied when someone listens to us. This important product of listening has been highlighted by Fleischman who argues that we all have 'the need to be seen, known, responded to, confirmed, appreciated, cared for, mirrored, recognised, identified' (1989: 8). Thus, listening is widely understood as a way of communicating caring and of validation. One of Myers' research respondents confirms its centrality: 'I feel good when I am being listened to because I know that person cares about me and what I'm saying' (2000: 158). This is one of the reasons why listening is such a vital element in coaching: it meets a real human need.

However, as Corradi Fiumara points out, our culture is very much one of 'saying without listening' (1990: 2). She argues that society tends to disregard exchanges that fail to provide immediate information, and describes how a form of habitual listening has become prevalent: 'a trend that acts as both a "norm" and a benumbing limitation' (1990: 84). In addition, in western society, speech appears to have gathered more power than listening. It is perhaps because of this tendency and a move towards habitual listening, particularly in the workplace, that coaching has gathered momentum: coaching, as much as anything, is a listening space.

Also, in coaching, listening plays another role. It plays an important role in building rapport and giving the client a space: it allows clients' articulations of their experience to be heard. Thus it is the first part of a dialogic process that will ultimately lead to the resolution of the coaching task.

In the field of communication, commentators trace the study of listening back to the seminal work of Nichols (1948), whose dissertation appears to have been the catalyst for the recognition of listening as a fundamental component of effective interpersonal contact. The importance of listening is similarly identified as important in many coaching texts, and coaches are constantly reminded of how necessary good listening skills are to the building of trust and rapport in the coaching alliance. Authors, like Skiffington and Zeus (2003: 27), identify active listening as central to a coach's role. Similarly, Hawkins and Schwenk (2010) explain how effective listening builds trust, and how coaching can help clients better when the coach listens at a deeper level. Coleman further acknowledges the paradox that coaches need to listen in order to 'see and understand how their clients perceive their own situation while simultaneously keeping in mind alternative ways of framing those situations' (2002: 20). He suggests that the active listening skills of paraphrasing and reflecting back can 'help them sort things out'.

Brockbank and McGill have a short section on listening that covers its importance, the possibilities for misunderstanding the message and a demonstration of attending using Egan's (2007) SOLER model (Squarely, Open, Lean, Eye-contact and Relaxed). These authors also discuss active listening, which is characterised, they suggest, by making the client aware of the listening as well. It involves 'listening to the whole person, not just the words he or she may be using at the level of intellect' (Brockbank and McGill, 2006: 177). So, active listening, they argue, is more than listening to content; it encompasses 'body messages and, often forgotten, the messages in the vocal channel – the tone of voice used' (Brockbank and McGill, 2006: 181).

Despite the emphasis on listening as a skill, the only coaching authors to devote a whole chapter to listening are Whitworth, Kimsey-House and Sandahl, who confirm that to be properly listened to is a rare experience. They claim that the importance of listening in the coaching alliance cannot be overstated: 'people open up when they know they're really being listened to; they expand; they have more presence. They feel safer and more secure as well, and can begin to trust' (2007: 31). Whitworth et al. also explain how, often in our everyday lives, we seldom need to listen at a deep level, and so our listening muscles are not toned.

However, even though the coaching literature recognises that listening is of the utmost importance, no text explains in any detail how and why listening works. Kemp (2008) comes closest to starting such an exploration when he discusses Reik's (1949) concept of 'listening with the third ear', a process that enables listeners to manage their own perceptions and biases so that, as Kemp suggests, 'less data from the client's unique perspective and context is lost through the coach's filtering process and more richness from the client's own experience can be harnessed' (2008: 42). Kemp's suggestion that the coach's subjective influence can be reduced through this process of bias-management is an idea that is explored later in the chapter.

This chapter on listening is therefore very significant, since it is the first time that a theory of listening for coaching has been attempted. The chapter is divided into five main sections: the first explores the levels of listening that have been presented by a number of authors in the practitioner guidance (Hawkins and Schwenk, 2010; Scharmer, 2008; Whitworth et al., 2007).

Following on from this, in section II, the idea of active listening is explored. Empathic listening is also mentioned frequently in therapy and counselling literatures, and so it is important to explore what is meant by empathy. Section III does this, and then in section IV the concept of generative listening, first introduced by Senge in 1990, is examined. Section IV also looks at the influence of Heidegger and Gadamer on the theory of listening, and considers the concept of authentic listening. In section V, an integrative model of listening for coaches is proposed.

I. Levels of Listening

Levels of listening are introduced by several authors, including Whitworth et al. (2007), Hawkins and Schwenk (2006, 2010) and Scharmer (2008). These three have probably been most widely adopted and are reviewed here:

1 Whitworth, Kimsey-House and Sandahl (2007: 34–39) have made a major contribution to our understanding of listening in relation to coaching through their introduction of three levels of listening:

   - Level 1 – Internal listening. At this level our listening is concerned with the content of speech and what it means to us personally. So, Level 1 listening is concerned with listeners gaining information for their own purposes. Whitworth et al. also suggest that if a coach is listening to inform what he/she is going to ask next, then this is Level 1 listening, too. So level 1 listening is essentially normal listening. In such everyday dialogue, meanings are mutually interpreted.
   - Level 2 – Focused listening. Here the spotlight is totally on the client and the listener will act as a mirror, reflecting back what comes from the client, but also maintaining an awareness of the impact the listening is having on the client. Whitworth et al. claim that in coaching most listening happens at this level: 'it is the level of empathy, creativity, clarification, collaboration and innovation'. They also suggest that 'the mind chatter virtually disappears' (2007: 36–37) in order to facilitate complete focus on the client. Thus, at this level, coaches are not attached to their own agendas, thoughts or opinions.
   - Level 3 – Global listening. Whitworth et al. describe this level as 'environmental' listening. They say it involves 'noticing the temperature, the energy level, the lightness or darkness' (2007: 39) and involves the use of intuition as an enhancement to level 2 listening. Coaches use their 'antennae' to look for energy and emotion, and also to read the impact they themselves are having on the client. They say the coach must be open and 'softly focused' for level 3 listening to happen. Gadamer uses a comparable definition, explaining that '...understanding must be conceived as a part of the event in which meaning occurs, the event in which the meaning of all statements – those of art and all other kinds of

tradition – is formed and actualized' (Gadamer, 2004: 156). So the conversational event itself and its context, the 'environment' in Whitworth et al.'s terminology, are as important as the words used, and are present in the softly focused listening.

2 Similarly, Hawkins and Schwenk (2010) list four levels of listening, which have some overlap with those described by Whitworth et al. The four levels are described as:

    i Attending. This level focuses on the demonstration of listening through eye-contact, posture and other activities that give the speaker the impression that he or she is being listened to. Hawkins and Schwenk point out that loss of eye contact can give the impression to clients that the coach is losing focus, and it appears to the client as if the coach has stopped listening. This situation is made worse, they argue, if the coach does not respond verbally in some way, even if only with Mmm or Ah! This attentiveness is important, and is displayed in a number of semi-verbal and non-verbal ways

   ii Accurate listening. The accurate listening level is described as including all the features of 'attending', but also brings in the accurate paraphrasing of clients' responses. This demonstration of accuracy is termed 'reflecting' in Passmore and Whybrow (2007), and as 'tape-recorder listening' by Egan (2007).

  iii Empathic listening. According to Hawkins and Schwenk (2010), empathic listening incorporates attending and accurate listening, plus it includes the matching of non-verbal cues, sensory frames and metaphors. This they claim helps show that the listener understands the speaker's 'reality'.

  iv Generative empathic listening. The fourth level incorporates the three preceding levels but includes the ability to playback and shape the emerging story that the coachee is sharing.

The first three levels in the Hawkins and Schwenk model are similar to level 2 in Whitworth et al.'s model, but level 4 seems significantly different in that it portrays listening that is potentially more resourceful and creative. However, the idea that the coach might shape the story is one that creates tension.

3 Scharmer (2008) also talks about four levels of listening. In his first level, listening is merely 'downloading', that is, listeners are reconfirming what they already know. In level 2, which he calls 'factual listening', listeners pay attention to what differs from what they already know. They let the new 'data' speak to them so that they notice what is novel in the conversation. In level 3, termed 'empathic listening', the listener's perspective is redirected, and they see the situation through the eyes of the speaker. The fourth and final level is generative listening, in which the listening connects to a deeper source of knowing. In Scharmer's terms this generative listening involves connecting to an emerging future whole, and requires a shift in identity and

self: 'Generative listening involves awareness of the deeper silences within, so that the mind can slow down and hear beneath the words to reach their meaning ... ' (2008: 53).

The term generative listening appears to have been first introduced by Senge et al., where they suggest that to listen fully means:

> ... to pay close attention to what is being said beneath the words. You listen not only to the 'music' but to the very essence of the person speaking. You listen not only for what someone knows, but for who he or she is. Ears operate at the speed of sound, which is far slower than the speed of the light the eyes take in. Generative listening is the art of developing deeper silences in yourself, so you can slow your mind's hearing to your ears' natural speed, and hear beneath the words to their meaning. (1994: 377)

In the coaching literature, Drake also talks about 'deep generative listening' in which the coach is mindful of his/her own impact on story formation and pays 'close attention to the nuances of what is said (and not said) in their interchanges' (2010a: 126–127). Like Whitworth et al. he describes listening as a 360 degree experience, and not as a dyadic transaction. Drake also identifies a paradox when he describes how coaches can be both 'fully engaged and wholly non-attached' (2010a: 127). This appears to echo what Whitworth et al. call being 'open and softly focused' in their description of level 3 listening (2007: 39).

Many helpers (therapists, counsellors, coaches and mentors) also draw on Egan's work. Egan (2007) describes how listening requires the listener to understand the messages communicated by the client, whether those messages are transmitted verbally or non-verbally, clearly or vaguely. His emphasis is on striving to understand the speaker in much the same way as level 2 in Whitworth et al.'s coactive listening levels and levels 1, 2 and 3 in Hawkins and Schwenk, as described above.

As well as creating tensions and paradoxes, the fact that these discussions of listening talk in terms of levels is somewhat misleading. I would suggest that levels of listening are better considered as 'modes' of listening that each serve different purposes, and that the coach can employ all or any of them at particular points in their coaching. In the next sections I shall draw on a variety of philosophical, psychological and neuroscientific theories to investigate active listening, empathic listening and hermeneutic listening in more detail, in readiness for proposing a simple, integrative model of listening for coaching that accommodates different modes of listening for different purposes.

II. Active Listening and the Feeling of Being Heard

Much has been written about active listening in relation to coaching and associated helping interactions such as teaching and counselling. The term appears to have been introduced by Thomas Gordon in the 1970s and has become a popular term for describing the skill of listening and then reflecting back to the speaker the meanings and feelings that the listener discerns. The aim is to test listeners' understandings of their message and arrive at mutual understanding. Gordon (1970) recalls how Carl Rogers referred to such testing as 'reflection of feelings' (i.e. actively reflecting back what clients have just said in relation to affect), and he includes previous research that shows how it does encourage clients to talk freely about their problems. Similarly, Weger, Castle and Emmett (2010) also trace active listening back to Rogers and identify how he saw it as an attempt to demonstrate unconditional positive regard.

In the general communications literature, Collins and O'Rourke describe active listening as requiring engagement of 'not only the intellect but the emotions as well' (2008: 10). These authors suggest that:

> As well as the content, the listener tries to understand the emotions behind what the speaker is trying to say and also draw conclusions about what the speaker is not explicitly stating. Active listeners ask questions to clarify their understanding. They reflect their interpretations of what's being said back to the speaker so that the speaker feels heard and has a chance to correct misunderstandings. (Collins and O'Rourke, 2008: 10)

Collins and O'Rourke are keen to point out that 'parroting' is not what is meant by active listening. In fact their definition of active listening involves blatant use of the listeners' own interpretations, and asking quite leading questions, which would not be appropriate in coaching. More recently, Passmore and Whybrow have described a process of reflective listening where 'the coach checks, rather than assumes' (2007: 165) the meaning of what the client is saying. However, they too explain that this reflection is not a passive process on the part of the coach, since he/she also decides what to reflect back and what to ignore.

Earlier, Whitworth et al. also described active listening as 'clarifying what the other person says, noticing body language, increasing … awareness of the feeling behind the words, and sharpening … sensitivity to the context of the conversation' (1998: 32–33). They suggested that there are two aspects to this: the first is attention, or awareness when coaches need to listen with all their senses and intuition, and the second is for coaches to be aware of the impact of listening on clients. Kraut et al. (1982) identified this second aspect as 'listener responsiveness' which focuses on feedback from listeners. Through it they claim: 'a listener can regulate a speaker's speech as it is happening' (1982: 718). So in active listening it is also important for coaches to be aware of the influence even their listening can have on the client.

Weger, Castle and Emmett (2010) describe active listening as a set of verbal and non-verbal skills, and Shotter has described this non-verbal aspect well, suggesting that 'nods, facial expressions, and "uhm uhms", indicate back to a speaker, while he or she is speaking, that [the listener is] "following" – and, perhaps, even anticipating – the speaker's speech' (2009: 29). So, to be effective, according to Shotter, the listener has to show response: 'all real and integral understanding is actively responsive' (2009: 30). Also, Shotter argues, clients may speak with expectations of indications of agreement, or sympathy, or even challenge on the part of the coach. This suggests that coaches have to remember that each encouraging response, by its very tone, expresses attitudes and values towards the client, and so it is important to be aware of over-sympathising or colluding.

Thus, what Shotter calls 'dialogically responsive listening' (2009: 39) is a developing process which 'can result in both speakers and listeners coming to share a set of determining surrounds for their utterances'. It is a process, he says, in which listeners, by taking 'an active, responsive attitude', reflect back to the speaker, in one way or another, moment by moment in the course of his or her speaking, what, uniquely, the speaker's speech is meaning to the listener in that particular circumstance, at that particular moment (Bakhtin, 1986: 68).

So, in a sense, the listener becomes a speaker. In Bakhtin's terms this means that no meaningful communication can occur without a response, and all understanding is imbued with response and necessarily elicits it in one form or another. So, although coaches are not talking, they are in fact 'speaking' all the time. Shotter further explains how listening is, in effect, a particular, albeit mainly silent, way of 'responsive talking'. He describes this 'talking' as important for allowing speakers opportunities to 'tell of, and to explore further, events and experiences that have mattered to them in their lives – but which can arouse within them a distinctive and recognizable feeling of being heard' (Shotter, 2009: 21). Generating the feeling of being heard is, it could be argued, one of the main functions of listening in coaching, and it is achieved through active listening.

In addition, Shotter points out that spoken and other bodily activities occur together 'in a unity' and cannot be separated, 'thus the listener who also sees as well as listens, will notice that various spoken words "touch" the speakers to such an extent that one can see them being moved by their own words' (Shotter, 2009: 35). Experienced coaches frequently bring this 'seeing while listening' into their next reply. For example, the coach may observe: 'When you said [such and such], I noticed that you seemed to have more energy'. Whitworth et al.'s level 3 listening is similar.

Shotter concludes that if, as a speaker, I sense you as

> not being responsive to me, but as pursuing an agenda of your own, then I will feel immediately offended in an ethical way. I will feel not only that you lack respect for our affairs, but a lack of respect for me too. In such circumstances, not only do I feel insulted, but I lack the social conditions necessary to express myself ... (2009: 40)

There is thus an ethical imperative to listening as well.

Egan (2007: 136) describes a whole range of activities covered by the term active listening and confirms that the aim of active listening is to build or demonstrate empathy by listening to clients' stories and their search for solutions.

The main function of active listening can therefore be viewed as a way to generate trust, understanding and the feeling of being heard (Myers, 2000). It suggests to the speaker that the listener is empathising with his/her situation.

III. Empathic Listening

The concept of empathy originated in aesthetics and related to 'the attribution to or projection into an art object of a viewer's feelings' (Jackson, 1992: 1626). Translated to human to human relationships, Adler and Towne describe it as 'the ability to project oneself into another person's point of view, so as to experience the other's thoughts and feelings' (1990: 400).

Collins and O'Rourke (2008: 10) argue that empathic listening is listening at its deepest level. Unlike in active listening, they say, when we listen empathically we try to step out of our own perspective and view things from the other person's perspective, not only understanding what the person is saying and feeling, but empathising with it. So it appears that empathic listening goes further than active listening, since it requires the coach to listen non-judgementally. This does not mean that a coach will agree with or condone what the client may be saying; just that he/she is willing to set opinions aside long enough to see how the client views the world.

Empathy is described most thoroughly by Rogers (1980), who was convinced of its utmost importance to the counselling relationship. He worked on the concept for many years and his early definition is worth noting:

> Empathy, or being empathic, is to receive the internal frame of reference of another with accuracy and with the emotional components and meanings which pertain thereto as if one were the person, but without ever losing the 'as if' condition. Thus it means to sense the hurt or the pleasure of another as he senses it and to perceive the causes thereof as he perceives them, but without ever losing the recognition that it is *as if I* were hurt or pleased and so forth. If this 'as if' quality is lost, then the state is one of identification. (Rogers, 1959: 210–211, emphasis added)

In this quote we see the 'distancing' that Rogers thought the counsellor could achieve. In his later definition, where he moves to a view of empathy as a process, he argues that the term has several facets:

> It means entering the private perceptual world of the other and becoming thoroughly at home in it. It involves being sensitive moment to moment, to the changing felt meanings which flow in this other person, to the fear or rage or tenderness or confusion or whatever, that he/she is experiencing. It means temporarily living his/her life, moving about in it delicately without making judgments, sensing meanings of which he/she is scarcely aware, but not trying to uncover the feelings of which the person is

totally unaware, since this would be too threatening. It includes communicating your sensings of his/her world as you look with fresh and unfrightened eyes at elements of which the individual is fearful. It means frequently checking with him/her as to the accuracy of your sensings, and being guided by the responses you receive. (Rogers, 1975: 4)

Rogers goes on to explain that the counsellor becomes a 'confident companion to the person in his/her inner world', and that by being in what he calls 'the flow of his/her experiencing' the counsellor helps the client to understand more fully and 'to move forward' (Rogers, 1959: 210–211). He also argues that to be with another in this way means that counsellors bracket their own views and values in order to enter the client's world without prejudice. He adds:

In some sense it means that you lay aside your self and this can only be done by a person who is secure enough in himself that he knows he will not get lost in what may turn out to be the strange or bizarre world of the other, and can comfortably return to his own world when he wishes. (Rogers, 1980: 143)

So, empathic listening as described above can be useful in the counselling or therapy relationship. However, its function in coaching may be limited. The descriptions above, suggest that clients' 'states' are hidden and must be discerned through empathic listening, and other forms of therapy work. It is almost as though the client is an object with static points of view that the therapist must try to understand. In a therapeutic setting the objectivity of the empathic approach has been useful because it has enabled the medical model of therapy to be applied: the therapist empathises with clients enough to gain trust and gather information about their state of mind, and is then equipped to make a diagnosis. Thwaites and Bennett-Levy describe how empathy is important, particularly in cognitive behavioural therapy, 'to communicate an awareness of the client's state, helping her to label it, modelling acceptance, and validating her difficulties in the context of her learning history' (2007: 598). However, in coaching, even such benign hypothesis testing is not generally acceptable.

The usefulness of empathy in the coaching process is much more limited: empathy may conceivably be useful during initial exploration and trust building, but it cannot assist hypothesis formulation, since coaching does not follow a medical model. Thwaites and Bennett-Levy (2007) present a model of empathy with four facets: empathic stance; empathic attunement; empathic communication skills; and empathy knowledge. This is helpful, for in coaching it is only the empathic stance, that is natural empathy, which is appropriate. The coach does not use empathy for diagnosis and treatment, as implied in the other three facets. In fact, I would argue that in coaching the use of empathy in the therapeutic sense is an anathema. Coaches remain non-judgemental in relation to the client throughout the process in order to engender a sense of the clients' ownership of their coaching issues. There is no room for any element of analysis on the part of the coach, and therefore total reliance on the therapeutic definition of empathic listening is misplaced in the coaching process. I am proposing, therefore, that empathy must play a different role in coaching, a more reflexive role. In coaching, I would suggest, there is less emphasis on attunement with the moment to moment psychological state of the client, and more on what is being constructed or produced between coach and client in the coaching room.

The previous accounts all described empathy as the conscious activity of putting oneself into the psychical state of the other person (Jackson, 1992: 1626). But Jackson too is critical of this empathic approach because of the seemingly positivist way in which empathy relies on an *accurate* understanding of the client's subjectivity: Rogers had confirmed that 'the ability to be *accurately* empathic is something which can be developed by training' (1980: 150, emphasis added). This emphasis on accuracy suggests that there is something specific within the client that needs to be considered and to be considered correctly.

Jackson's critique continues: 'the healer has listened in his special ways, but, all too often has heard mainly through the filters provided by his categories of investigative procedures, his diagnoses, and his technologically based interventions. And somehow the sufferer has been put at a distance' (Jackson, 1992: 1630). He mentions Schwaber's work (1981) where empathic listening is described as a form of analytic listening that tries to be independent of theories, to bracket them, and thus minimise the introduction of an outsider view. This, and other theories of empathy, could be seen as based on Freud's theory of listening which was founded on the notion of 'evenly suspended attention'. Underpinning this theory was the assumption that the patient's voice provides clues 'to revealing tensions or blockages in the unconscious drives that make up that person' (Lagaay, 2008: 54). However, as Lagaay reminds us, Freud 'warned of the danger that the analyst, perhaps in listening too attentively to what the patient says, might project unjustified meaning onto certain aspects of the narrative, thus letting conscious or unconscious intentions of his own interfere with the interpretation' (2008: 55). Thus, the 'evenly suspended attention' that Freud advocated appears to be his antidote to listener bias; it involves a kind of bracketing or 'laying aside', which is Rogers' terminology for describing how therapists should set aside their own values and judgements in order to grasp what the client is experiencing. Reik explains this process:

> if we strain our attention to a certain point, if we begin to select from among the data offered and seize upon one fragment especially, then ... we follow our own expectations or inclinations. The danger naturally arises that we may never find anything but what we are prepared to find. (1949: 158)

Interestingly, this notion is still evident in level 2 of Whitworth et al.'s model, when they talk of 'mind-chatter' disappearing.

Reik takes Freud's theory a step further, using Nietzsche's concept of the 'third ear' to describe a kind of listening that does not have as its focus the understanding of the words being spoken, but acts instead as a conduit for receiving signs and signals from the speaker that reveal aspects of their unconscious: 'it is not the words spoken by the voice that are of importance, but what it tells us of the speaker. Its tone comes to be more important than what it tells' (Reik, 1949: 136). Reik claims that for therapists to learn how one mind speaks to another they must learn to listen with this third ear, which he describes as 'a little known and concealed organ [that] receives and transmits the secret messages of others before [the helper] consciously understands them himself' (Reik, 1949: 146–147). The third ear 'can catch what other people do not say, but only feel and think; and it can also be turned inward. It can hear voices from within the self that are otherwise not audible because they are drowned out by the noise of our conscious thought-processes' (Reik, 1949: 146–147).

Thus, according to Reik, listening with the third ear also involves listeners embracing their own inner voices, rather than bracketing them, so that they can arrive at a deeper psychological understanding of others and of themselves (Reik, 1949). This notion has similarities with the level 3 listening of the Co-active Model expounded by Whitworth et al. (2007), and is perhaps one of the differences between coaching and therapy: whereas coaching maintains the client's right to be provided with an open sharing of such insights, the therapist might conceal his/her thoughts until a 'diagnosis' is sure, for fear of unsettling the client. So the coach needs to attend to the tone of the client's voice, and to notice changes and variations and report these to the client. The information is gathered in service of the client.

IV. Authentic Listening

I now want to develop an argument that suggests empathic listening can only ever be a partial approach to listening in the coaching alliance. The argument builds on the idea that the scientific basis of an empathic listening approach, already mentioned, is not in accord with coaching's constructivist ethos. To do this I examine Heidegger's contribution to listening theory, which emphasises human ontology. Dreyfus (1991: 47) noted that resulting from Heidegger's work, the notion of the separate or detached, meaning-giving, knowing subject becomes augmented by an embodied, meaning-giving, doing subject. Also, in his discussion of Heidegger's work, Hyde has suggested that a hermeneutic phenomenology of listening, such as that advocated by Heidegger, 'arrives at significant insights that are not reached by the dominant empathic approach' (1994: 179).

Following Stewart's (1983) discussion of interpretive listening, Hyde argues that the empathic approach to listening belongs to a reproductive model, since it attempts to reproduce for the therapist, a representation or reflection of the feelings and thoughts of the client. A phenomenological hermeneutic (interpretive) approach, on the other hand, views human understanding as productive: 'Rather than seeing the goal of interpretation as the reproduction of the text or speaker's inner meanings, this view posits that meanings are in fact "outer," created in interaction between text and reader, or between speaker and listener' (Hyde, 1994: 180).

This productive/reproductive dichotomy, as explained by Hyde (1994), is important: a model of communication based in hermeneutic phenomenology recognises that, because the meaning of a conversation is mutually created, both participants are involved in the creation of their world. So, the focus of the understanding is the communicative event, rather than clients' unilateral realities, or as Hyde terms them, 'the objectified psychological entities, the "reified selves" of the empathic paradigm' (1994: 180). This distinction seems to be pivotal to the definition of coaching. Coaching is a co-construction; it is a production rather than a reproduction.

Shotter suggests that when

> two or more forms of life 'rub together' … in their meetings, they always create a third or a collective form of life within which (a) they all sense themselves as participating, and which (b) has a life of its own, with its own voice, and its own way of 'pointing' toward the future. (2009: 26)

On this account, there is always a 'production' which consists of more than the sum of the parts. The coaching alliance is not just the coach trying to empathise with and understand the client. There is a dynamic imperative to create or produce a new understanding that can carry the client forward.

Hyde also argues that 'listening effectively to another means to be-with the other in a particular way' (1994: 181). He suggests a hermeneutic step back is necessary that entails that we look at how we arrived at our current understanding, since we are normally 'oblivious to our inauthenticity'. In Heidegger's words, 'we must first leap onto the soil on which we really stand' (1968: 41). This way of 'being-with' another can be characterised by the Heideggerian term *authentic*, which, Hyde argues, suggests a kind of 'mineness' or 'ownedness', where we are aware of our inauthenticities, and own them, accept them and make choices between them. Hyde calls this metacognitive identification of, but not with, our inauthenticity, 'the first authentic act' (1994: 182).

Hyde goes on to suggest that this more authentic approach to listening is interpersonal and is a way of 'listening generated by our way of being' (1994: 181). Empathy, he points out, only emphasises the difference between the coach and the client, and therefore belongs to a pseudo-positivist ontology, where checking of the others' mind-contents is deemed important. Empathy forms a bridge between subjects, and reinforces the idea of humans as isolated and different, requiring effort to understand. Hyde describes how that notion is based in Cartesian dualism.

In Table 4.1 empathic listening and authentic listening are juxtaposed in order to highlight the philosophical and practical differences.

Table 4.1   Comparison of empathic and authentic listening

	Empathic listening	**Authentic listening**
Ontology	Scientific Realism – where reality is apprehendable by the helper	Interpretivist – where meaning is constructed in concert with the client
Epistemology	Dualist/Objectivist – clients' feelings and viewpoints are true and can be known	Subjectivist/Relativist – clients and helpers create their own ever-shifting realities
Paradigm	Positivist	Constructivist; Hermeneutic
Proponents	Freud, Rogers, Egan	Heidegger, Gadamer, Marzano, Stewart
Methodology	Verification of hypotheses	Dialectical co-construction and interpretation of meaning
Synonyms	Reflective Listening; Accurate Listening	Hermeneutic Listening; Ontological Listening; Generative Listening
Mode	Reproductive	Productive
Focus	Client's internal experience	Client's and coach's verbal and non-verbal communicative action
Goals	(i) To try to understand the client (ii) To suspend prejudices in order to reproduce the client's experience in 'me' as helper	(i) To be present for the client (ii) To affirm and use both coach and client prejudices in order to produce meaning
Outcome	Understanding is an object The client's view is seen as a unit of objective knowing	Understanding is subjective, contingent and co-produced

Listening authentically (as can be seen in Table 4.1) belongs to a hermeneutic phenomenology which is socially constructed. Authentic listening reinforces sameness not difference, emerging from what Gallese terms 'the shared manifold of intersubjectivity' (2003: 171). Gallese draws on recent neuroscience to explain how the matching mechanism produced by mirror neurons in the brain would appear to enable significant intersubjective experiences. He argues that the capacity to understand others is grounded in the inherent relational nature of our interactions with the world: 'an implicit, pre-reflexive form of understanding of other individuals is based on the strong sense of identity binding us to them' (Gallese, 2003: 171). Schwartz's work (2009) also appears to confirm this relation, claiming that values are shared human constructs, which even have coherence across cultures. They are embedded at the visceral level of survival. This suggests that the coach and client will have shared values, although there may be degrees of emphasis. Thus, bracketing our own concerns, as in empathic listening, would fracture that relationship.

Hyde also talks about the existential priority of 'being-with' which gives the coach an inherent understanding of the client. This is not a psychological or empathic understanding based on acquiring information at the level of personal identity, rather it is an 'ontological understanding, based in shared being' (Hyde, 1994: 188). This echoes Merleau-Ponty's arguments that listeners do not need to interpret a speaker's utterances to grasp his or her thought, for 'the listener receives thought from speech itself' (1962: 178). Merleau-Ponty suggests that meaning is immanent in speech and that there is 'a thought in speech the existence of which is unsuspected by intellectualism' (1962: 179). This recognition of embeddedness is also evident in Gallese's (2003) notion of a 'shared manifold', whereby we recognise other human beings as similar to us.

Building on this notion, Hyde further suggests that 'a human being is a listening' – that is, listening is not something that human beings do; it is rather something that they are:

> One is never simply an empty vessel, a passive receptor into which another pours the content of his or her speaking. Rather each of us at every moment is always already listening in a particular way, listening from the ontological locus of our own particular set of values and concerns. Our way of being and our understanding of the world, given by these values and concerns, constitutes the listening that each of us always already is, the listening that determines the way the world occurs for us. (1994: 184)

In Heideggerian terms, the effort to be empathic suggests that there is an element of striving that is yet another inauthentic concern for the coach. The emphasis on imitation (and reproduction) in empathic listening was described by Heidegger as *ersatz* in its nature (Hyde, 1994). By *ersatz* he meant that it is a substitute activity that replicates inauthenticity. According to Heidegger, human beings, in their everyday relationships with one another, are 'thrown' into an inauthentic mode of being that is formed through our language and other socially and culturally constructed artefacts. Thus, authenticity becomes something that comes through awareness of alternative theories and perspectives, critical thinking and making informed and committed choices. It is something that can be achieved, but first, as Heidegger suggests, it is necessary to both recognise its lack, and yet no longer feel like a prisoner with no choices, which is the fate of the person trapped in an inauthentic way of being.

Heidegger further indicates there is no need to search for an authentic identity – we touch authenticity when we make choices from an informed place, when we author our lives. So there is a liberation about it, rather than a tension.

Authentic listening then involves helping clients to explore their values and beliefs in relation to the paradigms and theories that they hold fast to. In fact, Heidegger would say that such personalised theories are the root of our inauthenticity, and to be authentic as human beings we should knock holes in them, shake them up and reform them, ultimately abandoning them as sole controlling forces and making choices and commitments based on wider perspectives and a range of paradigms.

The Role of Bias in Authentic Listening

The authentic approach to listening recognises that humans necessarily use language and conversation to interpret, explain and make sense of their experience. According to Gadamer, conversation requires us to bring our own presuppositions and prejudices into 'play' (*spiel*) in order to begin the task of understanding. In fact, he argues, that the very act of understanding involves a process of projecting our prejudices. He explains how 'pure seeing and pure hearing are dogmatic abstractions that artificially reduce phenomena. Perception always includes meaning' (Gadamer, 2004: 80). Rather, Gadamer suggests, we should identify our opinions and biases so that we can then recognise the authentic questions of the other person (in this case the client). He also suggests that prejudices can be positive or negative, and so if we claim that all prejudices are unhelpful or misleading, this in itself is a 'prejudice against prejudice'. Gadamer's approach is to make prejudices and biases explicit in the search for understanding. For him, knowledge is a 'coping with' reality, and he defines human understanding as a type of practical understanding (phronesis) based on a social process of constructing justification. So, as White comments: 'interpersonal understanding is ... the result of the back and forth process of conversational understanding' (1994: 96).

This reading of Gadamer's theory suggests that coaching is a hermeneutic project: it is in the very process of communication that understanding develops. This suggests a different role for listening, rather than just communicating empathy. It also differentiates it substantially from therapy and counselling, which by their very nature adopt a scientific/objectivist approach, and from mentoring which implies some form of transmission of knowledge.

If as coaches we do not bracket off our prejudices, in the way empathic listening would propose, then our listening will inevitably be rooted in our own self interest and our own hypotheses. However, as Hyde (1994), explains honest self-reflection can reveal when we are listening for personal reinforcement or for the validation of our own perspectives. He suggests that the 'unconcealment of this all pervasive self-interest, and the degree to which, in the normal course of events we effectively conceal it from ourselves and attempt to conceal it from others is a first step in confronting human inauthenticity' (Hyde, 1994: 185). It is important too, he argues, to recognise a paradox that accompanies this: attempts to conceal self-interest merely reinforce it since any attempt will itself be an act of self-interest. Thus, bracketing and failing to recognise, confront and articulate our own values and meaning perspectives as they arise becomes an inauthentic act. The authentic coach uses his/her prejudices openly and productively in service of the client, seeking the support of a supervisor to help with the kind of candid self-reflection necessary in this process.

V. Summary: An Integrative Model of Listening

No research has been carried out to explore the function of listening in coaching, and so research theories from other disciplines, such as psychotherapy, have been uncritically adopted. Yet, as I have shown in this chapter, in therapy listening plays a quite different role than in coaching. For instance Myers (2000) confirms that in therapy settings listening overcomes the misunderstandings that hinder empathy. However, in coaching being misunderstood by the coach could have useful consequences for clients, since it causes both to examine their perspectives and beliefs, which in turn enables them to look more closely and constructively at what they intend.

In this chapter I have argued that although the levels of listening introduced by Whitworth et al. (2007) and Hawkins and Schwenk (2010) are useful, they give the impression of a hierarchy, where there are 'higher' or 'deeper' levels of listening. I have attempted to substitute an holistic model, based on evidence from philosophy and neuroscience, as well as psychology, which suggests that listening in coaching should follow a hermeneutic paradigm that allows for openness and authentic interpretation and combine this with active listening techniques in order to provide the feeling of being heard. I have tried to show how authentic listening is not a development from active listening, as suggested in some other extant models, but is fundamentally connected to it. It is not at a different level, it is incorporated in it. In the integrative listening model that I now propose, coaches need to look inside, even as they look outside. A Mobius strip is used to illustrate the integration and is shown in Figure 4.1. It is positioned within the shared manifold of human understanding that generates and produces meaning, and it works seamlessly with this through a combination of active and authentic listening.

This model of listening with its emphasis on reflexivity and openness would help clients to mitigate the tension between presenting identities that may be functionally and socially acceptable but may not be authentic.

In coaching, clients are frequently focused on their own concerns and interests, and the coaching task might well be something that helps maintain for them a potentially inauthentic position in the world. This could be something

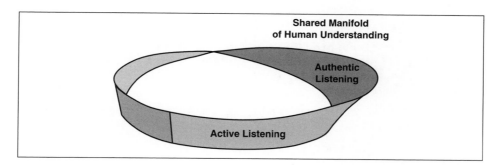

Figure 4.1   Modes of listening in coaching

they feel trapped by or ambivalent about. It is easy for anyone to get trapped by society, the workplace and relationships into the prevailing dualistic interpretations of reality, where absolutes reign: success vs failure, celebrity vs obscurity, right vs wrong, finding the right person for this job, finding the right job for this person. In this inauthentic condition 'everyone is the other and no one is himself' (Heidegger, 1962: 165).

Unfortunately, however, clients do not often ask for guidance on being authentic, since they are unlikely to be aware of the underpinning theory or the benefits authenticity can bring. So even if coaches are in touch with an authentic way of being themselves, they may wonder whether they even have the right to move the client towards that place. However, becoming authentic themselves in the way Heidegger proposes, and using authentic listening in their coaching, can be seen as a first, important step towards helping clients.

To use authentic listening I have suggested that coaches get away from trying to listen to what the client means through an empathic approach, which is essentially reproductive, and use coaching as a 'production' or an 'authoring', where meaning is created through what two people (client and coach) bring to the alliance. It would offer clients:

1) an experience of their paradigms as constructed realities as opposed to absolute reality, and

2) an experience of consciousness other than the 'I' that may be currently so embedded in their paradigms. (Marzano et al., 1995: 167)

From this, it can be seen that authentic listening is the more congruent approach for use in coaching since it is openly and mutually interpretive. It is also generative.

5
Clarifying

Chapter Aims:

- To examine clarification techniques as they apply to coaching
- To differentiate between paraphrasing, mirroring and reflecting back
- To understand the role of summarising

In Chapter 4, I argued that meaning and understanding are produced through a combination of active and authentic listening. In this chapter, I take the work of the coach a step further and examine the types of responses that the coach can make in order to clarify what the client has said, and also explore the purpose for doing so.

Gabbard (2009) describes clarification as an awareness-expanding intervention aimed at reducing distortion or pointing out patterns. In supportive psychotherapy, he says, the therapist clarifies frequently, and this is done by 'restating, acknowledging, summarising, paraphrasing or organising a patient's statements' (2009: 435). Thus, clarification enables the therapist to remain at the level of description without going beyond the data – it avoids interpretation. Clarification, according to Gabbard, 'reduces cognitive distortion or points out patterns by restating, acknowledging, summarising, paraphrasing or organising a patient's statements' (2009: 435). Gabbard's overtly realist description is not entirely congruent with a coaching approach, however, and in this chapter, I aim to explain how clarification techniques, whilst appearing to have a cognitive psychological origin, can also be useful for the coach, and support a constructivist philosophy.

Like active listening, clarifying techniques, such as mirroring, not only reassure clients that they are being listened to and understood but also help them to be sure of their own experiences and feelings. Thus, although clarifying necessitates active listening in order to generate a feeling of being listened to, it has a much wider function. It enables the coach to help clients understand their own words, and provides a basis for joint understanding in the coaching alliance. So, as well as creating initial empathy, which may be useful for rapport building, clarifying also promotes clarity of thinking, and keeps clients focused, helping them ultimately to reflect on and make meaning of their experience and the task they have set themselves. Clients may come to coaching because they are unable to make sense of their experiences and need help in putting things into perspective so that they can make choices and move forward. Their initial response, as discussed in earlier chapters, may include an admission of confusion or stuckness. So, clarification can be essential in order to create insights and promote thinking about other ways of approaching things.

In the coaching literature, Passmore (2006) suggests that clarifying is one of the most powerful tools, and identifies the skills of clarifying as: repeating back in different words; summarising; and reflecting back the exact words. Similarly Whitworth et al. suggest that 'the skill of clarifying is a combination of listening, asking and reframing, whereby the coach can offer different perspectives in order to help the client gain clarity' (1998: 40–45). Some authors also mention a clarifying 'stage' of coaching. Cope, for instance, maintains that: 'in the clarification stage we aim to delve further into the picture that the client has painted, to understand some of the deeper truths (both known and unknown) that might be preventing the client from resolving their issue' (2004: 74).

In fact, most coaching texts describe stages of coaching and include an understanding stage (see for example, Ladyshewsky, 2010; Starr, 2007). Sometimes in practice, however, this clarification stage is neglected or rushed, and the coach and client can continue working together, only to find later that the client becomes stuck or demotivated.

As with most coaching techniques, clarification methods are discussed in most detail in the literature from other helping fields such as counselling and family therapy. In the family therapy literature, for example, Conoley and Conoley (2009) suggest that clarification serves four purposes. When applied to the coaching context these purposes can be summarised as:

1 to create the feeling of being heard, already mentioned as being necessary but not sufficient in the coaching process;
2 to clarify for the coach what is important for the client thus resolving ambiguity;
3 to begin a process of self-discovery for the client; it enables the client to confirm or revise the paraphrase;
4 to guide the coaching process effectively, reinforcing the coach's role as the 'guide' or facilitator of the process. Thus there is an element of control of the process.

Ivey, Ivey and Zalaquett (2009) also explain how encouraging, paraphrasing and summarising involve saying back to clients what the helper has heard, using the client's key words. All three work by 'distilling, shortening and clarifying what has been said' (2009: 151).

Encouraging, however, really belongs to the active listening discussion, as it involves the variety of verbal and non-verbal methods that a coach might use to prompt clients to continue talking. These methods include hand gestures, nodding and using 'Uh-huh' type utterances. Encouraging might also involve the repetition of some of the client's key words. Restatements, Ivey et al.

explain (2009) are extended encouragers, involving repetition of two or more words exactly as used by the client. Paraphrasing, however, sometimes called reflection of content, captures the essence of what the client has said and involves the coach shortening and simplifying the client's utterances. Summarising is similar to paraphrasing, but is used to clarify and distil what the client has said over a longer time span.

It appears then that clarification approaches fall into two groups: those that repeat back the client's words with a focus on accuracy – echoing or mirroring – and those that attempt to gather or marshal the client's thoughts and ideas using interpretation by the coach: paraphrasing or summarising. I have therefore divided the remainder of this chapter into two sections that reflect these groupings: the first explores the purpose and effect of reflecting back content, or mirroring using the client's exact words. In this section there is also a discussion of clean language, since this is a strategy used by some coaches to reflect back to the client in order to gain clarity. The second section looks at strategies for clarifying that rework the client's response in some way: paraphrasing, the interpretation of emotion, and summarising.

I. Strategies for Clarifying that Repeat Clients' Words

(1) Reflecting Back as Mirroring

In Chapter 4, reflecting back was identified as an important part of active listening. In this section, the rationale for reflecting back is explored in more detail and in particular an inherent confusion is uncovered and explained.

Hardingham (2004) uses the term 'mirroring' to describe the phenomenon where the coach reflects back to clients what they are saying. She explains how, as a consequence, they begin to see themselves more clearly. Thus, reflecting back clients' words communicates to them not only that their coach has heard them, but offers up a mirror to those words so that clients can listen to what they have said. However, as Gavin points out, reflecting back of content is 'probably one of the most misunderstood and underestimated skills in the helping professions' (2005: 102). He identifies that some authors refer to paraphrasing as reflection of content, whilst others call it mirroring. He talks about reflecting back as using the exact words of the client. Passmore (2006) also appears to differentiate 'repeating back' from reflecting back, so there is some sense in the coaching literature that a distinction is being made. However, I would want to make a clear distinction between paraphrasing and reflecting back. Paraphrasing, as will be discussed in the next part of this chapter, involves an interpretation by the coach and use of different words to stimulate thinking and reflection for the client. By contrast, reflection of content, sometimes referred to as reflecting back, mirroring, or even echoing (Heron, 1999), uses the same words and repeats them back to the client.

In Gavin's own words, reflection of content appears to have a different effect on the client: 'by hearing their own words reflected back, they have opportunities to reflect on their thoughts and issues and to modify, evaluate, or acknowledge them for what they are' (2005: 102). This is different from paraphrasing: 'If the coach has used synonymous expressions, as in paraphrase, they may fail to capture the true meaning intended by the client' (Gavin, 2005: 102).

However, Gavin also identifies how reflecting content can be risky: 'the client may not realize what he has said, and upon hearing his own words fed back to him, he may reject the presentation as an inaccurate portrayal of the issues' (Gavin, 2005: 103). This emphasis again on accuracy suggests that reflecting back, or mirroring or echoing, is a strategy that has its origins in the scientific base of psychology. When Collins and O'Rourke (2009), for example, talk about reflecting back the content of a speaker's message, they suggest it is to ensure they are interpreting a message in the manner intended. They confirm that this reflection can take the form of perception checking. For Wilson too, reflecting means 'repeating someone's words back exactly as they were spoken, including tone and body language' (2007: 26). These references to true meaning, suggest a positivist view of knowledge, as discussed in Chapter 4. They suggest that the client has views, beliefs and perspectives that are 'true', and in a sense that implies something idiosyncratic and static, rather than something jointly created.

Sometimes early in the coaching alliance clients may agree with a paraphrase, rather than counter it with a different formulation of what they really mean – the trust in the coach may not yet have developed enough to counter the paraphrase. Coaches might therefore want to consider using reflecting back, and repeat back to the client his or her own words. This can have the effect of demonstrating listening and of showing that the client's words are valuable. It is also a useful technique at other times in the coaching process. For example, in my work with Jasmine, I used this to highlight to her when she was stuck in the drama triangle (Karpman, 1976):

Jasmine: It happened again this week, I was in the office and he came in, giving me surly looks. I can't bear it.

Coach: So, he came in giving you surly looks and you can't bear it.

Jasmine: That's right. I could tell he'd just been talking about me to Brian. He had that sheepish look.

Coach: OK, you could tell he'd been talking to Brian because he had that sheepish look …

Jasmine: Oh! I'm doing it again aren't I? I'm supposing because he looked at me strange, that he'd been talking about me. [pause] I expect there could be other reasons.

In the next section the concept of clean language is explored as an example of a stylised method of using reflecting back, which is designed again to acknowledge the value of the client's current perspectives.

(2) Clean Language

The concept of clean language was introduced in the 1980s by David Grove (Grove and Panzer, 1991), and aspires to uncover clients' personal metaphors without contamination of their view of the world. The use of clean language could be seen as an extension of reflecting back, since it also involves repeating the language used by the client. However, clean language takes the notion of reflecting content a significant stage further. Owen argues that language is a sixth sense 'through which we perceive the world and know meanings' (1991: 307). Thus, the words of a language enable us to categorise, to develop meanings, and to know our experiences. If this is the case, then how the coach responds to clients is very important.

Owen explains how using clean language invites clients to 'discover for themselves their internal processes' (Owen, 1996: 314), and describes a process whereby questions are asked of the client, using the client's words, that only the client can answer since they relate directly to the experience as described by the client, not as paraphrased by the coach.

Bracketing and purification are achieved by the attempt at exclusion of the coach's current assumptions, beliefs, biases and presuppositions of the coach.

Owen also suggests that Grove's model of clean language uses an awareness of the interconnection between speech and what it normally does to change the meanings of a person's lived experience. Clean language is characterised by the use of bland repetitive questions which create a 'synchronic and diachronic phenomenology' (Owen, 1996: 273) that aims to capture 'alive' the metaphorical answers from ordinary speech. Repetitive questioning elicits clients' meanings and experiences, together with any associated subjective experiences. Thus, the technique is information based and questions are developed that seek information about the symbolic way in which the client makes meaning of the world. In a simple and repeatable interaction, it structures and elicits descriptions of lived experience and reveals new information about the client's language and its relation to their experience. It is argued that it does this through a self-reflexive and partially closed system of feedback between what is interpreted as 'outside' and what is maintained and created 'inside' through the construction of language (Owen, 1996). Thus it is assumed that language and experience are intimately connected. Language is assumed to influence pre-reflective experience, not just when an experience is made manifest in thought or speech.

The main tenets of clean language can be adapted for a coaching context, in a similar way to focusing, discussed in Chapter 2. Since it requires clients to change from direct non-reflective involvement with the world (their everyday interactions) to begin to reflect about everything and anything, the nature of their intentional acts is clarified and forms the sole focus of subsequent questions. Questions are used to elicit how clients perceive, interpret and impose their representations of the world through metaphor and symbolic language.

Clean language assumes a transcendental phenomenological epistemology. Owen explains how the psychological and transcendental phenomena produced in clean language exchanges are claimed to be pure psychic verbal representations of phenomena, which are not interpreted or made abstract by intellectualising them. The method imposes as little meaning as possible on to the descriptions being produced. Consequently, there is no analysis or discussion during the process. Clients remain at a level of description and can attend to any signifiers, aims or intentional awarenesses (Owen, 1996). The method elicits descriptions of their experience in their own terms, via their own metaphors, ideally with the smallest amount of disturbance from the questioner.

Lakoff and Johnson (1981) suggest that metaphors provide important clues to the way the brain conceptualises things, claiming that thought is based on unconscious physical metaphors, and that our beliefs are then determined by the metaphors in which our ideas are framed. They argue that metaphor is not an occasional foray into the world of figurative language, but the fundamental basis for everyday cognition:

> In all aspects of life, we define our reality in terms of metaphors and then proceed to act on the basis of the metaphors. We draw inferences, set goals, make commitments, and execute plans, all on the basis of how we in part structure our experience, consciously and unconsciously, by means of metaphor. (Lakoff and Johnson, 1981: 158)

Put simply, it could be argued that metaphors are in fact our own paraphrases of our experiences; they are the only way we can put things into words to be understood. Metaphors saturate our language, and, according to Pinker, 'spin off variations that people easily understand (such as "We need to step on the brakes")' (2006: 24). Furthermore, when a client uses an expression, especially one that contains a metaphor such as 'My boss is a tyrant', Owen would say that these words have 'a great physical quality because they are born of felt experience' (1991: 308). They are not rationalisations of the felt experience. Jasmine may talk about being 'stabbed in the back' or about the office environment as a 'vicious circle', and these words allow the dynamic nature of her experience to be described. Consequently, a paraphrase of such terms would be unacceptable, potentially destroying a fundamental relationship between experience and word.

The clean language process involves asking questions that repeat the words used by the client, as this dialogue illustrates:

Client: The board meetings wear me out. It's like all the energy has been sucked from me.

Coach: And when you're worn out and all your energy has been sucked from you, that's like what?

So already the coach has identified a metaphor and asks the client to expand the metaphor in order to understand it better. The client may answer:

Client: It's like I'm a limpet, clinging on, no backbone.

and the coach can continue to repeat questions that begin 'and is there anything else about that limpet?' or 'what happens when you are clinging on?' in order to reach a place, which, as Wilson (2007) describes, features calm and positive symbols. It is claimed that this process helps clients to work through their anxieties on a subconscious level, and that the repetition of questions allows self-knowledge to emerge.

There is little empirical evidence relating to the use of clean language. However, Hyer and Brandsma (1997) do report on a proposed intervention of Eye Movement Desensitization and Reprocessing (EMDR) in which they propose clean language as an element of intervention in trauma situations. Clean language, they explain, involves the therapist's use of 'non-leading language that keeps the focus on the target in an uncontaminated way' (1997: 519). Hyer and Brandsma argue that 'by the mere act of the "clean" loosening the infrastructure of the trauma (as with penetrating oil), the stuck symbol, idea, sensation, or feeling evolves – if enough components are involved, an epiphanic moment results' (1997: 519). Interestingly, speaking of her own experience as a coach, Wilson (2007) also claims that after coaches have used clean language, any repeated emotional reactions that the client may have experienced before the session will have stopped, with no conscious effort on the part of the client.

Wilson (2007) further points out that because people develop their own symbols or metaphors, the coach's interpretation of the symbol may not be the same as the client's, but in clean language this is less of an issue: the coach would follow the client's metaphor instead of introducing symbols of his/her own. The premise is that minus interference from the coach, the client can be led by his/her own subconscious mind. However, in Lakoff and Johnson's (1981) theory these discoveries usefully undermine the essentially western notion of a conscious, universal and detached reason based on logic and fact. Conversation becomes a succession of metaphors made necessary by our inability to frame and share our feelings and experiences in anything other than a poetic, creative language. According to Lakoff and Johnson, this inability to couch our thoughts in any way other than metaphor demands that we repeat back to our clients the words they have said so that we avoid contamination of the metaphors that they are struggling to express.

However, it could be argued that if we allow clients to go round in their own metaphor loop, there is a danger that they remain trapped in their own conceptions: their perspectives only ever remain their own. Also, in spite of Lakoff and Johnson's inherent critique of objectivism, there is a latent realism in their theory. The clean language position assumes that the client's symbolic language is correct and demands that the helper uncover that metaphor, purely and without contamination, so that it can be expanded further. In a sense this is an over-emphasis of the client's existing perspectives and world view, which may limit the potential for creative thinking and transformative learning. So, at some point, the coach would need to move from a clean language perspective towards a more authentic, generative exploration. For Jasmine, I reinforce her drama triangles and her frozen script if I stick with her metaphors in a kind of exaggeration exercise. Once I have acknowledged her concern and helped her see how she might be trapped, it is time to move on to reworking her responses. The strategies outlined in the next section do just this.

II. Strategies for Clarifying that Rework Client Responses

(1) Paraphrasing

Ivey et al. suggest that paraphrasing involves using all the key words that the client has used, and that an accurate paraphrase will enable the client to 'go on to explore the issue in more depth' (2009: 158). In fact they say that the goal of paraphrasing is to facilitate the client's exploration and clarification of issues, and that 'accurate paraphrasing can help clients complete their storytelling'. They further suggest that there are four dimensions to the paraphrase (2009:158):

1 A sentence stem, sometimes using the client's name;
2 The key words and main ideas used by the client; this is different from the encouraging restatement;
3 Capturing the essence of what the client has said in a briefer and clearer form; the skill being to keep true to the client's ideas but not to repeat them exactly;
4 Checking for accuracy by asking a brief question at the end of the paraphrase, such as 'have I got that right?' or raising the voice at the end of the final sentence as if the paraphrase was a question.

Similarly, Conoley and Conoley suggest four justifications for using paraphrasing in a session: firstly to reassure the client that he/she is being listened to: 'After a restatement, we should pay careful attention to the client's reaction so that we know the client felt understood' (2009: 38). Coaches might seek confirmation themselves by asking 'is that right?', or sometimes the paraphrase is presented in a questioning tone which gives an opportunity to obtain more information if necessary. Secondly, the paraphrase indicates to the client what the coach finds most important about the client's statement. Not all information is restated: there is a selection by the coach that may well indicate to the client what the coach sees as important for progress. Thirdly, the coach is modelling effective listening, which may help clients in their working relationships. Fourthly, the coach guides the coaching process, taking responsibility for the session. Like Ivey et al.'s conceptualisation, these reasons also suggest a search for accuracy.

By contrast, Quine's explanation of paraphrase is more in line with dictionary definitions where the term is said to have its origins in the Greek term *'para phraseïn'* which means 'additional manner of expression' or additional phrasing. According to Quine (1960: 38), a paraphrase aims to be clearer, more informative and perhaps simpler than the original utterance. If, for example, a client says that her manager is good and she means that she likes the manager, rather than that the manager is doing a good job for the company, then clarification of that difference is important for both the client and for the coaching alliance. Quine argues that words that allow truth values to vary between speakers and contexts 'must be supplanted by unambiguous words or phrases before we can accept a declarative sentence as a statement'. He says that it is 'only under such revision that a sentence may, as a single sentence in its own right, be said to have a truth value' (1960: 182). The following quote from Quine appears to sum up the responsibility of the coach in relation to paraphrasing:

> Paraphrasing is what we are up to when in a philosophical spirit we offer an 'analysis' or 'explication' of some hitherto inadequately formulated 'idea' or expression. We do not claim synonymy. We do not claim to make clear and explicit what the users of the unclear expression had unconsciously in mind all along. We do not expose hidden meanings ...; we supply lacks. We fix on the particular functions of the unclear expression that make it worth troubling about, and then devise a substitute, clear and couched in terms to our liking that fills those functions. (Quine, 1960: 258–259)

The key point is that since more than one paraphrase can meet these criteria, no unique meaning can be assigned to the words and sentences of the client. Thus paraphrase in Quine's assessment has less emphasis on accuracy, as suggested in Ivey et al., and is a generative technique that complements the generative, authentic listening discussed in Chapter 4.

Kee, Anderson, Dearing, Shuster and Harris (2010) argue that paraphrasing is the least used communication skill, but that it provides the opportunity for greater clarity and *movement* of thinking. As well as creating a safer environment for people to express their thoughts they also claim that one of the purposes of paraphrase is not so much to benefit the listener as to benefit the speaker. It has the potential to 'serve as a gift to the speaker while at the same time creating permission to move forward with more details ...' (2010: 107). This claim may seem counter intuitive at first, but in a coaching context we can see that rephrasing the client's words according to how another (in this case the coach) interprets them, whether 'accurate' or not, can be very useful for helping the client acknowledge other perspectives.

Hearing their own words paraphrased helps clients to hear themselves differently and to think about themselves and their situations differently. One of Myers' respondents used the phrase 'It was coming back the way I meant it' (2000: 160) – suggesting that the therapist, in this case, was able to capture the client's meaning better than she could herself. Another respondent, talking about the therapist said:

> I may take five minutes to tell him something and he could sum it up and give me the words that would say the same thing. But they were, the words were given back to me in a different way ... in a *different perspective* for me. (Myers, 2000: 160–161, emphasis added)

Myers' respondents confirm that paraphrasing encouraged them to tell more of their story. One explained: ' … then I would talk and tell him how I [experienced it], like it was just a variation of what he said' (2000: 160). So, in this more generative form of paraphrase, opportunities are provided for clients to examine themselves from a new vantage point.

According to Kee et al. (2010: 111–113) there may be three levels of paraphrase:

1 acknowledging and clarifying ('identifying and calibrating content and emotions')
2 summarising and organising (offering 'themes and containers that shape the initiating statement or separate jumbled issues') and
3 shifting conceptual focus.

These authors also suggest that 'metaphors, analogies, perspective taking, and reframing shift the focus upward or downward' thus helping to move thinking 'to a higher, more conceptual level or to a lower, more logical level, based upon observed need' (Kee et al., 2010: 113). They explain that: 'a shifting-up paraphrase illuminates large ideas or categories, often leading the speaker to new discoveries. A shifting-down paraphrase focuses and clarifies, increasing precision of thinking' (Kee et al., 2010: 113).

Examples of 'shifting up' might be moving the emphasis to a discussion of values, beliefs or goals:

Client: I have great difficulty starting work in the morning without checking the news website and having at least two or three cups of coffee.
Coach: So, one of your goals might be to overcome procrastination?

In shifting down the coach might respond:

Coach: So, you're noticing that you are not able to focus on this particular project until you've made yourself comfortable.

A paraphrase that shifts to a higher level of abstraction is often particularly effective in problem-solving situations. Initially, more abstract language widens the potential solution set and encourages broader exploration of ideas and strategies for problem solving. However, as suggested by these examples, it could be argued that shifting up or down is actually shifting away from paraphrase *per se*, as it involves an element of challenge. Challenge is discussed in more detail in Chapter 7.

Related to paraphrase, is the notion of interpreting or reflecting back emotion. Gavin makes an important distinction, though, between reflection of content and reflection of feeling: 'Reflection of feeling, feeds back the emotional or feeling dimension of the client's message' (2005: 102). He suggests that it is an 'accurate restatement of the emotional or affective part of the client's message. The coach must distinguish here between emotions that a client talks about having experienced as part of a story and those that the client is experiencing in the moment' (Gavin, 2005: 104). However, since it can only ever be an interpretation, reflections of feelings, whether originally expressed through the client's story or whether they are more immanent, can be seen as a kind of paraphrasing of the client's affective response. As such reflection of affect is useful for acknowledging and clarifying the feelings.

In the field of counselling, Cormier and Nurius (2003) have identified five purposes of reflection of feeling. Adapted for the coaching context, the first is that reflection of feeling helps clients identify their emotional experiences (either positive or negative) in relation to the situation; secondly, it enhances a client's capacity to cope with and manage emotions. The third purpose would impact the coaching relationship itself: by taking the risk of identifying evidence of resistance (shown through expressions of emotion), coaching can enable clients to deal with obstacles to progress. In fact Gavin (2005: 105) says that a critical competency of coaches is their ability to face a client's emotionality towards them, and to overcome this in order not to impede goal attainment. The fourth purpose is educational, in that the coach can help clients differentiate between the emotions they are experiencing and the feelings that are arising because of this. The fifth purpose is to communicate empathy and understanding, through the recognition that the client has feelings.

(2) Summarising

Ivey et al. describe summarising as encompassing a longer period of conversation than paraphrasing. The coach attends to 'verbal and nonverbal comments from the client over a period of time and then selectively attends to key concepts and dimensions, restating them for the client as accurately as possible' (2009: 159). Ivey et al. confirm that facts, thoughts and emotions are included in a summary and that there should be a checking for accuracy at the end. Summaries may be used at the beginning of a session to recall what happened previously, in the middle of a session to marshal ideas, and then again at the end of the session. Gavin also explains how 'coaches can bring together diverse topics of discussions at strategic moments in a session' (2005: 109). Thus, summarising can be used at the beginning or end of a session in order to move the client towards a new topic, or to clarify some complex issue. Most important, according to Ivey et al. (2009), is that summarising assists both the client and the helper to organise thinking about what is happening in the session. Such synthesis of the client's experience provides a helpful new perspective on that experience (Myers, 2000), resulting in what Perry (2008) calls a perspective enhancing relationship.

Summarising is also a way of bringing together themes or topics in the client's response that have been repeated or referred to with a particular emphasis (Cormier and Nurius, 2003). However, as Gavin cautions, this should not be a mechanical or 'rote process' that merely sets out all the details of the conversation. He describes four significant reasons why a coach may summarise. The first would be to confirm a general understanding of the client's message and validate any assumptions. The second is to identify the specific focus of the client's communication. He argues that when the same issues recur the coach will attribute additional weight to those issues, and, at the right time, will 'bring together the different references to this single theme and through summarising enable the client to consider the significance of the theme and how it relates to plans and processes' (Gavin, 2005: 109). This second type of summary has a different effect on the client, as Gavin also explains: the 'first is an overview of various themes', whereas the second is like 'shining a beacon on a particular area of the client's messages' (2005: 110).

A third function is when the coach uses summarising to slow down the coaching process to allow more time to think and reflect. Gavin suggests that in the 'paralinguistic' dimensions of the client's speech, such as speed or volume, coaches will be able to find cues about exactly how to rate a summary that will enable them to pace the response to match that of the client. Thus coaches use the skill of summarising to 'slow down the process and give the client room to reflect without the pressure of moving forward' (Gavin, 2005: 110). The fourth purpose of summarising he proposes is 'to bring all the themes and issues of a session together toward the end' (2005: 110). Such a review confirms all that has been discussed and provides an opportunity to look at future action points. An example of one such summary might be:

Jasmine: Well then I'd feel sorry for the speaker, but if I was chairing I might want to say something to Brian right there and then so that the speaker could finish – a good chair would do that. Or I might do that anyway, or I might say something to him later, if I felt it was a recurring thing that was holding him back.

Coach: So, it seems that you have identified two options for speaking to Brian: to tackle him directly in the next meeting, or to take him aside afterwards.

So, summarising is not a mechanical process used merely to pull together all the details of the coaching conversation. It is, in fact, a deliberate and skilful strategy for moving discussions forward. It captures key elements of the conversation and offers examples of organisation to which the client can react.

Summary

This chapter has explored why and how the coach uses clarification techniques during the coaching conversation. Two categories of clarifying activity were identified: those that repeat back the client's words, and those that rework client responses. Each was found to have a specific usefulness in the coaching process. In the first category, reflecting back and clean language were discussed as methods of staying true to the client's values, beliefs and perceptions. In the second, paraphrase was explained as useful for the reduction of ambiguity, since it allows the coach to offer an interpretation of what has been said. Similarly, summarising is an interpretive activity, whereby the coach can marshal and interpret the client's statements, and provide some form of organisation that may help the client move forward.

In this chapter, I have suggested that paraphrasing, which allows the coach's own interpretation, appears to provide a more fertile ground for expansion of ideas and perspectives, than does echoing, reflecting back or using clean language. In fact there appear to be three different clarification techniques available here: paraphrasing, where the coach uses different words to provoke a response from the client; mirroring, where the coach uses the same words to show recognition and perhaps solidarity; and reflecting back, which we might distinguish as going further than a rational or logical paraphrase. Reflecting back appears to include an affective element, whereby coaches would include observations on how they perceive the client to be feeling, or whereby they share their own feelings evoked at that point in the session. These three techniques form a continuum of clarification approaches, each serving its own purpose, from those involving no interpretation by the coach to those that involve significant interpretation. This continuum is shown in Figure 5.1.

This chapter has also suggested that there is a difference between the use of these techniques in therapy and counselling and their use in coaching. From a counselling perspective, Cormier and Cormier (1998) suggest that clarification ensures that what the helper has understood is accurate. However, as suggested earlier, accuracy suggests a 'right' answer, and I would argue that in coaching the benefit of clarification at any stage in the alliance is to ensure that clients have made their message explicit, so that they understand it themselves, and then for the coach to help them elaborate if necessary. In coaching, clarification is there to help clients, not the coach, and it provides the basis for the alliance to move forward. In therapy, the main function is to enable the helper to gain an accurate picture of the client's reality in order to make decisions about what course of 'treatment' to provide. In coaching it is clients who need to order and reorder their thoughts and create a picture, and so they need to be provided with opportunities to discover new ways to do this.

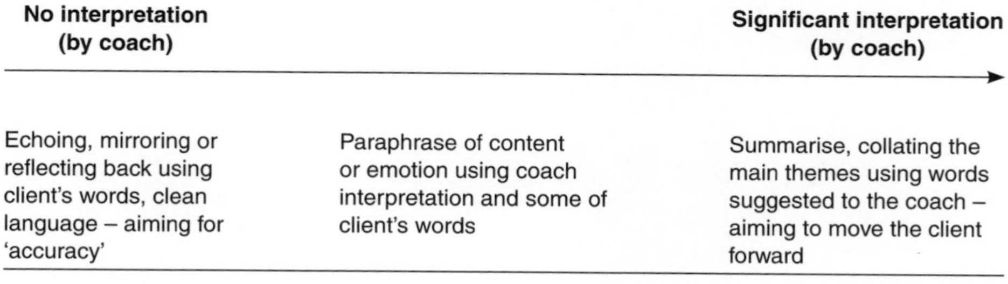

No interpretation (by coach)		Significant interpretation (by coach)
Echoing, mirroring or reflecting back using client's words, clean language – aiming for 'accuracy'	Paraphrase of content or emotion using coach interpretation and some of client's words	Summarise, collating the main themes using words suggested to the coach – aiming to move the client forward

Figure 5.1   Continuum of clarification approaches

All clarification involving echoing and clean language suffers from the underlying assumption that what the client presents is central, and this is in line with most coaches' espoused wish to adopt a person centred approach. But reflecting back, mirroring, echoing and clean language, rather than proposing alternative perspectives for clients to consider and so expanding their meaning perspectives (Mezirow, 1991), may lead only to an elevation of their own modes and styles of thinking or expressing themselves. Some reflecting and mirroring is useful as a starting point, but the generation and incorporation of wider, fresher, new ideas that lead to a broader understanding of themselves and the world in which they operate is also vital. Paraphrase, I would suggest, begins this more developmental challenge.

As in the previous chapter, where two distinct types of listening were compared, one empathic and one authentic, it can be noted that clarification strategies also fall into these categories. Coach identification with, and imitation or repetition of, the client's language generates empathy, but may elevate existing perspectives. It may have some utility at the start of a relationship. However, the interpretation of the client's response by the coach through paraphrase or summary, offers new horizons that have a more generative function. This approach is important as the coaching relationship reaches its productive stage.

6
Reflecting

Chapter Aims:

- To examine reflective practice models and their benefit for working with clients
- To distinguish between phenomenological reflecting and critical thinking as part of the Experiential Coaching Cycle

In the coaching literature, although reflecting is recognised as important, there has generally been little in-depth examination of the theories of reflection that inform its application. As a consequence there is nothing in the coaching literature that makes the link between practices and techniques that encourage reflection and the theories that underpin the concept of reflection. For example, despite Skiffington and Zeus referring to reflection as 'a new thinking approach' (2003: 81) and describing a 10-step process where the coach invites the client to explore self limiting beliefs through reflection on specific behaviours, they give no more information about why this process might work. Similarly, Clutterbuck (1998) recognises the importance of reflecting, talking about the difference between personal reflective space and dyadic reflective space, where individual reflection is augmented by external dialogue. He recognises the value of having someone like a coach to help contribute other perspectives and other experiences, but does not explore how this might be facilitated.

In earlier work (Cox, 2006) I described how authors such as Brookfield (1987) and Mezirow (1991, 2000) advocate reflection as a form of personal learning. I similarly commented on how coaching can create the conditions for reflective learning, and suggested that this is best done by creating a psychological space that allows clients to withdraw from the workplace in order to stand back and think, thus enabling them to gain some perspective on their experiences and on their tasks. I have also described how reflective practice tools or models lead to knowledge and wisdom about ourselves and would be useful for both coach and client: 'Reflection, then, is where professionals come to terms with their feelings, learning from their mistakes, explore their successes, and develop empathy and understanding. It is an important practice for both the client and the coach' (Cox, 2006: 199). More recently, Oliver (2010) looked at reflection from a systemic perspective, summarising the influence of Dewey's work

(1910, 1934, 1938), and noted that he presents reflection as a creative process that enables us to make meaning when we make connections between our experience and the potential consequences of that experience in the future. Because Oliver is looking at systems, she also proposes that reflection is particularly useful at the individual level where meaning can be explored and subsequently connected to social processes and discourses.

In this chapter and in Chapter 7, I want to discuss the two different modes of reflecting that are used in coaching, although this may be the first time they have been separated and discussed in this way. The first mode is phenomenological reflecting (Bitbol and Petitmengin, 2011), which involves the bracketing of what Husserl terms the 'natural attitude'. The second is critical thinking, which is distinguished by its emphasis on challenging existing perspectives. In distinguishing these two modes I hope to explain the progression from: (a) beginning to understand experience through describing feelings and events, and (b) making meaning from these events through thinking critically about them. Making this distinction also allows me to focus in this chapter on the importance of phenomenological reflection as a strategy that does two jobs for the coaching alliance:

1 It allows the client to reveal the nature of his/her subjective experience.
2 It enables the coaching alliance to hold a descriptive account of such experience, without premature analysis or evaluation.

As discussed in Chapter 2, experience forms the bedrock upon which knowledge is built. In that chapter, immersion in experience was portrayed as embracing and foregrounding the natural attitude, bringing experiences in all their fullness into the now (Tolle, 2005). This chapter describes the next stage in understanding the client's experience, which involves bracketing or suspending the natural attitude temporarily, in order to focus differently on perceived reality. This follows Zahavi's (2011) explanation that immanent immersion in experience and the expansion of our field of attention are different from the mental operations by which we detach ourselves from our own judgements and actions.

I begin this chapter by reviewing the concept of introspection, which seems to have been a catalyst for Husserl's development of a more structured methodology for examining experience. This will help with our understanding of the phenomenological undertaking outlined in the sections that follow. In section II, I include a discussion of the bracketing process advocated by Husserl, and its function in a phenomenological reflection model. In part III, there is a discussion of how the quality of reflection on experience shifts over time, as the experience recedes in the memory and becomes mediated by intervening events. After this, in section IV, I examine models of reflective practice, which appear to share an underpinning phenomenological philosophy, and identify the ways in which they support the process of reflection. In all sections I discuss the implications for coaching clients, but in the final section I draw these together to present a table summarising the coach's role in relation to phenomenological reflecting for the client.

I. Introspection

Husserl's commitment to the phenomenological method came seemingly from a reaction to criticism of the concept of introspection (Gallagher and Zahavi, 2008). Introspection is a method of examining subjective experience. It can be described as the systematic study of mental events undertaken by contemplating the processes of our own conscious experiences. Vermersch explains how the immediate recollection of lived experience is often 'poor, anecdotal, and soon exhausted' and that there is a 'fundamental gap between what the subject believes he [sic] knows about his lived experience and what he could in fact produce, particularly when he is guided by introspection/explication aid techniques' (1999: 15). Thus Vermersch advocates explication interviews that encourage introspection. These appear to be similar to some forms of counselling dialogue where clients are invited to uncover more past information than they expect, and are often amazed to discover things that they recognise as having experienced, but that are only remembered after the fact. Counsellors might use encouragements such as 'Can you think of another instance of where you felt like that?' Vermersch describes this process for an individual:

> It is as though, at the moment when he was experiencing them, he did not know them, and that at the moment he was about to talk about them, he did not know in advance that he would have something to say about these particular points, and that as a result he seems to be discovering it as he names it, while recognising it without hesitation as his own lived experience! (1999: 15)

One of the criticisms of such introspective accounts is that they focus not on the experience itself, but on the personal processes of consciousness that reflect on that experience, creating links within the memory, rather than examining the experience at hand. Consequently, as Pronin and Kugler (2007) explain, introspective information automatically includes value judgements made at an unconscious level. This propensity to operate non-consciously means that bias is often hidden from introspection. They further explain how there is an over-valuing of 'thoughts, feelings and other mental contents, relative to behaviour, when assessing their own actions, motives and preferences, but not when assessing others' (Pronin and Kugler, 2007: 566). Their findings reveal how the faith we often place in the diagnostic value of our introspections is, therefore, misplaced, and hinges on a totally subjective, and therefore circular, activity.

Pronin and Kugler (2007) also refer to what they call the 'introspection illusion'. This illusion is caused by adherence to the metaphysical fallacy that locates the phenomenal realm within the mind. and suggests that the only way to access and describe it is by 'turning the gaze inwards (introspicio)' (Gallagher and Zahari, 2008: 21). The concept of introspection then, endorses the Cartesian idea that consciousness is inside the head and the world is outside.

Gallagher and Zahari summarise the dilemma by making a comparison with phenomenology, where the focus is directly on experience:

> Whereas the introspective psychologist considers consciousness as a mere sector of being, and tries to investigate this sector as the physicist tries to investigate the physical world, the phenomenologist realises that consciousness ultimately calls for a transcendental clarification. (2008: 23)

Husserl's own explanation of the difference is pivotal here:

> The objectives of which we are 'conscious' are not simply in consciousness as in a box, so that they can merely be found in it and snatched at in it; ... they are first constituted as being what they are for us, and as what they count as for us, in varying forms of objective intention. (Husserl, 2001: 275)

According to Husserl then, in order to explore our experiences without interference from such illusion or bias, we need to disengage temporarily from the natural attitude, which is a non-reflective position, and apply a more phenomenological stance in order to facilitate reflection. Husserl recommends bracketing to allow 'objective' descriptions of behaviours. It is a vital component of phenomenological reflection and it is to this descriptive endeavour that we now turn.

Before moving on to look at phenomenological reflection in more detail though, I want to clarify two points. In Chapter 4, I suggested that if coaches bracket their own concerns as in empathic listening, then it may not be productive for the coaching alliance. However, as a mechanism for encouraging clients to detach from experience prior to analysing that experience, bracketing is useful. It allows 'fracturing' of the experience so that attempts can be made to gain a better perspective prior to rationalisation and analysis. This process is also different from phenomenological research, where the researcher uses phenomenological interview techniques in order to get closer to the object of study, the 'thing in itself'. There the focus is on the phenomenon. In coaching and in phenomenological reflection as described here, we are concerned with using the process only as a means of development for the client.

II. Phenomenological Reflection

In Chapter 2, I referred to Damasio's model that suggests how pre-reflective experience and emotions shift to awareness in consciousness, and I highlighted the need in coaching to consider how the initial dilemma can begin to be understood. The first conscious awareness of the shift from pre-reflective to reflective is a feeling or uncertainty that often cannot be put into words. Frequently, the client requires time to 'sit with' and try to re-experience the experience in order to become familiar with it and accept it as indicating something valuable.

The purpose of phenomenological reflection is to accept the essential meaning of that experience, thereby gaining insight into the essence of the phenomenon, which as van Manen explains, involves a process of 'reflectively appropriating, of clarifying, and of making explicit the structure of meaning of the lived experience' (1990: 77). So the process following 'sitting with' the experience is to try to describe the experience, including naming the behaviours, feelings, emotions and dilemmas. This conscious activity is aimed at enabling clients to describe their experiences as objective phenomena, but to avoid any kind of evaluation or analysis. In the coaching session this form of phenomenological reflection is an attempt to bring the client's current feelings and experiences that have been brought into intuitive awareness through focusing, for example, into a more conscious, yet detached and non-judgemental, awareness. It is a reflective activity that is separate from the critical evaluation and analysis that comes afterwards (discussed in Chapter 7).

Working in a sports context, Downey states that when working phenomenologically, coaches 'bring into awareness what is inchoate or unconscious' (2008: 3). He also explains how important the process of description is, but that this is not an easy or quick process. If we contrast phenomenology with our natural attitude, where there is no deliberate reflection and no attention is given to making meaning of our daily experiences, the distinction becomes clearer. Many phenomenologists point out that most of us function most of the time at this pre-conscious, natural attitude level of understanding: 'in other words, we take things for granted without reflecting about their meaning' (Greenfield and Jensen, 2010: 1189). But a 'phenomenological attitude' refers to a conscious effort to recount and understand lived experiences by suspending the natural attitude (our habits of mind, in Mezirow's terminology), and just describing behaviours and experiences. Such description involves acceptance rather than any form of censorship or analysis. The process should allow perceptions, feelings and emotions to emerge and be pictured and presented whole, rather than being judged. Pure reflection is thus a conscious process that brings the client's experience into the open, into a clearing, presenting it objectively without analysis.

Although phenomenological reflecting is often claimed as a first-person process that does not recognise mind–body dualism, Husserl (1952) did consider it to involve a form of 'self-fission'. He suggested that there needed to be a distance between the *reflected* self and the *reflecting* self. So, Husserl further argued that reflection is a 'modification of consciousness' (Husserl, 1952: 148), where the field of attention can broaden so that it is aware of both the 'pure' object of description and, separately, the intentional perceptions of that object. Bitbol and Petitmengin describe this self-fission as a process, not a state: 'a functional dualisation within a unique flux of experience, rather than a duality' (2011: 27), and one that involves a 'receptive observing openness of the subject' to what is given. They further suggest that this receptiveness has is origins in the basic proto-reflective element of consciousness which makes reflection possible 'by exhibiting a domain of experience that could be objectified later'

(2011: 28). This distancing is important in coaching because it encourages the client to reflect in a seemingly objective way, without the preconceptions normally associated with reflecting.

Phenomenological Reduction and the Epoché (Bracketing)

Husserl calls the bracketing of the natural attitude, the epoché, which in Greek philosophy means suspension of judgement. We have seen how an important aspect of phenomenological reflection is the ability to bracket, or set on one side, the prejudices and judgements that we would ordinarily bring to any verbal explanation of events, in order to create a clearing. In this section I will explain this process in more detail so that when we explore reflective practice models later in this chapter we have a reasonable understanding of the concept.

Husserl used the term 'phenomenological reduction' to identify the complex process involving two moments: bracketing and acceptance. The first moment, the bracketing, involves suspending the natural attitude and the 'reduction proper' to enable a focus on the ways in which things appear to us. Gallagher and Zahavi (2008: 25) describe the process as:

> a reflective move that departs from an unreflective and unexamined immersion in the world and 'leads back' (re-ducere) to the way in which the world manifests itself to us. Thus everyday things available to our perception are not doubted or considered as illusions when they are 'phenomenologically reduced', but instead are envisaged and examined simply and precisely *as perceived* … In other words, once we adopt the phenomenological attitude, we are no longer primarily interested in *what* things are – in their weight, size, chemical composition, etc. – but rather in *how* they appear, and thus as correlates of our experience. (2008: 25, original emphasis)

Depraz et al. (2003: 25) usefully explain that there are three 'folds' within the complete process:

1 The suspending fold is the intent to arouse an experience without its accompanying value laden baggage. In this phase clients need to reject the idea that what normally appears to them is truly the state of the world. Phenomenologists claim that this is the only way we can change the way we pay attention to our own lived experience; in other words we must break with the natural attitude.

2 The reflective or redirecting fold involves redirecting our suspended attention towards a neutral stance. Here is it necessary to substitute the unexamined, natural attitude for a more discerning act of unbiased perception, where descriptions of experience are metaphorically laid out, not as facts, but as perceptions – just features of one person's reality. Folds 1 and 2 are closely linked.

3. The letting-go fold is acceptance. Depraz et al. describe this fold as moving from looking for something (an interpretation to cling to), to letting something come or letting it be revealed. They suggest that what is difficult here is that the client will have to go through an 'empty time', a time of silence and not 'grab onto whatever data is immediately available' (2003: 31) in order to fill the gap.

The double correlation effect of the process of suspending and redirecting, followed by letting go is illustrated in Figure 6.1.

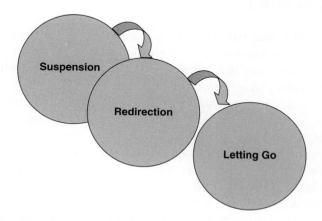

Figure 6.1   The two moments of phenomenological reduction

An example of this three-fold process can be observed in part of a coaching dialogue with Jasmine.

Coach: So can you describe the event in more detail?
Jasmine: Hmm, well, it was Tuesday afternoon, 4pm start as usual. Eight members of the team had turned up and Brian was chairing. It was a long agenda, so I knew we were going to go late into the evening. My name was by one of the agenda items near the end, and I was stunned to see it there [long silence].
I thought that item had been put there to catch me out because I'd not been asked to report on it. I felt like running out there and then. I felt sick.
Coach: So your perception is that the team leader or whoever compiled the agenda had wanted to catch you out?
Jasmine: Definitely, that's why I had to leave before the agenda item.
Coach: Could there have been any other explanation? [SUSPENSION]
Jasmine: Well, it could have been an admin error, I suppose [long silence] – yes it might have been a genuine mistake. Perhaps Jane (administrator) was sitting there feeling embarrassed.
Coach: Any other explanation?

Jasmine: Well if Brian put it there deliberately it was either to catch me out or [pause] maybe to challenge me. [REDIRECTION]

Coach: Why might Brian want to challenge you?

Jasmine: Oh, he likes to do that sometimes. He did it with someone else at the end of last year. Caught them out as well.

Coach: So we have an item on the agenda that you found discomforting, but that equally might just have been an admin error or it might have been the team leader's idea of legitimate challenge?

Jasmine: Yes, I suppose. [LETTING GO]

Coach: [long silence]

This example illustrates part of an ongoing process of learning to reflect for Jasmine. During the bracketing of her experience of the team meeting, she begins by describing only the experience that she has of it and within it. Only Jasmine's subjective perception of the phenomenon is described. This makes it possible to set out her relationship with the team, particularly the team leader, ignoring any temptation to edit, repress or modify her perspectives, and remembering not to judge them in any way. There is no right or wrong. Thus we get closer to the 'thing itself' by setting out how she is experiencing it. However, through the suspending, redirecting and letting-go process she is enabled to distance herself from her feelings and meaning making and see them as only one reality. Her experience of this team meeting is real for her, but may not be the same for others. By stepping back from her own subjectivity and looking at it dispassionately she allows herself to take on board the possibility of other perspectives.

This method of descriptive bracketing, or 'epoché' is different from the attempts to get in touch with experience that were discussed in Chapter 2. Visualisation or focusing, for example, are much more about staying with the experience in order to feel it and get close to it in a completely natural, subjective and visceral way. Highlighting that subjectivity then paves the way for what emerges following descriptive phenomenological reflection, which is an opportunity for expanding perspectives. The whole experience is put into the coaching space for examination and the natural attitude towards that experience suspended and redirected. At the 'letting go' or acceptance phase existing perspectives are examined and possibly compared with others, and the client would be encouraged to hold or 'sit with' the loss of her perspective – not to immediately grasp at a different explanation.

It should also be noted that Heidegger (1962), who was Husserl's pupil, argued that our very being in the world, our 'thrownness', precludes us from ever being able to successfully bracket the world. However, as I have argued here, there is benefit to be gained for clients in trying to observe their values, beliefs and perspectives through the use of a reflective practice model that helps to separate out subjective material. For novice reflectors the exercise can be revolutionary.

III. The Time Factor in Reflective Processes

Reflective self-consciousness, as proposed by Husserl, provides an understanding of pre-reflective experiences and subjectivity that is always after the fact. Such reflection takes pre-reflective experience as its object, and so is always limited by the same temporal structure: it is a retrospective activity that can never be contemporaneous. Merleau-Ponty explains how 'temporality contains an internal fracture that permits us to return to our past experiences in order to investigate them reflectively, but this very fracture also prevents us from fully coinciding with ourselves. There will always remain a difference between the lived and the understood' (Merleau-Ponty, 1962: 397–399). There will always be a time gap, at least a momentary delay between the reflection and the pre-reflective object of that reflection.

One of the first people to recognise the temporal differences in reflection was Schön (1983). Schön argued that in our daily lives we demonstrate what we know through our actions which are usually spontaneous and intuitive. However, when situations arise that are more uncertain or unstable, what he calls 'reflection in action' occurs. This is the immediate 'thinking on one's feet' response to instability. Thus he introduces two points of reflection: reflection in action, which is almost immediate; and reflection on action, which happens after the event, allowing time for consideration of experiences. Smith summarises the process:

> We have to take certain things as read. We have to fall back on routines in which previous thought and sentiment has been sedimented. It is here that the full importance of reflection on action becomes revealed. As we think and act, questions arise that cannot be answered in the present. The space afforded by recording, supervision and conversation with our peers allows us to approach these. Reflection requires space in the present and the promise of space in the future. (Smith, 1994: 150)

More recently, Depraz et al. have also suggested that learning is generated 'by continually re-enacting the act of becoming aware, and that each step is more sedimented and incarnated than the one before' (2003: 20). This pattern, they suggest, provides for 'different scales of temporality, from the fraction of a second which it takes for a trigger mechanism – an essential facet of becoming aware – all the way up to the historical temporality of the transmission of the act between generations' (2003: 20).

Griffiths and Tann (1991) also identified the qualitative differences between reflection at five different temporal removes or 'eras':

1 *Rapid reaction*: which involves an instinctive and very immediate response.
2 *Repair*: where reflection may entail a slight pause to gather the thoughts, but action is still fairly immediate. This could be seen as similar to Schön's reflection *in* action.

3 *Review*: necessitating time out to re-assess, usually some hours or days later. Similar to Schön's reflection *on* action.

4 *Research*: a systematic, sharply focused approach to reflection, taking place over weeks or months.

5 *Re-theorise and reformulate*: the abstract, rigorous, clearly formulated contemplation which occurs over months or years.

Each form of reflective thought, however much delayed by time, is valuable and an indispensible part of a learning process. The progression from rapid reaction to re-theorisation suggests that reflection over a long time span has benefits, and that the eras of reflection each enable a different quality of understanding. It has also been suggested that such staged use of reflection can help identify recurrent issues and problems (Cox, 2006) which is useful – reflecting on earlier experience with a coach could produce important insights. Orange, Burke and Cushman (1999) suggest that through each era, individual knowledge and expertise is progressively refined and enhanced. Interestingly, in Chapter 10 it will be suggested that the effects of reviewing, re-theorising and reformulating do eventually become integrated into the 'Rapid Reaction' response repertoire, and thus complete a learning cycle.

IV. Models of Reflection

As we have seen through the discussion of phenomenology in this chapter, the reflecting process is one that ultimately leads to clients being liberated from restrictive thought patterns that can limit their lives. Dewey summarised the interconnection as including 'the reflection that sets us free from the limiting influence of sense, appetite, and tradition' (1910: 156).

One way in which to encourage reflection and also ensure that the benefits of the phenomenological method are achieved is to use a reflective practice model. On inspection, most models appear to use a clear process that facilitates detachment, and so could be interpreted as being founded on Husserl's phenomenology. Many of them also attempt to segment everyday interpretations of experience into an objective part and a subjective part. This section then, discusses existing models of reflection that are commonly used for capturing and deconstructing reflections in professional situations. All aim to enhance the metacognitive processes involved in learning from experience, and include Kolb's learning cycle (1984); the SOAP model (Dye, 2006); Johns' MSR model (2009) and Mezirow's levels of reflectivity (1991).

Probably the most well known, and most emulated, model of reflection is Kolb's (1984) learning cycle, which has reflection as the second step in an experiential learning process. Other models similarly begin with experience as the genesis of understanding, and move through a cycle of objective and subjective accounting together with analytical exploration. The models that appear to owe a debt to Kolb include Johns (1994, 2009) and Gibbs (1988). These models are process oriented and move sequentially from describing actual events through subjective reflection, to analysis and subsequent action or recognition of learning. There are other seemingly simpler models, for example Pearson and Smith (1985) and Borton (1970) where the concern is also with describing events and feelings and extrapolating meaning.

In a review of reflective practice models within health professions, Mann, Gordon and MacLeod (2009) observed that reflective practice has both an iterative and a vertical dimension. The iterative dimension involves a cycle of disruption to normal, everyday experiences, followed by a re-ordering of experience to create new understanding, which is then translated into an intention to act differently in future. Mann et al. identify Boud, Keogh and Walker (1985) and Schön (1983) as particular models that follow an iterative pattern. The vertical dimension that Mann et al. identify involves reflection on different aspects (or levels) of the experience. Within the vertical plane they describe the difference between surface levels and the deeper levels: 'Generally the surface levels are more descriptive and less analytical than the deeper levels of analysis and critical synthesis. The deeper levels appear more difficult to reach, and are less frequently demonstrated' (Mann et al., 2009: 597). They identify the models of Dewey (1910), Mezirow (1991) and Moon (1999) as ones that focus on the depth of reflective thinking.

An example of an iterative model, as described by Mann et al. (2009), would be the SOAP model of reflection. This model is widely used in healthcare and medical contexts, and involves the use of a 'self-SOAP note' (Dye, 2006). It is a reflective practice framework that parallels the iterative learning process of Kolb's cycle (1984). The model requires the practitioner to record information in four sections, the first two of which differentiate between subjectively recorded information and objective accounts. These are then drawn together in an analysis phase:

'S'   records Subjective information;
'O'   documents Objective information;
'A'   is Analysis of detail recorded in 'S' and 'O', drawing out alternative perspectives and information;
'P'   is the resultant Plan of action based on learning acquired during the process.

There are also a number of Reflective Practice Models that encourage thinking at different 'vertical' levels. For example, Johns' model of structured reflection (MSR), first designed in 1991 (Johns and Freshwater, 1998), gives cues for reflection that enable progression of thought. Johns argues that 'with use, the reflective cues become embodied and shape the … gaze moment by moment in mindful attention' (2009: 51). He describes the dynamic of the model, not as the hierarchy that Mann et al. identified in certain other models, but as a spiral that moves the practitioner 'from perception (significance – what lies on the surface of the experience and what may seem obvious) to insights that lie enfolded within …' (2009: 52).

In earlier research (Cox, 2005) I used Johns' MSR cue questions with adult learners. The cues are designed to organise the cognitive, affective and temporal aspects of experience, a process which is particularly helpful for those new to reflecting. Johns' argument for this structure is that reflecting on an incident without a structured format is difficult. The model helps by forcing thinking about other options, perspectives and approaches, and so ameliorates the effect of preconceptions. One of the main findings from the 2005 study was that considerable self-understanding can be generated for people who may not normally reach this level of self-awareness:

> Using reflective practice techniques began to make students conscious of the potential for learning through their work, and could even actively encourage them to seek new experiences from which to learn. Rather than being troubled by change and discord, or being condemned to repeat their mistakes over and over, reflective learners could begin to view each new challenge as a learning opportunity. (Cox, 2005: 471)

In 1991 Mezirow introduced a theory of reflection that comprised consideration of content, process and premise, each of which he considered to be qualitatively different. He proposed that each represented a different level of reflection on a continuum of increasing complexity. The first level, content reflection, is described as a process in which we 'are not attending to the grounds or justification for our beliefs but are simply using our beliefs to make an interpretation' (1991: 107). Thus, content reflection would appear to invite subsequent phenomenological reduction.

The next level, process reflection, focuses on the success of the approach chosen to work out the problem. So the coach might simply ask: 'How effective were you in solving the problem?' The aim is to help clients consider whether what they have been doing so far is working, and allowing them to reflect on the way in which they work. Thus, metacognitive strengths are encouraged.

Kreber and Castleden (2008) explain how in the first of Mezirow's two levels of reflection there is a move towards questioning knowledge within the boundaries of existing beliefs, but these beliefs themselves are not yet questioned. It is in the final level of premise reflection where core beliefs are questioned. Questions then might include 'Why is it that you identified this as a problem at all?' Kreber and Castleden point out how at this level, as in process reflection, evidence for validating new insights is obtained through either formal knowledge or through personal experiences. This is a move away from phenomenological reflection towards a more critical exploration. Thus, in both process and premise reflection questions are being asked, but it is through premise reflection that perceptions and core beliefs are questioned and reworked to construct new knowledge (McAlpine et al., 2004). In the coaching session, such questions can provoke a disorienting dilemma and so give the opportunity to work with outmoded habits of mind. Mezirow (2000) claimed that following this three-part reflective process could lead to the potential for people to transform meaning perspectives which have been uncritically acquired in childhood, and to make them more permeable, inclusive and discerning.

The third level of reflection can also be emancipatory, as the fundamental beliefs that underpin how a client currently interprets their world begin to be questioned (Mezirow, 1991). The process may enable clients to question why particular performance indicators, for example, are valued above others, and, with the help of a coach, such clients can critically examine the processes and conditions by which such indicators have evolved within their organisation.

Often proponents (and detractors) of reflection have not recognised the value of this early, phenomenological reflecting and fail to include it as part of a complete reflective process.

Interestingly, in Mezirow's (1991) 10-stage transformational learning model, for instance, once a disorienting dilemma is identified, the next stage in the transformation process involves self examination of feelings, values and judgements. In fact all the stages, apart from the disorienting dilemma that initiates the process, appear to involve evaluation and assessment or analysis of some kind. However, it could be argued that there is an important stage missing here. The phenomenological reflection is absent. Furthermore, having introduced the idea of content and process reflection, Mezirow appears to dismiss them as less important than the more analytical premise reflection. In fact, both Mezirow (1991, 2000) and Cranton (2006) tend to exalt the benefits of premise reflection. However, I would argue that the content and process reflection undertaken prior to premise reflection is essential, as it renews the contact with experience, enabling a full description to emerge prior to analysis. In Table 6.1 I have suggested how all three types of reflection can be seen as equally important:

Table 6.1   Benefits of content, process and premise reflection

Type of reflection	Benefit in coaching
Content reflection	Promotes full portrayal of events and experiences. Enables identification of patterns and general principles in relation to the way in which content is described.
Process reflection	Encourages active self-monitoring and aids metacognitive abilities.
Premise reflection	Helps the understanding of motivations and assumptions that underpin experiences. Promotes reflection on values and beliefs. Prompts expansion of meaning perspectives.

V. The Role of the Coach

From what has been discussed so far, coaching could be seen as a method of communicative learning, where the meaning and relevance of values and beliefs are questioned in relation to current experience. Indeed, Johns (1994) has argued that reflection should always be coached or supervised, to prevent meanings from being distorted, and my 2005 study participants confirmed that for *self*-confrontation to occur, regular individual coaching that focused on reflections and influencing factors would have enhanced the whole experience. Mezirow (2000) also explains how knowledge is corroborated through dialogue with others in order to distinguish, for example, patterns of similarity. Thus, the role of the coach in relation to reflecting and critical thinking becomes clear.

In coaching it also interesting to note that two types of bracketing occur. I have discussed this concept mainly in relation to the client, to enable the client to describe his/her experience separately from evaluating it or imputing meaning. But there is also a form a bracketing that is required of coaches themselves. In the field of therapy, Greenfield and Jensen describe bracketing as a filtering process where the helper sets aside his/her own personal values and beliefs 'to focus on the values and beliefs of another individual' (2010: 1192). They explain how the process requires commitment and ongoing self-reflection. Kemp (2011) also explains how it is important for the building of the coaching alliance that the coach spends time reflecting on and exploring his/her own 'self' before beginning the coaching process with a client. The purpose of this exploration is to surface existing values, beliefs and prejudices, and Kemp argues that if these are not identified and surfaced prior to the start of the coaching, 'the potential impact on the client's developmental direction and process can be significantly compromised' (2011: 166). So, he suggests, the coach must 'actively surface these subjective biases to prevent them from actively confounding the content and direction of the coaching engagement' (2011: 166). Kemp further explains how supervision aids insights and enables coaches to be what he calls 'present' and 'selfless' in the process of supporting the client's development. This then could also be seen as a type of phenomenological reflection.

In Table 6.2, I review the Coach's role in relation to phenomenological reflecting.

Table 6.2   Phenomenological reflecting – a coach's role

Phase	Coach activity	Possible questions to ask the client
1.	Coach is aware of own prejudices throughout the coaching session and brackets values and beliefs about what he/she believes should be the experience of someone in this situation.	
2.	Coach facilitates factual descriptions of experience by the client to leave the natural attitude and encourage suspension and redirection.	Tell me about what happened next? Was there anything else going on at that time? Who else was there?
3.	Coach strengthens the client's ability to describe and name emotions whilst in the suspended attitude.	Was there anything you were feeling at the time? What emotion were you feeling?
4.	Coach helps clients identify themes and structures within their experience, being careful not to assess or evaluate experiences as trivial or important.	Which particular features of this event have occurred before? Can you describe a similar event?
5.	Coach encourages further descriptions of experience, including encouraging metaphors that describe experiences and capture complex thought processes.	If this experience was a natural phenomenon, which one would it be?

Summary

The coaching literature recognises the value of reflecting, but detailed examination of why it is beneficial and how it operates in practice has been lacking. In this chapter I focused on the shift from pre-conscious to conscious awareness via a reflective activity which is phenomenological. I have shown how the reflective process that began with trying to touch experience has then to progress to a stage of describing subjective experience, but describing it 'objectively' without discriminating or evaluating the subjectivity that surrounds it.

A number of existing models for facilitating reflection and critical reflection were also discussed. These models invariably begin with a brief descriptive account of the phenomenon. My suggestion for coaches and clients would be to spend more time on this aspect so that clients have an opportunity to see their personal experience from a distance, free from value judgements and emotional entanglement. The bracketing of such judgements and meaning making allows clients subsequently to see their idiosyncratic interpretation as just one possible perspective. The processes of phenomenological reflection and critical reflection, then, are not separate stages, but only displayed and discussed in this way for practical purposes. Sometimes the relationship between describing and analysing is so close that in practice they will occur in close succession, perhaps iteratively. There is a symbiotic relationship between the two.

In some professional spheres the descriptive form of reflection may not hold such importance. In mentoring, for instance, because mentors are focused on sharing knowledge, there is less focus on the meaning mentees make of their previous experience. In counselling it is different too: the counsellor is concerned with articulation of experience in so far as it reveals information about the client that can inform clinical knowledge. For these clients there is less emphasis on self-development and transformation and more on healing and change. Similarly, in some coaching assignments there may be less need to incorporate in-depth phenomenological reflection, particularly if the emphasis is on the achievement of practical goals, and the client is already clear, and has done some reflection.

Reflecting is, however, an important activity for practitioners in any field. Those nurses, lawyers, teachers, coaches, managers or leaders who simply respond in a habitual, pre-reflective way and never stand back to consider other ways in which events may be perceived or conceived may significantly restrict their ability to develop personally and professionally. The reflective process that underpins that development is therefore important for coaches and clients to grasp.

7
Becoming Critical

Chapter Aims:

- To explain the importance of critical awareness
- To examine the role of critical thinking in coaching

In the Experiential Coaching Cycle introduced in Chapter 1, I suggested that Reflection on Experience is a space within coaching where the deconstruction and articulation of experience through a process of reflective description can begin. Such exploration can help clients start to understand their experience, and ultimately facilitate more and better understanding. In Chapter 6, I stressed the importance of enabling clients to 'lay out' descriptions of their experience prior to focusing on those descriptions as catalysts for further exploration. Bitbol and Petitmengin described such laying out in terms of first- or third-person functionality, proposing that 'reflection can concern either: (a) experience as it is lived in the first person, or (b) acts, thoughts and intentions as they are evaluated in the third person (irrespective of whether they concern oneself or another)' (2011: 26). In this chapter, therefore, having focused on the first person, I move to an examination of the more evaluative and critical function of reflection. It is here that I want to begin to examine the role of critical thinking (sometimes referred to as critical reflection) that involves a third-person evaluation of events and experiences.

One of the few authors to mention reflective practice and critical thinking as separate activities is Price (2004). Price, working in the field of nursing, states that critical thinking is 'the ability to deconstruct events and to reason the origins of situations'. Like reflection, she suggests, there is a retrospective dimension to it, but there is also a prospective and a creative dimension as well: 'critical thinking involves considering the relationship between events – whether this is cause and effect or whether there is a more general process underway' (2004: 46). As well as the generative dimension, however, there is also a symbiotic relationship between phenomenological reflection and critical thinking that I want to stress. Both draw on various levels of cognitive processing, and each is dependent on the other.

In Table 7.1, I show the role of experience in developing understanding, from the initial phase of pre-reflective experience, discussed in Chapter 2, through to final transition from critical thinking to integration, which will be the subject of Chapter 10. Table 7.1 highlights how critical thinking is a dependent process that relies on reflection. The important aspect to stress is that a description of the client's dilemma is essential first, before analysis begins; otherwise it is like writing a management report before all the information has been gathered – spurious conclusions and recommendations result!

In the table I also indicate the cognitive activities at each phase (based on Bloom's taxonomy, 1956) and include some of the coaching activities that may facilitate each phase.

In this chapter I am concerned with the two phases that involve encouraging clients to think critically: the transition from phenomenological reflection to critical thinking, and critical thinking itself. The chapter looks at the challenge created for coaches by the phenomenological descriptions of experience, which, as we saw in Chapter 6, involved bracketing the natural attitude in order to expose values, beliefs and assumptions. The aim of thinking critically is to observe those values and beliefs, and examine the assumptions they embrace. This is done in the light of all available information: previous experience, vicarious experience, extant knowledge, logic and reasoning. Ultimately, it enables the coach and client to explore what the coaching task might be in relation to that experience.

Like other chapters, this one begins by reporting on how the coaching literature addresses this subject. I first present any existing discussions of how

Table 7.1   Coaching and cognitive activity in the coaching cycle

Phase in the coaching cycle	Cognitive activities	Coaching activities
Pre-reflective Experience	No conscious activity in this phase	Intuitions, hunches, uncertainties and other non-cognitive events may begin to surface
Transition from Pre-reflective Experience to Phenomenological Reflection	Remembering, recalling	Focusing, recollective visioning
Phenomenological Reflection	Describing	Detailed description of events and naming of feelings, but with no evaluation or analysis
Transition from Phenomenological Reflection to Critical Thinking	Comprehending, understanding	Acceptance (letting go) and growing awareness of the existence of assumptions underpinning events or feelings, exposure of context
Critical Thinking	Knowing, analysing, synthesising, evaluating	Examination of assumptions and alternative perspectives, development of healthy scepticism
Transition from Critical Thinking to Integration	Application	Support for transfer of learning and integration

and why thinking is encouraged in coaching, and follow this in the second section with a more detailed explanation of critical thinking, drawing on Brookfield's seminal work in the adult learning field. Finally, in section III I discuss Brookfield's four components of critical thinking, integrating an exploration of the role of the coach and potential strategies for generating criticality.

I. Critical Thinking in the Coaching Literature

Critical thinking is often mentioned in the coaching literature as an activity that the coach should be undertaking as part of professional practice. It is also promoted as imperative for the coach in order to support evidence-based practice. For example Drake, Brennan and Gørtz argue that: 'if coaching is to fully emerge as a true field of study, we need to adopt a greater discipline in engaging with and in sound scholarship and critical thinking' (2009: xxiii). Grant points out that 'in addition, coaches need to have well-developed critical thinking skills, the ability to analyse and reason from first principles, and the ability to construct arguments and hold robust and well-reasoned discussions' (2005: 6). Yet another example of this emphasis on the development of the coach appears in Campone who describes how the learning inherent in reflective practice is most important for coaches, and charges coaches to see coaching engagements as 'opportunities for judgement artistry' (2011: 11).

However, it is hard to find coaching texts that specifically explain the value or benefit of critical thinking for clients. If critical thinking is considered such an important activity for coaches, why is there no parallel drawn between coach development and client development – after all, most clients are also working professionals? Even my own chapter in the *Evidence based coaching handbook* (Cox, 2006) fails adequately to discuss how critical thinking promotes an exploration of beliefs and assumptions for clients that can subsequently lead to transformation and change. However, some coaching texts do recognise the value for clients of related activities such as challenge or reframing. Brockbank and McGill (2006), for example, present a discussion of challenge to clients' thinking, and most other coaching books at least mention the importance of challenging clients' assumptions.

The reason for the lack of in-depth discussion of this important area for client development has been, I would argue, because of the emphasis on psychological theories to explain coaching practice. For example, Dryden (2010) expounds cognitive behavioural strategies, such as the rational-emotive approach, as a way of dealing with emotional problems for clients. Other coaches use the downward arrow model, or variations of it, which have been adapted from Beck et al. (1979) for use in coaching, but that all involve examining the negative, automatic thoughts that accompany assumptions made in response to critical incidents. The result of this emphasis on psychotherapeutic models is that critical thinking, rather than being recognised as an integral part of coaching, has been marginalised by being relegated to a technique embedded in cognitive-behavioural coaching, or criticised as being too cerebral to be part of an holistic coaching process. I want, therefore, to stress that coaching is a learning process, informed fundamentally by learning theory, and attention needs to be paid primarily to theories of learning, with the applications and adaptations from psychotherapy being an important, but secondary, touchstone.

II. Critical Thinking

One of the fundamental, but usually unspoken, aims of coaching is to facilitate clients to become critical. This means helping them to compare and contrast their own experiences with the experiences and expertise of others. As well as challenging assumptions, activities might involve creating opportunities for them to consider a range of different perspectives within or indeed outside of their organisation, reframing a career trajectory in the light of new information, or discussing some reading material that challenges views and beliefs about aspects of their situation. The outcomes of this expansion process are then used to inform decision making.

Ntuen and Leedom (2007) define critical thinking as a structured process involving reasonable and reflective thinking about ideas, concepts and beliefs. They suggest it is also described as 'thinking about thinking' or 'thinking out of the box'. The difference between critical thinking and just thinking is summed up by Dewey who said that 'to think of a thing is just to be conscious of it in any way whatsoever' (1910: 1). Critical thinking, on the other hand, involves reasoning, conceptualising and analysing currently held tacit knowledge.

The main champion of critical thinking in recent years has been Brookfield (1987, 2005), working in the field of adult education. According to Brookfield, thinking critically involves 'calling into question the assumptions underlying our customary, habitual ways of thinking and acting and then being ready to think and act differently on the basis of this critical questioning' (1987: 1). This description confirms the distinction between the phenomenological reflection described in the previous chapter, and critical thinking which is a more probing and questioning activity. The difference can be further highlighted by thinking of reflection as a dressing-room mirror that surrounds the client and enables an objective, yet in-depth, description of what is seen within the dressing cubicle. Critical thinking, on the other hand, more resembles what can be viewed through a camera obscura – in which a lens provides an exciting outside perspective, perhaps not seen before. So the critical approach involves comparison, distancing, and other techniques. Some of these will be discussed in this chapter.

Brookfield has explained that critical thinking is one of the most important activities in adult life:

> When we become critical thinkers we develop an awareness of the assumptions under which we, and others, think and act. We learn to pay attention to the context in which our actions and ideas are generated. We

become sceptical of quick-fix solutions, of single answers to problems and of claims to universal truth. We also become open to alternative ways of looking at, and behaving in, the world. (1987: ix)

Thus critical thinking impacts our lives in many ways. In relationships we are more tolerant as we begin to see ourselves through the eyes of others. At work we can take control and initiate new projects. Politically, as Brookfield also suggests, 'we value freedom, we practice democracy, we encourage a tolerance of diversity and we hold in check the demagogic tendencies of politicians' (1987: ix). He places critical thinking 'at the heart of what it means to be a developed person living in a democratic society' (1987: 14). For Brookfield, 'being a critical thinker involves more than cognitive activities such as logical reasoning or scrutinising arguments for assertions unsupported by empirical evidence' (1987: 13). It is in this way that we scrutinise our own assumptions and beliefs, as well as other aspects of life. We can then justify our choices because we have looked at alternatives.

Brookfield further points out that the various phrases used to describe critical thinking, such as critical analysis, critical awareness, critical consciousness and critical reflection are often vague, and he describes how the concept has been interpreted differently in different contexts. In philosophy and education it is seen as synonymous with developing logical reasoning ability. In psychology, criticality focuses more on manipulating thought processes, such as beliefs or values, or enhancing metacognitive understanding. Brookfield refers to these different interpretations of critical thinking as 'traditions'. It is worth exploring these in more detail.

Analytic – In the first tradition, according to Brookfield, critical thinking follows the work of Argyris (1982), with its use of lateral, divergent thinking strategies and double loop learning methods. Executives, for example, are said to learn critically when they examine assumptions that govern their business decisions by 'checking whether or not these decisions are grounded in an accurately assessed view of market realities' (Brookfield, 2005: 11). This tradition has its basis in analytic philosophy and logic. Traces can be seen in the work of Argyris, and other business or research models where accuracy of evidence and subsequent analysis is sovereign, and there is no requirement to question assumptions. This tradition works on the basis that critical thinking must be sensitive to the context, reliant on criteria, and be self-correcting (i.e. reflexive).

When coaches are recommended to become critical via reflective practice, it is often within this analytic frame of reference. As a coach developer based in Higher Education, the critical thinking I expect from student coaches in their essays and written papers requires an internal coherence between the evidence they present and the conclusions they draw. Similarly, a director of an organisation needs to examine the evidence underpinning decisions made. This is critical thinking, but it is not necessarily transformative, since no challenge or reframing is generated. Students are encouraged to become critical researchers and evidence-based practitioners, but the criticality works within the system, uncovering inconsistencies rather than questioning their premises. It is not transformational – although it has the potential to be so. It encourages the kinds of mind working that is eventually required to examine assumptions.

Doddington (2007) writes from within this tradition, suggesting that critical thinking is a type of logical thinking that 'helps us to analyse and make sense of, or interpret, all forms of situations or information so that the conclusions we draw from our interpretations are sound' (2007: 449). She argues that critical thinking is seen as 'vital to any *developed* life' (2007: 450, original emphasis). Such a critical thinking disposition is prized, she explains, and is achieved through the critical examination of underlying assumptions and the constant evaluation of beliefs and actions. The implication is that coaches must be critical thinkers in order to promote critical thinking in their client: 'to induct them into a stance towards the world in which information, problems and experience can be probed to form sound beliefs, decisions and judgements for a flourishing and well-grounded way of life' (Doddington, 2007: 450). Much of business, academia and science works with this analytic conception of critical thinking: it is not always appropriate or desirable to question the system, but it is always appropriate to question! As Brookfield points out, this form of criticality works *within* a specific culture, leaving the status quo unchallenged.

Democratic – However, criticality in business can also relate to the explicit critique of capitalism, where clients may recognise and be prepared to challenge the ethical issues involved in, for example, the relocation of global organisations to countries where labour is cheap, unions are not allowed and resources can be easily appropriated. In this tradition, criticality is required to challenge what Mezirow (1991) would term socio-cultural assumptions, where transformation begins with an identification of the cultural systems within which we operate and that are otherwise taken for granted. Brookfield presents the critical learning tasks for this tradition as challenging ideologies, contesting hegemony, unmasking power, overcoming alienation, learning liberation and reclaiming reason, and practising democracy.

However, such aspirations are not without their pitfalls for coaching. For many coaches there is a conflict between wanting a supposedly better, more democratic world for themselves and their clients, and the need to earn money to support their families. To encourage clients to question the system in which they live and work in the way this critical tradition suggests, requires the coach to hold an agenda for the client, which is generally an anathema for coaches: it also jeopardises livelihoods, since international organisations do not want their profitability challenged. Ironically, underpinning such a desire for a better world lies the assumption that everyone should become a critical thinker, including people currently exploited in other countries, and it could be argued that merely by facilitating the critical thinking capacity in other ways, via other traditions, it can ultimately have a similar liberating effect, without any immediate, overt confrontation.

In the above descriptions it can be seen that Brookfield has identified two contrasting 'traditions' of critical thinking: the analytic (basing decisions on extant

evidence) and the democratic (challenging authority). These two are sociologi-
cally grounded. But, there are two further traditions that he sets out, which
could be seen as psychologically grounded.

Psychotherapeutic – This tradition is encouraged by psychoanalysis and psychotherapy, which for the most part work with beliefs and inhibitions that are
uncritically acquired in childhood. This is the critical tradition underpinning a
good deal of coaching practice at present, and it uses cognitive behavioural and
rational emotive strategies to change thinking. Rational Emotive Behaviour
Therapy (REBT), for example, is used by a number of coaches. It was first
explained by Ellis (1957, 2003), who argued that thinking, emotion and action
are not really separate processes – they overlap; and much of what we call emotion is actually a biased, prejudiced, or strongly evaluative kind of thought. The
'pure' emotional experience (like our recall of experience) picks up value as it
emerges into consciousness. These values, preferences, biases (whatever we
may call them) in turn affect our thinking and subsequently our actions. REBT
is premised on the notion that beliefs are formed rationally and can be changed
through thinking. In REBT clients are encouraged to think about their problem
or issue using the A-B-C model, where 'A' is the activating event that brings
about the undesired consequence 'C', whether that happens to be emotional or
behavioural. Between the event and the consequence is a belief (B), which is
involved in evaluating the activating event. If the belief is fixed, inflexible or
seemingly dysfunctional, then the consequence can be negative and unhelpful
to the client. If the belief is efficacious and flexible the emotional or behavioural consequence is likely to be constructive and helpful. Thus, challenging
inflexible beliefs can have extremely beneficial and often transformational
effects. It can be seen, then, that REBT relies on a purely cognitive, rational
attempt to modify a client's thinking.

Constructivist – The final tradition identified by Brookfield is what he calls
'pragmatic constructivism' which emphasises the way people 'learn to construct and deconstruct their own experiences and meanings' (2005: 15).
Constructivism, as Brookfield explains, 'rejects universals and generalisable
truths and focuses instead on the variability of how people make interpretations of their experience' (2005: 15). In this tradition, evidence is still the starting point, but instead of using it to justify a position as in the analytic tradition,
it is tested in practical settings and the findings are then used to enhance
knowledge and understanding about the subject and the world. In this sense it
has a transformative capacity that is lacking in the analytic tradition.

Developing Brookfield's arguments further, I propose that thinking critically
about experience can be seen as operating in two paradigms, as shown in
Figure 7.1. The first paradigm involves validating where the client is now
(through reflection). This happens in two spheres: the psychological and the
sociological. In the psychological sphere, as suggested above, the client's experience is explored in an attempt to reveal his/her values and beliefs and shed
light on what the coaching task may be. Experience is examined in order to

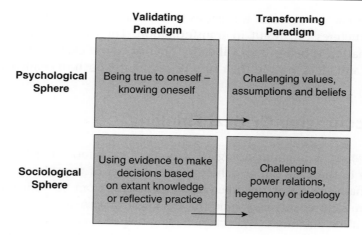

	Validating Paradigm	**Transforming Paradigm**
Psychological Sphere	Being true to oneself – knowing oneself	Challenging values, assumptions and beliefs
Sociological Sphere	Using evidence to make decisions based on extant knowledge or reflective practice	Challenging power relations, hegemony or ideology

Figure 7.1   Critical thinking paradigms

look for meaning, which in turn will validate experience. In the sociological sphere, the validating paradigm is manifested in the search for evidence-based practice, such as statistics, to justify research and reports, or competences to justify ability.

However, exploring experience from within the validating paradigm means that experience is only ever compared with existing knowledge. That paradigm, although it provides value-based judgements upon which to make decisions or choices, does not question whether such knowledge is beneficial or indeed useful in a wider context. It could be argued that the paradigm supports a status quo. By contrast, the transforming paradigm includes a challenge to current values and perspectives through the consideration of alternatives. As Brookfield argues:

> when we think critically we become aware of the diversity of values, behaviours, social structures, and artistic forms in the world. Through realizing this diversity, our commitments to our own values, actions, and social structures are informed by a sense of humility; we gain an awareness that others in the world have the same sense of certainty we do – but about ideas, values and actions that are completely contrary to our own. (1987: 5)

In Figure 7.1 these two forms of working critically (validating and transforming) are mapped against Brookfield's framework of psychological/interior focus and sociological/exterior focus to create quadrants that encompass these ideas. In coaching, although the validating paradigm is useful for creating trust and showing support for clients, it needs to be enhanced, first by acceptance that existing values and beliefs are OK, and then by a shift to the transforming paradigm through becoming critical, and challenging the client's assumptions; looking for opportunities to challenge the status quo. In the context of the workplace, moving from the validating paradigm in the sociological frame involves neither accepting evidence at face value nor relying on traditional practices to achieve results. It suggests that a challenge to extant ideologies or power structures can result in transformation. The assumption here is that transformation is better than validation, but of course even transformed perspectives and ideas must in their turn be constantly open to challenge.

III. Encouraging Critical Thinking

The move from phenomenological reflection to a more objective, critical approach to thinking can be achieved in a number of ways. In particular the transformative processes described here as emerging from the validation of the client, can help clients overcome the stuckness that sometimes accompanies significant life dilemmas. The coach, having helped clients identify and name their experiences, leads them to accept that their subjective involvement with their experience is only one interpretation. Then, through the use of particular challenging strategies, clients are carefully guided towards a place where more insight and meaning can be adduced.

Brookfield talks about two types of trigger that prompt transformative critical thinking. The first type could be an external trauma like a serious accident or illness, which can cause people to question the very bedrock of their lives and how the world works. Such events do not have to be negative: sometimes positive events, such as a promotion at work or the birth of a child, can have the same effect: 'In such circumstances we begin to reinterpret our past actions and ideas from a new vantage point. We begin to wonder if our old assumptions about our roles, personalities, and abilities were completely accurate' (Bookfield, 1987: 7). The second type of trigger is internal events aroused by our sceptical scrutiny – repeatedly testing our decisions and ideas against reality as we understand it. Our commitment to certain beliefs and values, rather than being weakened by such scepticism, is, Brookfield argues, 'all the more strong because it has passed through the fires of this critical analysis. Our commitment is informed and rational, balanced by a recognition of its possible falsity' (1987: 23).

According to Brookfield, there are four main components of critical thinking: becoming sceptical; identifying assumptions; challenging the influence of context; and exploring alternatives. Some of these components have been mentioned in the coaching and self-help literature (for example, Kline, 1998; Passmore, 2011), but are not reviewed comprehensively. I will therefore consider how each of these components applies in coaching and supports the shift from validation to transformation.

(1) Becoming Sceptical

When Brookfield talks about scepticism he is not talking about outright cynicism, rather it is a 'cautious intelligence' that examines all claims to an ultimate truth: commitments to the 'truth' are made only after 'a period of critically reflective analysis, during which we establish the validity of the apparently ultimate or final truth by examining its congruence with reality as we perceive it' (1987: 21). Brookfield describes critical thinking as a process, not an outcome. He explains that 'If we felt that we had reached a state of fully developed or realized critical awareness, we would be contradicting one of the central tenets of critical thinking – namely, that we are sceptical of any claims to universal truth or total certainty' (1987: 6). Uncertainties or dilemmas, then, are generated in two ways – either by external events or traumas, or by coach-engineered challenges to values and belief systems. In either event a coach needs to tread carefully and help generate full descriptions of the nature of the uncertainty, as described in the earlier parts of this book.

Scepticism is often thought of negatively. Sceptics are viewed as people who question everything and are certain of nothing. However, Denham-Vaughan and Edmond have described how 'it is only by holding one's own opinions and judgments lightly, that we can remain in contact with "what is" and allow new interpretations to emerge' (2010: 14). Citing Brothers, they talk of how when the certainties we cling to are revealed as unreliable, the trauma often 'plunges us into chaos, disorientation, terror and shame' (Brothers, 2008: 49–51), but when we hold our choices lightly we are better able to let go and to change. Hart suggests how this can result in insight: 'the dynamic tension of holding opposing views simultaneously may produce a shift in our normal waking state, catalyzing the development of a new schemata, and opening to intuitive insight or synthesis', adding that 'if we can hold the tension of the incompatibility or discrepancy long enough, a new perspective may break through' (2009: 77).

(2) Identifying Assumptions

Brookfield (1987) reminds us how important it is to be able to identify and challenge assumptions, but points out that the task is often difficult. He says that admitting that our assumptions, our perceptual filters, may be 'distorted, wrong, or contextually relative is often profoundly threatening, for it implies that the fabric of our personal existence might rest upon faulty foundations' (1987: 89). The coach then has a tricky task, because challenging the way in which clients make sense of the world will call into question the very beliefs and values that help them to cope with their lives. Coaching provides an ideal, safe, 'powerless', yet empowering environment. However, it should be noted that the task can be affected by the culture of the client's organisation. Forneris and Peden-McAlpine (2009) found, for example, that power and culture affect critical thinking in adverse ways: the ability to think clearly and critically is negatively impacted by helplessness and anxiety.

Brookfield also suggests that 'the right to challenge someone must be earned' (1987: 91). Clients, as we know, will only come to trust their coach enough to accept a challenge after a reasonably long period of contracting and getting to know each other. Thus, the groundwork provided by phenomenological reflection, listening and clarifying activities provides a starting point for challenge. Confidence to undertake challenge comes from knowing the situation in which clients find themselves – that is, knowing them well. Since the coach needs to challenge clients by suggesting they consider alternative strategies or approaches, it is not adequate to remain at a superficial, detached level of challenge 'with no accurate or specific knowledge of the viability of the alternatives facing the client' (Cox, 2003: 13).

In Chapter 4, we saw how authentic, hermeneutic listening also involves the identification by coaches of prejudices and taken-for-granted assumptions that underpin both their own and their clients' perceptions and actions. In normal conversation these assumptions would seldom be heeded, but coaches need to pay attention and be aware of them. In the move towards identifying assumptions, unlike in normal conversation, there will be significant interruption to patterns and habits of response which have hitherto been unquestioned. The following example from a session with Jasmine illustrates the disturbance the coach may create during a challenge.

Coach:	So it seems that you are suggesting that you can't sleep because you need to work until 11 o'clock every evening just to catch up with paperwork and administration.
Jasmine:	Yes, that's just the way it is at our place.
Coach:	Does this mean that everyone works in the evenings? Do you have evidence for that?
Jasmine:	Well, no. Some people seem to get away with it.
Coach:	Get away with?
Jasmine:	Yes, get away with. They get away with giving their work to other people, like delegating it or maybe they just don't have as much work?
Coach:	So you're assuming you have more work than anyone else and that you can't delegate any of it?
Jasmine:	Hmm [long pause]. I suppose I have been thinking that way.

From this example, it can be seen that challenges are made that would not normally feature in everyday conversation, or indeed in the validating paradigm described earlier. The coach has encouraged the client to think carefully about the claims she is making about the workplace. Often this is all the coach needs to do to activate a change in thinking by the client. The success of the dialogue hinges on developing an incisive question (Kline, 1998). In the dialogue above, if Jasmine didn't reach this point on her own, the coach might continue with:

Coach:	If you knew you had the same amount of work as everyone else and that you could delegate some of it, what would you do?

Similarly, another strategy, that Sintonen (2004: 261) discusses, is recognition of anomalies. If the client gives a response that contradicts the rest of the story, that then becomes significant. Anomaly awareness is particularly important to the coaching alliance because it may indicate goal violation: anomalies may be detected through diversionary behaviour by the client at any point during the coaching, and suggest that the client's motivation supports a different goal/task than the one articulated. It may be that the dilemma first discussed was in fact imprecise, perhaps because it related to workplace demands rather than personal needs and ambitions. However, coaches and clients are more likely to notice and discuss the anomaly if the phenomenological description of the initiating experience has been attended to.

Various strategies exist in psychotherapy and other spheres that can assist identification of assumptions. For example, Transactional Analysis is useful for thinking about relationship issues. 'Drama triangles' can often be identified where a client has a problem that has its origin in difficult relationships with certain others. The drama triangle comprises three roles that are unconsciously adopted in turn by participants in the drama. These roles are identified as persecutor, rescuer and victim (Karpman, 1968). The people in the drama are all in some kind of distress and occupy one of the roles, but frequently switch to another role as distress increases. A rescuer for example, may try to help someone in the office, to give that person the confidence to speak to a tyrant boss (currently the persecutor), but such help can get in the way of resolution, and can in fact reinforce dependency. Often a rescuer can become a victim, if the original victim perceives that advice was not sound or sincere, for example. In this way a victim can become a persecutor, attacking or blaming the rescuer.

Burgess describes how, in the rescuer role, anger at the lack of appreciation or response of the victim, can shift them into the role of persecutor, or the victim can move into the persecutor role, getting 'angry at the way others will not take away their problems, or even angry at the way they do' (Burgess, 2005: 101). Similarly, the person who is originally seen as a persecutor may become the victim when the current victim gains confidence to speak out. A victim is the over-adaptive wounded party who feels hurt from being blamed or 'victimised'. Thus it can be seen that the drama triangle becomes a self-fulfilling and self-perpetuating cycle that can be very difficult to break. Burgess (2005) explains the dynamic inherent in the drama triangle: people flip from one role to another, either pushing or being pushed by the others in the game. Unfortunately, despite this movement of roles, people can stay for a long time within the destructive dynamic of the drama triangle, and it sometimes takes the intervention of a third party to resolve it.

From the coach's perspective, something needs to be done if clients' assumptions consistently suggest a drama is being played out. However, as in the challenge dialogue with Jasmine above, often all that is needed is for clients to be made aware of the existence of the triangle through discussion with the coach. It then becomes easier for them to break the cycle of blame by becoming more objective and resisting the temptation to be part of the drama.

(3) Challenging the Influence of Context

Brookfield (1987) argues that context is vitally important to critical thinking, since it is manifest in all attitudes and behaviours. For coaches, this means helping clients become aware of how hidden and uncritically assimilated assumptions are embedded in all they and others do, thus shaping all perceptions and interpretations. Sometimes, in the process of developing a critical outlook, clients may still feel they have no choices. The coach's role then is to find ways of helping clients see that everything is in fact culturally or contextually conditioned, and is therefore arbitrary and mutable. A skilful coach can help clients understand that developing the capacity to take account of context helps them extend their choices and so empowers them. Clients become liberated when they understand that there are choices of culturally and contextually bound alternatives. It is at this point that they can assert their authority, albeit a different quality of authority – one that encompasses humility.

A strategy that may be helpful for thinking critically about context is counterfactual thinking. Kray et al. (2010), for example, report on how thinking counterfactually or hypothetically about the past, can be instrumental in creating awareness. Coaches can ask questions that help the client explore what might have happened differently had the context been different. This 'what if?' approach has two functions: firstly it helps heighten the meaningfulness of the client's life experiences, and secondly it enables different perspectives to be examined and considered. The second function can lead to some useful reframing. Reframing, as Conoley and Conoley explain is an 'interpretation that describes some bit of data accurately but with a slight twist. It is meant to insert some new information for ... review that could lead to a more helpful understanding of a particular ... truth or dynamic' (2009: 40). Lee refers to it as 'a shift in perspective – a new way of seeing and experiencing that takes in new possibilities and that opens the door to change' (2003: 124).

(4) Exploring Alternatives

According to Schlick (1932) knowledge of something requires comparison with something else. So one of the important aspects of critical thinking is exploring alternatives. Again, this begins with the comparison of the hard-won phenomenological description of the client's dilemma with other experiences and events. By linking recent experiences to earlier ones and looking for commonalities and differences, the client can begin to view things from alternative perspectives, and set down more complex and interrelated mental schema that will ultimately lead to transformative learning and significant, lasting change.

Clients who feel trapped and think that there are no alternatives, invariably keep circling around the same problem. They feel stuck, and are unable to generate new options for behaving differently. The questions that the coach asks can help them view the problem from a completely different perspective. A simple question such as 'What would you do if you had a personal assistant to delegate to?' or 'What would you do if you had your evenings free?' could prompt the client in the scenario introduced earlier, to generate alternatives that could lead to a motivating action plan, as well as an enhanced capacity for critical thinking. Such questions have the power to increase the variety of options available.

Critical reflection also requires evaluations and categorisations of such alternatives to be made. When people think in these ways it enriches their experience and things become more meaningful. Discussion that involves only descriptions, such as the anecdotes exchanged at a social gathering or indeed the phenomenological descriptions encouraged earlier in the coaching process, are validating and useful as starting points, but they are not constitutive of learning unless they subsequently explore meanings. Furthermore, in the workplace most people do not get the thinking time to analyse, evaluate and synthesise their experiences. This is the reason why the space provided by coaching is so vital.

The Role of Emotions in Critical Thinking

Emotions, traditionally, have been held to be a hindrance to critical thinking. However, Brookfield argues that critical thinking is emotive as well as rational. He suggests that in critical thinking 'we cannot help but become aware of the importance of emotions to this activity ... Asking critical questions about our previously accepted values, ideas and behaviours is anxiety producing' (1987: 7). He explains:

> We may well feel fearful of the consequences that might arise from contemplating alternatives to our current ways of thinking and living; resistance, resentment, and confusion are evident at various stages in the critical thinking process. But we also feel joy, release, relief, and exhilaration as we break through to new ways of looking at our personal, work and political worlds. As we abandon assumptions that had been inhibiting our development, we experience a sense of liberation. (1987: 7)

Brookfield also says that as we come to realise that we have the capacity to change aspects of our lives, we are 'charged with excitement. As we realize these changes, we feel a pleasing sense of self-confidence' (1987: 7). This suggests that helpers, such as coaches, should not ignore these emotions.

The advent of Dual Process Theory (Evans, 2003, 2008) has recently given long-overdue respectability to the place of emotions, the practice of reflection, and any associated attempts to bring the pre-reflective into a more cognitive, reflective space. The Dual Process Theory celebrates an interplay between reasoning and reflection. Whereas the descriptive process of phenomenological reflection is designed to lead clients inductively towards a subjective picture of their experience, the critical thinking process is channelled towards leading them away from that subjectivity towards a more deductive or objective viewpoint. This move is important. It is vital to avoid the natural tendency to dwell on emotional hurts and preconceptions. In ordinary conversations with friends and colleagues we tend to stay in this place and not apply our powers of criticality to the situation. However, it is not the role of the coach to be a friend or a colleague. Thinking at this point in the Experiential Coaching Cycle becomes more overtly objective and critical. Its focus is objective analysis, and that is what the coach should encourage to generate critical thinking.

Summary

In this chapter and the previous chapter I have explained two different, but intricately interrelated types of reflection, a descriptive phenomenological type that tries to get as close as possible to the experience and accept it without judgement, and an analytic, thinking type that accepts nothing and takes a critical approach to making meaning from that experience. Their relationship is interesting because it is not causal in the way I have needed to suggest in these two chapters; rather it is symbiotic, as described above – each is incomplete without the other. Some of the models of reflection discussed in Chapter 6 recognised this inter-dependency, and indeed in workshops with students where such models have been tested, I have found that they invariably comment on how the models cannot be used linearly.

In this chapter I also pointed out the difference between reflection that validates in the same way as a mirror might, and critical thinking which exploits different lenses in order to provide the option of transforming current thinking. This differentiation has implications for the tools and techniques that coaches use, with life history exercises, journaling and concept maps seeming to sustain a status quo unless used critically. The role of critical thinking in coaching is to encourage the client's thinking towards three main outcomes:

1   an objective understanding of intuitions, dilemmas and perceived goals;
2   rational thinking to aid decision making and problem solving;
3   evaluation of incidents (own and vicarious) in order to create conditions for intuitive, rapid decisions based on experience.

The dynamic of the shift in emphasis from validation to transformation helps to highlight a difference between coaching, mentoring and counselling. We can see how the coach, through encouraging critical thinking, tends more towards being a self-directed learning specialist, which is in contrast to common definitions of a mentor as a knowledgeable expert, and a counsellor as someone who helps clients understand their current situation, rather than transform it. Critical thinking may be encouraged by the mentor, but it is often enhanced by the vicarious experience and judgement of the mentor, rather than being generated by the client. Critical thinking in the counselling literature is discussed only in relation to developing criticality for the counsellor, rather than for the client (see for example, Feltham, 2010).

One area that I have deliberately not touched on in this chapter is the potential for cognitive development stimulated by critical thinking. It can be noted, for example, that a shift from the subjective activity of phenomenological reflection to the more objective focus on critical thinking, is suggestive of the subject/object dynamic in Kegan's work (1982, 1994). Adult cognitive development is a complex and contentious area of adult learning, and there was not space here to consider the issues and implications in detail. However, these have been discussed at length elsewhere (Bachkirova, 2010; Bachkirova and Cox, 2008; Cox and Jackson, 2010).

The chapter did, however, stress how, as clients begin to think critically about their values, beliefs and behaviours, they do begin a precarious journey of considering new perspectives and actions. Critical thinking is an iterative process: it is an interplay between experience, phenomenological reflection on and description of that experience, acceptance, and subsequent critical reflection and analysis of the experience. It can be challenging and emotional for coach and client, but if coaching only encourages reflection it undersells itself. Clients need to reach beyond individualistic aims and visions. If coaching fails to help them bracket and then accept their views as contingent, to see their experience differently and then challenge their original perceptions, then it isn't coaching! In the next chapter I explore the part that questioning plays in this challenge process.

8
Questioning

Chapter Aims:

- To examine the function of questioning in the coaching context
- To explore how coaching questions originate
- To review various typologies of questions and their application to coaching

Many novice coaches ask 'How does the coach know what questions to ask?' Indeed, in my experience the quality and power of their potential questioning is the one thing that worries new coaches most of all. However, although the coaching literature extols the effectiveness of questions, it fails to mention just why they are so valuable or to stress the idiosyncratic way in which questions arise. This chapter, therefore, draws on theories from cognitive science, philosophy and the learning sciences in order to examine the purposes and functions of questioning for the coach and the client. It explores where questions come from and the different types that exist, including the significance of the 'why' question, which is often held to be problematic. Through the chapter, I hope to begin to explicate a theory of questioning that reveals why it is considered to be one of the most powerful elements of coaching; useful for helping the client reflect on experience and for encouraging criticality.

Almost all texts that introduce coaching mention the importance of the different types of questioning. For example, Bresser and Wilson describe questions as 'the precision tools in the coach's toolkit' (2006: 18) and, in describing their CLEAR coaching process, Hawkins and Smith suggest that powerful questions are core as they 'enable the coachee to explore the situation from different standpoints and generate new perspectives and possibilities' (2010: 239). Kemp also identifies questions as vital, suggesting that what he terms 'insight-driven questions' (2008: 42) can stimulate deeper personal awareness and reflection. He suggests that questions such as 'If you were to change your view of the current situation, what would that allow for?' and 'What may be possible if you were to make the change you are describing?' invite clients to free themselves from self-limiting beliefs and thought processes. Oliver too gives examples of questions that are useful in generating reflexivity in a coaching context (2010).

Skiffington and Zeus (2003) and Whitmore (2009) probably give most space to explaining the importance of questioning. Skiffington and Zeus look at three types of questions that are based on Argyris and Schön's (1978) levels of learning. Single loop questions are those that explore issues on a superficial level. The questions tend to focus on what actions the client will perform to resolve a problem. Double loop questions go beyond the surface to look at assumptions and ask why events have happened and what has contributed to them. Such questions invite reflection and may look at issues such as the status of the individual in the organisation, or inherent structures of the organisation that indirectly impact on performance. Torbert (1999) goes beyond Argyris and Schön, describing first-, second- and third-person questioning that involves perspective taking and generates single-, double- and triple-loop feedback. Whitmore (2009) devotes a whole chapter to the notion of effective questions – discussing the effect of different questions, and also hinting at the importance of questioning in, for example, helping the client to bring vital subconscious factors into awareness.

However, as Alexander (2006) acknowledges, coaching interactions always need to be appropriate to the individual, and need to take account of and relate to his or her unique position. Thus, even though a lot of texts do try to list different types of questions as a guide, the coach cannot fall back on a predictable set of tried and trusted questions. This chapter shows why lists of questions are inadequate in the coaching context. It explains how questions arise and how they are effective in different ways. Once the coach understands the underlying principles then lists are unnecessary.

The chapter has four main sections. It begins by looking at who is doing the questioning and introduces the concept of the coaching alliance as a particular system of knowledge acquisition which extends the cognitive function of the coaching relationship. In section II the purpose of questions is discussed and from there I discuss how questions arise from partial knowledge, and also look at what constitutes a good question. This section also explores the role of the coach's existing knowledge in question formulation. Types of questions are discussed in section III and section IV briefly discusses answers.

I. Coaching as a Form of Extended Cognition

In order to explore the purpose of questions and look at how they are formed and used in the coaching context, it is useful first to think of the coaching alliance as a form of extended cognition. Extended cognition has been defined as cognitive processing that extends into the environment surrounding the organism (Rupert, 2004). It is the notion that the brain, the body and the external world are dynamically coupled, and that mental states and cognitive functions might be viewed as extending spatio-temporally beyond the human organism (Chemero and Silberstein, 2007).

If we think of coaching as an alliance that is a form of extended cognition, then we can talk about the alliance itself as learning in an incremental way, due partly to the ignorance (or in certain contexts the authoritative doubt) of the coach, but also due to the client's continued unlearning and relearning prompted by the coach's necessarily naïve questions. In this way, as Ram (1991) suggests, the 'understander' (in this case the alliance) changes even as its questions change. So the coaching alliance learns: by noticing interesting aspects of the client's story the coach generates questions and the alliance fills in the gaps in its conjoined memory that correspond to questions unanswered from previous experiences. Like any other learner, the alliance learns by acquiring a new piece of knowledge or by organising its existing knowledge differently. A new piece of knowledge may result in either a new explanation or it may be used to fill a gap in an existing explanation, but both help the alliance come a little closer to a more complete understanding of the task and its resolution. Each type of learning may also result in a new set of questions as the alliance realises what else it needs to learn.

It may also be helpful here to think of the alliance as a coupled system. Clark and Chalmers define a coupled system as one where a human organism is linked with an external entity (in this case the created coaching alliance) in a two-way interaction that can be seen as 'a cognitive system in its own right' (1998: 29). Because the coupled system of the alliance does not have a 'memory' at the start of the coaching, the client, with the help of the coach, has to populate it with data. Cavanagh explains what happens when such information is put into the space between the coach and the client, in what he calls the external space:

> The knowledge that is elicited is new knowledge – we coaches see it in the connections between what the client is experiencing and our own experience and understandings. When we are truly engaged in the conversation, this emergent knowledge has the character of insight, rather than of the mechanical overlay of our pre-existing models on the client's situation. (2006: 339)

In an ideal scenario, both the coach and the client enter the alliance with a degree of ignorance or tentativeness that allows them to sublimate their existing knowledge, biases and presuppositions to the questioning emptiness of the alliance.

In Table 8.1 the role of the coach and client in forging an extended cognitive alliance is made explicit. Following Ram's (1991) model, the process of knowledge acquisition for the alliance is shown in six stages.

So it can already be seen that question generation is an idiosyncratic and dynamic process – questions are contextual and arise based on the requirements of the current task. In addition, as Ram suggests, questions may be 'indexed' in what he calls 'opportunistic memory' (1991: 287) suggesting that the coach (on behalf of the alliance) can 'hold' questions, like hypotheses or pending questions that represent what is still not understood or verified. Then, as the client tells of further experiences, the alliance 'remembers' previously unanswered questions. The alliance's understanding of the task is gradually refined as more questions are answered. In addition, as the alliance learns more

Table 8.1   The coaching/client alliance: a model of question-driven understanding and learning

Stage	Client	The alliance	Coach
1.	Tells story – maybe constructing it for the first time	Construction of the story provides basis for the coaching work	Hears the client's story (may be some minimal representation in own memory) and tries to build an understanding of the situation on behalf of the alliance.
2.	May be hearing the story for the first time – sometimes the answers are there already in the telling (learning occurs)	The story becomes a reference point	Hears how the story relates to the client's aim for the coaching – the task.
3.	Begins to formulate own questions	Questions formulated tentatively provide focus	Retrieves and reflexively assesses questions from own memory that might be relevant. This understanding produces questions – usually simple ones at the outset.
4.	Answers own and coach's questions to move the task forward (learning occurs)	Shared history of questions and answers facilitates rethinking	Hears the answers and considers whether they move the task forward. Adopts position of ignorance (authoritative doubt) to devise further questions.
5.	Answers more questions, based on new input from coach	A bank of relevant information is built to help clients with the task	Generates new questions, based on next inputs from client. Makes the inferences required to match the answer to the question, but also considers further pieces of information that are likely to be relevant to the task.
6.	Constructs explanations and new routes forward	Summaries and checks ensure continuity, congruence and relevance	Summarises, paraphrases, provides feedback (see Chapter 5)

about the task, the coach can ask better and more detailed questions and the client can give more informed answers. The aim is integration, which is directed by the task, and questions focus attention on aspects of the client's story that allow the understander (the alliance) to learn something of interest to its needs. As Sintonen explains: 'questions are precisely the means of focusing on a particular issue, and of making important contrasts. To put it metaphorically, questions are cognitive pegs in which relevant background knowledge can be hung' (1999: 131).

Another additional benefit of thinking about the coaching relationship as a coupled system and as an extended cognitive alliance is that Payne's (2006) concerns about threats or interrogation are vastly reduced. It is not the individual that is being questioned, but the knowledge held by the alliance formed between the coach and the client. The client chooses what to input into the alliance space, via his/her agenda, story and responses to questions, and both parties work with what is available. Openness is therefore key in the process.

II. The Purpose and Origin of Questions

The only reason why a coach asks questions is to move the client closer to some resolution of the task. With this single aim in mind, it is possible to see how explanations about questioning that have their basis in other disciplines, such as psychology and education, may fail to fit with a theory of questioning in coaching. These theories presuppose that the questioner has an agenda of his/ her own that drives the questioning. In what follows I show that questioning in coaching is different.

Ram, working in the field of cognitive science, suggests that 'questions arise from an interaction between the interests of the goals of the understander and the information provided by the environment' (1991: 275). He describes a theory of a dynamic understander being driven by its own questions or goals to acquire knowledge. Thus, at the centre of Ram's theory are the knowledge goals of the question asker. However, in coaching, the actual question asker is the coach and yet it is not the coach's knowledge goals that are being satisfied. In coaching it is the knowledge goals of the client that are paramount in the effort to achieve the task, and yet the client is not asking the questions: the questions the coach asks need to serve the interests of the client and not satisfy his/her own curiosity, as suggested by Ram's theory. This indicates that we need to modify this theory of questioning for coaching.

Ram further suggests that all questions are founded on four types of knowledge gleaned from storytelling (Ram, 1991: 303–304). Made relevant for coaching, the four are:

1 Parser-level tasks, related to the construction of language and grammar;
2 Integration of facts, with what the understander (in this case the alliance) already knows;
3 Detection of anomalies in the client's story (that may identify flaws or gaps in the alliance's developing knowledge of context, or may reveal contradictions in the story that are worth questioning with the client);
4 Formulation of explanations (for the alliance) which resolve anomalies and confirm or refute earlier explanations. Such formulation is used as the basis of new explanations for use in understanding by the alliance of future stories and situations. In formulating explanations the alliance needs to know more about the situation than is explicitly stated, and so questions will be generated.

It is true that at the outset, the coach has to integrate the facts of the client's story in order to situate the task in a context, and so there is a dual aspect to the coach's questioning: the information required to understand the context at the outset is help on behalf of the alliance. It is purely instrumental and leads to the formulation of the more strategic questions needed to move the client forward. This progression is similar to the little questions and big questions referred to by Sintonen (2004). Sintonen suggests that questions actually come in two sizes – large and small – where small questions have the instrumental role of bringing in information needed in the construction of the big question. Thus, a seemingly small question may turn out to be influential in generating a larger, more important question later in the coaching sequence.

We can see, then, that at no point do coaches ask questions to satisfy their own learning needs or curiosity. In coaching the situation is different. So, unlike in Ram's theory (1991), a theory of questions in coaching would need to exclude the coach's need to know and substitute the coach's need to clarify the task and ask questions that help the client to know. Ram's basic assumption that asking questions is central to understanding still applies, but applies in a different way. The coach is still the 'reasoner' in that he/she asks the questions, but is not the 'understander' in Ram's sense of the word. The understander in the coaching context is, as I reaffirm throughout this book, the alliance formed between coach and client, and ultimately the client, who constructs the explanations in response to the questions.

Role of the Coach's Existing Knowledge

The coach is interested in the client's task in order to help the client, and as such it is a requirement for the coach that his/her knowledge demands be sublimated so that the requirements of the situation (the client task) can be attended to. As Block Lewis claims, 'in truly cooperative work, personal needs can function only as they are relevant to the objective situations; the common objective in other words is more important than any personal objective' (1944: 115). In this sense the coaching relationship is asymmetrical, since the personal objectives of the coach are diminished, while the task-goals or even ego-goals of the client are highlighted. Learning in the coaching alliance is also unbalanced, since it can only focus on the interests or questions that are relevant to the client task. This suggests that the coach should only ask a question when the client needs to acquire a piece of knowledge, or the coach, acting on behalf of the alliance, needs information to enable construction of further questions that can help the client acquire such knowledge.

Without the above modifications, Ram's argument would suggest that understanding comes from relating what we hear to the questions that we already have. That is to say, if coaches have an understanding of the context already, then their questions (for better or worse) will be based on that understanding. In reality, many coaches will have more knowledge of a context than their clients. Internal coaches, for example, may have significant knowledge of how the organisation operates. So coaches in these situations often act as if they do not have the knowledge. But they do it not from a position of pretence or subterfuge; they do it from a position of authoritative doubt (Oliver, 2010) whereby they facilitate the 'right answer' to come from the client through questioning, even though they may have an understanding of the answer themselves. One of the dangers of having background knowledge is that the coach may actually anticipate admissible answers. However, what happens in practice is that coaches attempt to ask the questions on behalf of the alliance that they judge are ones that will help the client with his/her understanding, using 'authoritative doubt'.

It is often argued that it is better if coaches have no prior understanding of the client's context. Indeed, this is often seen as one of the differentiating features of coaching, and now we can see why – if questions are dependent upon the knowledge coaches already have, then the less prior knowledge coaches have, the more current information they will need to gather on behalf of the alliance, and the 'purer', less contaminated, more naïve and innocent the questioning is likely to be.

Interestingly, Kemp identifies how Overholser (1996) has argued for the adoption of a position of ignorance by therapists within counselling relationships. This position of ignorance can be interpreted as the adoption of a mindset of an inquisitive and curious learner, underpinned by genuine interest, concern and unconditional positive regard. By adopting this position, Kemp argues, a coach creates the conversational and psychic space to allow for the client's needs and reflections to surface. The coach in effect occupies the empty space of the alliance which is devoid of information at the start of the coaching (see Table 8.1).

The empty space metaphor could be useful for novice coaches to utilise in preparing for their coaching. If they step into the alliance space at the outset they can adopt the position of knowing nothing about the client or the task and are free to ask simple questions. The subsequent new questions will be based on the client responses, not based on their own prior understandings. Hopefully too, the client will not repeat well rehearsed arguments, but will also enter the space with creativity.

In coaching, some questions (particularly small questions) act as starting points – they are heuristic guides. The initial questions build sufficient knowledge for the coach to be able to pick out something salient that requires the special attention of the alliance. It is argued that in a successful process of inquiry new questions are generated from an original question (Ram, 1991; Sintonen, 2004). Sudden flashes or perceptual reorganisations are made possible by a series of transformations in the organisation of knowledge. These could be what clients see as 'good' questions, and they appear to be entirely serendipitous. Sintonen asks about the criteria for a good question: ' … good questions have plenty of gosh value, where gosh value depends on the cognitive gains obtained if conclusive answers can be found to them' (2004: 255). Sometimes clients do exclaim 'Gosh that's a good question; I've not considered that before'. So 'gosh value' in the coaching context means that a question has some perceived cognitive gains for the client.

Pending Questions

Ram (1991) also introduces the notion of pending questions, which are those that the questioner (in this case, the alliance) will find answers to incidentally, or opportunistically, when it is thinking about some other question. A specific question can prompt an unexpected answer to turn up in the discussion (see example dialogues later in this chapter, where the client realises that Jones may not be picking him out for bad treatment). This theory suggests that a question raised during a specific coaching session may be one actually formed earlier in the session, or even in a previous session, and the delay in answering represents the imminent knowledge goal of that particular coaching alliance at that point in time.

Similarly, Ram (1991) suggests that the process of question transformation leads to understanding, so that the understander actually uses questions to focus the reasoning process. This suggests that coaches use the development of their own understanding of the domain/task through a series of questions, in order to help the client rethink their understanding of the domain/task. This is another function of questions and another function of the coach – to rework the needs of their own understanding in service of the alliance and the client's task.

Charged Questions

Wilberg (2004) talks about charged questions, highlighting that questions are a way of articulating an absence or obscurity of connection: 'a verbal question – any question – is essentially a way of representing this absent relation, this missing connection between two things and two people' (2004: 46). This is an interesting idea and may account for one of the perceptible, but as yet unarticulated, strengths of coaching. If 'real' questions, that is those that come from a genuine curiosity, create an absence of connection because the answerer (client) discerns an apparent lack of understanding, then it would follow that a coach is better not to ask 'real' questions. In bracketing his/her own curiosity in favour of asking questions that shift the client's thinking in the space of the alliance, what the coach is creating is not a gap or absence of connection, but a significant link. A connection is created by the fact that the question is really the client's question. The question is charged by its very relevance to the client and the client's coaching task. Research would be needed to consider whether this 'charge' is what creates the trust and rapport that is evident between so many coaches and their clients.

Coach Bias

Unfortunately, however non-judgemental and uninformed the coach might set out to be in the coaching engagement, all people are necessarily biased: 'they interpret stories in a manner that suits them' (Ram, 1991: 278). So coaches cannot help but sometimes put their own interpretive spin on the explanations that clients give. There will always be instances when even the experienced coach may jump to conclusions, compromising the effectiveness of the alliance and also affecting the quality of the questions. Ram explains that there are two ways in which this 'jumping to conclusions' happens:

1 *Variable-depth parsing.* 'People concentrate on details that they find relevant or interesting and skim over the rest' (Ram, 1991: 289). So it is likely that coaches could home in on points in the client's story that interest them, based on prior knowledge and experience. For instance if a coach was once by-passed for promotion and now the client is being considered for promotion, the memory of the unsatisfied goal may lead the coach to focus questions on the most relevant details (to the coach) of the client's story. So it appears that domain knowledge might hinder the coach and the task of the alliance, despite their best intentions. Similarly, if the coach has organisational goals in their memory, following, for example, an initial meeting with the Human Resource Department of the client's organisation, then questions are inevitably going to be influenced to some extent by the goals of the organisation as well as the task of the client.

2 *Learning and change.* According to Ram, people change as they read, or in the case of the coaching alliance, listen. If this is true, the implications for coaching are immense. It suggests that the coach on behalf of the alliance has to be alert to the progress of the client, and not assume that what seemed the case at the start of the coaching is the same three or four sessions in.

III. Types of Questions

Open and Closed Questions

Open and closed questions are probably the most familiar types of questions. Closed questions require clients to recall facts, experiences or behaviours, make a decision between a limited selection of choices or offer no response at all. Open-ended questions encourage speculation and have the potential for sustained, shared thinking and talking. Nicholson et al. (2006: 65) make the distinction between open questions (ones that begin 'How', 'What', 'Why', 'Who', 'When', or 'Where') and closed questions that have a 'Yes' or 'No' or one word answer. They suggest that a series of closed questions can sound like interrogation, and argue that the most effective pattern is to ask open questions and then follow up with closed questions if more information is needed. They also highlight leading questions, such as 'I suppose you're thinking of leaving now?' that are both closed and suggest the right answer. Thus, differences in the wording of a question can have a significant effect.

Coaches tend to use open-ended questions to elicit a longer, fuller answer. In the coaching literature, Hawkins and Smith (2010) list types of questions, including: closed questions that seek data or facts; open questions that seek information about a topic; leading questions that seek information, but indirectly suggest how the question is to be answered; and inquiry questions and transformational questions that both invite active investigation.

Munch and Swasy, working in the field of marketing communications, argue that differences in the grammatical structure of questions (e.g. the open/closed dichotomy) can create different pressures for respondents: 'the most coercive questions leave the fewest options open to the respondent, whereas the least coercion occurs when discourse constraints are at a minimum (e.g. open questions)' (1983: 211). Research in courtroom settings also seems to suggest that responses to open-ended questions produce greater commitment and realisation than responses to closed questions. However, it is important to note that before clients feel able to answer an open question such as 'What's important to you about x?' they must perceive the coach as safe and, above all, trustworthy. Open questions can seem invasive unless trust is established, but trust can be achieved through the use of small, closed questions which, as suggested earlier, can be used as heuristics that get closer to the big question. Only when trust has been established can the coach use open questions to good effect.

Graesser, Person and Magliano (1995: 511) propose six types of open questions that have an application to coaching:

1 Antecedent questions (why? how?): What caused an event? What logically explains or justifies a proposition? These need to be used cautiously in coaching since exploring causation or justifying actions can frequently be non-productive.
2 Consequence questions (what if? what next?): What are the causal consequences of a state or event? What are the logical consequences of a proposition? These are useful questions to use both retrospectively and hypothetically.
3 Goal orientation (why?): What are the goals or motives behind certain actions? Looking at motivation for the task is useful at various points in the alliance as it allows clients to revisit their original impetus in the light of ongoing learning and change.
4 Enablement (why? how?): What object, state or resource allows an agent (the client) to perform an action? What state or event allows another state or event to occur?
5 Instrumental-procedural (how?): What instrument or plan would allow the client to accomplish a goal?
6 Expectational (why not?): Why did an expected state or event not occur? Why did the client not do something? This use of the 'why' question may sound accusational and should therefore be used carefully.

The Why Question

Brockbank and McGill (2006), and others, are cautious about using 'why' questions in coaching. Questions such as: 'Why do you want to change your job?', they argue, can be interpreted as an attack on assumptions. In the Neuro-Linguistic Programming (NLP) meta-model there is also a concern to avoid asking the 'why' question, mainly because of the perceived tendency to feel the need to defend what has been said or done, or to make excuses or rationalise behaviour. It is often felt that a 'how' question provides better understanding and is less confrontational. Sintonen (2004) explains that why questions have a peculiar quality. They can indicate that the questioner's expectations are not being met and so can be cognitively challenging for the respondent. Nicholson et al. also argue that why questions can lead to the interviewee 'feeling attacked, or making up an answer ...' (2006: 65). They urge consideration of the difference between 'Why are you scared of x?' and 'Can you say what scares you about x?' The second of these examples allows the client to objectify the response, making it less of a personal admission.

It is also thought that the question 'Why?' automatically puts clients in defence mode, and they try to justify the problem or behaviour, with the effect of possibly reinforcing or emphasising it. Substituting 'why' with 'How can we approach this stuff differently?' or 'What can we do to understand the problem?' is considered better in some circumstances.

However, in coaching the why question may be useful. Coaches are not looking for the cause in order just to know it. As suggested earlier, they are not seeking answers to their own questions, they are acting on behalf of the 'alliance' and are looking for answers on behalf of the client. The cause and the possible assumptions underpinning the cause, that can be identified through use of the why question, do need to be examined if the client is to be adequately challenged. So the why question has its uses, particularly, I would argue, to stimulate challenge in performance or goal-focused coaching.

The resistance to the why question probably has its origins in Aristotle – where the request for an explanation using 'why' implies a link with causation. Bromberger discusses this scientific use of the why question at length, the problem being that it can 'call for and countenance very different answers' (1992: 19). Clients may produce different rationales, so looking for a cause, according to Bromberger's logic, is often self-defeating. However, not all why questions are requests for an explanation that identifies a cause, especially not a cause in the sense implied by Aristotle. McClure and Hilton (1998), in their research, show how the why question can in fact be very useful. Their study reveals that by framing a causal question as an 'explain' question (using 'what', 'how', etc.), rather than as a 'why' question (as many coaches tend to do in avoidance of why), actually increases the use of preconditions or factors that need to be in place before goals can be achieved. Using 'why', on the other hand, actually encourages goals to be given as explanations more than preconditions. The results of this research suggest that if clients are asked why an action occurred, they select their goals as explanations, and these are considered to be better explanations than the preconditions, since people can more easily change those conditions around. For the coach, the outcomes of this research are important and demonstrate why the 'why' question plays an important role in questioning. The why question reaches the heart of the answer – pulling out the true goal or value from the client, whereas pussyfooting around, changing the why question to something less penetrating, may result merely in a list of preconditions for the goal, rather than shedding light on the goal. The why question is important because it uncovers 'strategic principles' – it may be better to ask 'Why have you come to coaching?' rather than 'What do you want to achieve through the coaching?'. With the why question clients have more options (for example, my boss sent me; to become a better decision maker; to be more likeable), and the explanation provides vital information about what is important to the client and the ultimate task of the coaching.

Socratic Questions

Many coaching and education texts mention the Socratic Method as the underpinning approach to questioning in coaching. Davey Chesters (2010), for example, describes the seven steps in the Socratic Dialogue Method: choosing an appropriate question; choosing a personal experience to apply to the question; finding a core statement; identifying the experience in the core statement; formulating a definition; testing the validity of the core statement; and, finally, finding counter examples. She states that these steps must be followed rigorously in order to finish the dialogue, and that through this process Socratic questions aim at increased understanding through a constant striving for consensus.

Neenan (2009) also champions the method, describing it as indispensable for raising awareness, promoting reflection and improving problem solving. Brockbank and McGill similarly make the claim that helpers use the Socratic Method to 'enable their clients to generate their own goals and address the prevailing discourse, their assumptions and the taken-for-granted (tfgs) in their lives' (2006: 215).

This infatuation with the Socratic Method appears to be based on the enabling nature of the questions, which it is suggested are different from interrogative questions – although equally probing: 'questioning aims to enable clients to struggle with the issue under consideration, challenging embedded paradigms and encouraging consideration of possibilities, without restricting the range of possible solutions and without providing a ready-made solution' (Brockbank and McGill, 2006: 215).

This type of questioning, Brockbank and McGill insist, mirrors the style of inquiry in Plato's *Meno* (Jowett, 1953: 282),where Meno challenges Socrates to demonstrate his maxim that 'All inquiry and all learning is but recollection'. Allen (1959: 167) explains how the Socratic dialogue in *Meno* offers a dramatic demonstration of the validity of the first argument put forward for *anamnesis*. The idea is that when people are questioned, if the questions are well formed, they will always answer correctly, because they have the knowledge and the correct account already within them; it is only sleeping. The slave-boy in *Meno*, is ignorant of geometry, and yet succeeds in establishing the truth of a difficult theorem with only the assistance of intelligent questioning. The argument is that since the boy had never been taught, but only questioned, it implies that he 'had some recollection of a truth seen before he entered human form, a truth locked and forgotten in the recesses of personal memory' (Allen, 1959: 167). Socrates' method was therefore to help recover the individual's knowledge of certain forms: ' … when we come to explicit awareness of the nature of a Form, it is not a discovery of something wholly new, but the recollection of something already known. Learning is recollection' (Allen, 1959: 172). However, coaching is not about recovering knowledge of forms or even facts for the client: performance coaching is about achievement of specific goals, and developmental coaching is about the achievement of wider perspectives and understandings.

It is the emphasis within the Socratic Method on questions that challenge assumptions, together with the fact that answers appear to come from the learners, that is appealing to coaches. However, despite its attraction and apparent synergies with the client-centred humanist tradition, when looked at carefully it can be seen that the Socratic Method is not strictly appropriate for coaching because it is founded on the philosophical notions of *anamnesis* and *elenchus*, which are actually at odds with a coaching ethos. In addition, as Gronke (2010) argues, the method suffers from three weaknesses; the main one being that Socrates determines the content of the dialogue, and any alleged self-knowledge of the learners is produced by him. Gronke argues that the motivation of learners to realise any insights suffers as a consequence, as they have not worked out the ideas independently. Thus the Socratic Method essentially depends on leading questions.

It should also be noted how in his dialogues, Socrates uses his method of *elenchus*, or refutation, which intends to induce an experience of emptiness or not knowing in the learner. Through the questions posed to him in *Meno*, the boy is led purposively towards the answer that Socrates knows is already within him. Dialogues also often conclude with *aporia* – an inconclusiveness that frustrates the once confident respondent. Thus it would appear that Socrates' aims and method are not those expected in coaching. The effects of *elenchus* left the slave boy 'numb and speechless', as well as the subject of ridicule and amusement for bystanders (Allen, 1959). Socrates also does much more talking and telling that would be expected in coaching. It seems that in the absence of a theory of questioning for coaching, and proper models on which to base their practice, writers and coaches have clung to the Socratic Method as a drowning man would to a straw.

Systemic Questioning

Tomm's (1988) classification of four types of questions, has, I would suggest, much more application to coaching than Socratic questioning. Indeed, Huffington and Hieker (2006) used the questioning types to illuminate Dilts' (1996) change management framework, and so demonstrated their workplace application. A systemic approach is better suited to coaching since it focuses on information gleaned from the client's networks and environments rather than a spurious data set held internally. Tomm's classification has its origins in family therapy, and recognises the systemic nature of most client issues. The four question types (lineal, circular, strategic and reflexive) are described below and examples given from a hypothetical coaching scenario which illustrates their use and effect:

1 Lineal questions – which seek clearly defined causes of explanations of actions, events or feelings.

Coach: How did the meeting with the director go last week?
Client: Not as well as I had hoped.
Coach: What could have been better?
Client: Jones was there, up to his usual trick and the atmosphere wasn't great.
Coach: Does Jones always have this effect on meetings?
Client: Sadly, I think he does, yes.

The lineal questions are useful for extracting information, but because the questioner is overtly directing them, the answers are reactive. Lineal questions reinforce an investigative, memory-based model. Lineal questioning might also include a number of closed questions.

2 Circular questions – also gather information, but are more exploratory. They assume that everything is connected and so aim to reveal recurring patterns rather than lineal causality.

Coach: How has this week been?
Client: It's been OK, but the meeting didn't go so well.
Coach: Who else thought the meeting didn't go well?
Client: Well, Art was there and he thought Jones was being obstructive.
Coach: What does Jones do to make Art think he's being obstructive?
Client: He talks over me.
Coach: What do others in the meeting do when he tries to do that?
Client: They just appear 'gob-smacked'.
Coach: What do you do when they do that?
Client: I just clam up.

The examples above suggest clients might become more aware of their interactions with others and so enable them to disrupt unhelpful patterns.

3 Strategic questions – these emerge during the coaching process after some 'hypothesis' has been formed by the coach. Thus they build on the information revealed by answers to lineal or circular questions.

Coach: What would happen if you just talked louder to make sure you got your point across?
Client: I expect he'd be surprised.
Coach: Wouldn't you like to make sure that you were heard and for Jones to see that you had something important to say?

Client: Yes, but I'm not sure I would want to be seen to get agitated or angry in the meetings.

Coach: What would happen if you were seen to be agitated?

Client: I suppose people would see that I wasn't going to be a 'pushover'.

Coach: What other strategy could you use?

Tomm (1988) suggests that strategic questions are useful when the process becomes stuck, but that they are a double-edged sword. They can mobilise the conversation, but might jeopardise the alliance if the client refuses to accept the challenge they present (Ryan and Carr, 2001). Peavey (1992), however, describes strategic questioning as a process for creating a path, explaining that it is not a psychological process, but is, instead, political, because it is a way of actually transforming attachment to goals. Strategic questioning opens up alternatives in a social context and gives people ideas about which strategies are embedded in the way they are currently working, and hence how they might overcome them. So this type of questioning appears to have a particular affinity with coaching.

4 Reflexive questions – Tomm argues that reflexive questions are the family therapist's key tool for resolving problems, and are superior to strategic questions for promoting a therapeutic alliance because they marshal individual problem-solving resources. This holds true for coaching. Reflexive questions are not directive or confrontational and the questioner's own views are not imposed in any way. Reflexive questions allow a client to reframe his/her thoughts by reflecting on beliefs and making new connections. In the example that follows the client begins to ask himself questions as well.

Coach: If you were to talk to Jones about his butting in what do you think his reaction would be?

Client: I don't know, maybe he doesn't know he does it.

Coach: Let's imagine we are in another meeting and you are chairing the meeting and Jones interrupts someone else, how would you feel then?

Client: I've not seen him do it to anyone else, so does that mean he has something against me, or I just missed seeing him doing it to others?

Coach: If you did see him interrupting someone else what might you do?

Client: I'd feel sorry for the speaker, but if I was chairing I might want to say something to Jones there and then so that the speaker could finish – a good chair would do that. Or I might say something to him later, if I felt it was a recurring trait that was holding him back.

According to Tomm (1988), lineal and circular questions have an orienting intent, whereas strategic and reflexive questions have an influencing intent. We can see this difference in the examples given.

IV. Answers and the Importance of Common Ground

Munch and Swasy describe how questions that involve more than simple direct memory (recall) are actually process questions, in that 'higher order memory processes are needed to answer them' (1983: 213). There is greater control of mental construction, and respondents have less perceived pressure exerted by the question. In a coaching setting, the strategic and reflexive questions illustrated above would enable the client to use knowledge principles and concepts in relation to their problem solving.

Furthermore, in order to make sense of questions people rely on two interrelated resources. These are described in Schober (1999) as *audience design* and *grounding*. Audience design relates to how the question is couched, and whether it will affect how a particular client interprets what is being asked. The design is bound up with the common ground (the alliance) that exists between coach and client. The client therefore infers the coach's intentions against the common ground that he/she assumes is shared, and answers accordingly. Invariably, coaching literature will talk about building trust and rapport, and discuss the role questions play in that process. If the alliance is not well formed, that is, if the grounding is not there, a question will be perceived differently and the answer will be affected.

Schober further argues that people assume common ground with each other on two main bases – cultural and personal. At the cultural level, he argues, 'people can assume that they share relevant kinds of mutual knowledge with other members of the many communities to which they belong' (1999: 80). At the personal level, the coach would need to work at ensuring that trust is being built and that the client has a stake in the alliance that is forming. Both cultural and personal common ground come into play as a client interprets the coach's questions and his/her answers will be constructed according to that interpretation.

In addition, Schober (1999: 77) describes a number of cognitive and linguistic processes involved in answering questions. He points out how it is necessary to parse questions into words, which necessitates phonological knowledge: a knowledge of the grammatical structure of the language is needed in order to understand the form of the question and its component parts – nouns, verbs, etc. It is also necessary to understand conventional meanings of words in the question and how they are being used in the current context. So, a variety of technical and contextual information is needed in order to make the question intelligible. He further confirms that 'making sense of questions involves more than just individual processes like computing syntactic structure or accessing conventional word meanings. Making sense of questions also involves an *interactive* element' (1999: 78, original emphasis). The client will make inferences about the coach's questioning intentions through his/her assumptions about how the social world works and will rely on the coach to help interpret the question in subsequent dialogue. So the question enters the 'ground' of the conversation.

Summary

Questioning could be viewed as *the* key component of the coaching process, so it is surprising then that no specific theory of questioning for coaching has been proposed. In this chapter we began to explore the purpose of questions for coaching, and to think about how they arise in practice. The chapter started by claiming that lists of questions were not possible, and I argued that some of the most incisive questions emerge in the context of dialogue, since it is there that both coach and client are attuned to the content of previous conversations within the alliance. The chapter then examined the relationship between questions and the coach's knowledge base, and also analysed the efficacy of several typologies and theories of questioning that might be used in the coaching context. For example the usefulness of Socratic questioning was queried, since it is premised on the ancient philosophical notions of *aporia* and *enchulus*, which in turn are based on Plato's theory of forms. More appropriate models and approaches to questioning were then considered, including Tomm's (1988) questioning model, which introduces a 'logic of questions' that could begin to build towards a theory of questioning for coaching.

In the chapter it was proposed that coaching be considered as a form of extended cognition where questions are formulated when the 'coupled system' of the coach/coachee alliance requires an answer in order to facilitate achievement of the coaching task. The coach's questions in this argument are always in service of this alliance. Questions therefore need to be functionally useful to meet the needs of the overall aim/goal of the alliance. A model of the coach/client alliance was presented here that suggests that information is not available to the alliance at the start of the inquiry, but is constructed from a position of ignorance adopted by both the coach and the client. The alliance is the empty place from which the coach and the client explore all that is necessary to achieve the task. So, the model is of a dynamic alliance driven by questions between the coach who prompts conjoined thinking through questions, and the client who owns the task. The search for the coach is for questions that satisfy the alliance, not those that satisfy themselves. For the client it is not a search for appropriate answers to satisfy the coach, but for answers that satisfy themselves.

One of the most important conclusions emerging from this chapter is the difference between questioning in coaching, and in other disciplines, such as mentoring, counselling and teaching. It was argued that even if coaches have some knowledge of the client's context, they can still operate from a position of ignorance through the space of the alliance, and so ask questions that serve the client's learning. This demarcation is important and helps to further identify coaching as significantly different from counselling and mentoring. In counselling and therapy, helpers may operate from a position of authoritative doubt, but can never claim a position of ignorance due to the client assessment knowledge that underpins their work. Similarly, in mentoring the key differentiator is that mentors have more knowledge in a specific area than their learners, and so again the position of ignorance cannot be attained.

9
Being Present

Chapter Aims:

- To examine the nature of mindfulness and presence
- To explore the concept of being present for the client

In some fields, such as nursing and therapy, the 'presence' of the helper is seen as an important factor in successful treatment (Felgen, 2011; Geller and Greenberg, 2002). In coaching there is a similar consensus. Flaherty for instance talks of the benefits of: 'staying present and attentive to our conversational partner, which means – in practice – returning ourselves from self-conscious inner worries, or self-criticism, or wild speculations about what might happen next in the conversation' (2010: 101). Flaherty also notes how it is easy for coaches to respond automatically and thus 'miss being present' with what they are encountering (2010: 64).

The significance of presence has further been recognised by professional bodies. For example, the International Coaching Federation sees presence as a core competence for coaches, and their definition of it has been set out as the '[a]bility to be fully conscious and create spontaneous relationship with the client, employing a style that is open, flexible and confident' (ICF, 2011). In the field of coaching supervision, Patterson has described presence as sitting 'at the very head of our ability as coach supervisors to work with what is in new, fresh and exciting ways' (2011: 117).

However, as Patterson also notes, it is easy to confuse presence with mindfulness:

> Where mindfulness is defined as a total awareness of what is happening in the moment, it is a precondition for the state of presence but does not of itself guarantee presence, which is a wider, deeper and more encompassing state of bringing the whole self and being – and all of who we are – to the work. (2011: 117)

She explains that mindfulness is the 'solitary, personal and individual awareness that we bring to ourselves, to others and to our experiences', whereas presence is a 'wider embodiment of mindfulness in action' (2011: 119). Thus presence is seen as a broader concept, with mindfulness being just one aspect of it. Patterson illustrates the complexity of presence by introducing a long list of components, which include: awareness; curiosity; generosity; compassion; abundance; courage; respect; tolerance; permission; authenticity; honesty and openness; trust in self, in others and the process; safety; space and spaciousness; spontaneity; humour; and equality.

In this chapter, I want to explore the nature of both mindfulness and presence, and consider their differences, their close relationship and the part that each can play in successful coaching. The chapter is therefore divided into two main sections: as mindfulness could be seen as a necessary precursor to presence, I begin with that, exploring other related concepts as I go, and then in the second section I examine presence. Finally I summarise the discussion and introduce a model of 'Being Present' that captures the interplay between these two important theories, but takes the whole concept of presence a stage further.

I. Mindfulness

In the Buddhist tradition the term mindfulness is associated with specific methods of meditation that focus on emptying the mind. In Buddhist practice, such meditation focuses thoughts on a single idea or experience, like the breath, and this builds the capacity for focused attention, which in turn can be used to build the complete awareness needed for mindfulness. In western psychology mindfulness is more often defined as 'the awareness that arises through intentionally attending to one's moment to moment experience in a nonjudgmental and accepting way' (Shapiro et al., 2008: 841), that is, without cognitive interventions such as evaluation or analysis.

Although early western theories of mindfulness, such as that proposed by Langer (1989), did include active cognitive operations such as an emphasis on multiple perspectives or the creation of new categories, more recent conceptualisations have moved away from a focus on cognitive activity. Brown, Ryan and Creswell see mindfulness as distinct from self-referential phenomena, and go on to explain the difference between self-awareness as a concept that concerns 'reflexive consciousness, in which attention is in the service of self-relevant thought' (2007: 272) and mindfulness, which they describe as 'an open, unbiased awareness of and attention to inner experience and manifest action' (2007: 273). Brown et al. also refer to how mindfulness is 'essentially about waking up to what the present moment offers' (2007: 272). Rather than generating mental accounts about the self, it offers instead 'a bare display of what is taking place' (Shear and Jevning, 1999: 204). Thus mindfulness (despite its name) does not involve cognitive operations of aspects of the self through self-examination.

One of the key differentiators between self-awareness and mindfulness is that mindfulness is non-judgemental and unbiased. Brown and Ryan's earlier definition emphasised an 'open, undivided observation of what is occurring both internally and externally, rather than a particular cognitive approach to external stimuli' (2003: 823). They confirmed mindfulness as 'pre-reflective', and as such it resounds with the phenomenological arguments made earlier in this book that advocated the need to be in touch with experience before inviting cognitive activity. The implication is that cognitive intervention can interfere with the reality of the present moment (or the past in the case of phenomeno-logical reflection) by making interpretations or analyses that may be premature or inappropriate. Cognitive activity has its place, but needs a reality check! In a coaching session, when the coach reminds the client to focus on what is hap-pening for them in the moment, it is not an invitation to be reflexive, rather it is an opportunity to make contact with aspects of experience that are other-wise missing or missed.

Probably the most cited definition of mindfulness comes from the clinical setting, where Kabat-Zinn defines it as 'the awareness that emerges through paying attention on purpose, in the present moment and non-judgmentally to the unfolding of experience moment by moment' (2003: 145). Other defini-tions have built on this and all appear to place an emphasis on mind–body interconnectedness. Collard and Walsh, for instance, report how 'mindfulness is about being fully awake, about being in the here and now, about being con-nected to the flow of every experience and enjoying a sense of oneness between mind and body' (2008: 33–34). They suggest that the opposite of mindfulness is a feeling of being lost, disconnected, 'feeling obsessed with the past, or fear-ing the future or maybe functioning in an "automatic pilot" mode' (2008: 33–34). This emphasis on somatic awareness is picked up by Todres, who argues that the 'truth value' of mindfulness has been identified as 'a faithfulness to the bodily felt sense that opens or touches the holistic presence of the phenome-non as it is experienced'. He suggests that if this felt sense is not considered, 'the opportunity for a rigorous connection to the fullness of the phenomenon-as-experienced has been lost' (Todres, 2007: 38).

Black concludes that mindfulness can be contrasted with 'experiences of mindlessness that occur when attention is scattered due to a preoccupation by past memories or future plans and worries, in turn, leading to limited aware-ness and habitual responses to experiences' (2010). Brown and Ryan have also suggested that it captures 'a quality of consciousness that is characterised by clarity and vividness of current experience and functioning and thus stands in contrast to the mindless, less "awake" states of habitual or automatic function-ing that may be chronic for many individuals' (2003: 823). They explain how attention to and awareness of current experience or present reality is usually restricted. For example, 'when people are occupied with multiple tasks or pre-occupied with concerns that detract from the quality of engagement with what is focally present' (2003: 822).

Shapiro et al. (2008) are critical of Brown and Ryan's 2003 study for not assessing all the facets of mindfulness. They claim that any assessment of it needs to include the three components of intention, attention and attitude, and take account of the process of decentring or reperceiving, which they claim allows people to disidentify from the contents of their consciousness (thoughts and feelings), and view their momentary experiences with greater clarity and objectivity. So, as Diaz also notes, mindfulness operates by modifying attention in order to reduce reactive modes of thinking and enhances attentional capacity through the 'inhibition of rumination, improved self-regulation, improved ability to choose and switch between competing tasks, and improved vigilance' (2010: 97).

From these definitions it would seem that mindfulness has a grounding role for both coach and client, ensuring that each is fully aware of what is happening cognitively, somatically and environmentally in the moment. There is a role for the coach to help clients see the values of aligning body and mind in one place and observing the result.

Recently, Aldao, Nolen-Hoeksema and Schweizer also reported on another feature of mindfulness that most researchers tend to agree upon – the non-judgemental acceptance of emotions: 'mindfulness has been conceptualized as non-elaborative, non-judgemental, present-centered awareness in which thoughts, feelings, and sensations are accepted as they are' (2010: 218–219). Interestingly, this allowing of emotions to come into consciousness, be attended to, accepted and then let go, seems to fit with Frankl's observation that 'emotion, which is suffering, ceases to be suffering as soon as we form a clear and precise picture of it' (1984: 95).

Furthermore, when this acceptance of emotions occurs in the coaching session it demonstrates to the client that emotions are normal. Traditional suppressive workplace attitudes towards emotions (Bachkirova and Cox, 2007) can cause anxiety, as Gavin notes: 'when people continually repress, deny, rationalize, or otherwise contain them, they take on proportions far larger than the realities they represent' (2005: 105). Badiee (2008), on the other hand, argues that being in the present moment, being allowed to accept what the senses are revealing without judgement, allows clients to be more self-aware, and pushes them to accept themselves and their surroundings. In coaching, encouraging clients to accept their emotions, as well as their other thoughts and anxieties, helps them to accept themselves and to accept others too.

Benefits

Much has been written on the benefits of mindfulness. Authors tend to agree that it can lead to increases in well-being and performance, enhanced self-regulation and goal attainment, with resultant gains for both the coach and the client. Marianetti and Passmore, for instance, discuss the health benefits of being mindful, and suggest that it is only by engaging in moments of inner stillness that opportunities are created to 'step out of this overwhelming flow, regain composure, strength and clarity of thought' (2010: 190). Research by Shapiro, Schwartz and Santerre (2005) also shows the physiological and psychological health benefits.

The advantages claimed for mindfulness are highlighted across a number of disciplines. Zen philosophy, for example, affirms that mindful attention and awareness has beneficial effects 'through insight into present realities, a loosening of attachments to outcomes and to a solid sense of self, and greater clarity in thought and action' (McIntosh, 1997: 38), while in western psychology, Fodor and Hooker (2008) summarise the benefits of mindfulness as increased self-management, relaxation and acceptance. Weinstein, Brown, and Ryan report that mindful individuals made 'more benign stress appraisals, reported less frequent use of avoidant coping strategies and reported higher use of approach coping' (2009: 374). They suggest the ways in which mindfulness may produce salutary effects: it may promote a less defensive approach to challenges and experiences, which in turn can reduce perceptions of stress; and it may encourage the capacity to cope with situations perceived as 'challenging, threatening or harmful' (Weinstein et al., 2009: 375). Thus, Weinstein et al. hypothesise that mindfulness is related to a reduced tendency to construe events as stressful, and more adaptive coping in stressful situations.

Brown et al. also point out that mindfulness has been associated with health benefits, whereas private self-consciousness, surprisingly, has been linked with 'negative mental health' (2007: 273). Indeed, Greeson reports on research suggesting that mindfulness training can change the brain and the immune system, and so provide some resistance to disease. It is thought to do this by promoting health 'in part, by attenuating stress reactivity and stimulating parasympathetic tone, perhaps more strongly than relaxation techniques' (2009: 4). Recent neuroscience research further confirms how methods that act via the body, such as mindfulness, access limbic structures that have innate abilities to find balance and well-being.

In their study of the integration of mindfulness training and health coaching, Spence et al. (2008) similarly acknowledge the role that mindfulness plays in effective human functioning and well-being. They recognise that most progress can be made when there is 'greater acceptance of mental events (via mindfulness), rather than the pursuit of greater control (through cognitive restructuring)' (2008: 148). Spence et al. explain how attention and awareness are 'key to weakening the potency of impulses and other psychological states that initiate unwanted responses' (2008: 148). Citing Brown and Ryan (2004), they further argue that when consciousness is brought to bear on present realities, an element of self-direction is introduced into behaviours that would otherwise be non-consciously regulated.

Earlier, Ryan and Deci had pointed out how mindfulness may be important in separating people from their automatic thoughts, habits and unwanted behaviour patterns. They suggested this could play a key part in fostering increases in informed self-regulation, which has long been associated with well-being enhancement (Ryan and Deci, 2000). In self-determination theory, open awareness is seen as valuable in facilitating the choice of behaviours that are consistent with needs, values and interests (Brown and Ryan, 2003). The claim is that automatic processing can prevent consideration of options that might be more compatible with current needs and values, but that awareness facilitates our attention to the 'prompts arising from basic needs' (2003: 824), thus making us more likely to regulate our behaviour in a way that fulfils those needs. Mindful attention to these prompts appears to provide a regulatory function that has beneficial effects in many life areas – health, relationships as well as work situations.

Awareness and attention then are identified as instrumental in the maintenance and enhancement of psychological and behavioural functioning:

> The power of awareness and attention lies in bringing to consciousness information and sensibilities necessary for healthy self-regulation to occur. The more fully an individual is apprised of what is occurring internally and in the environment, the more healthy, adaptive, and value-consistent his or her behaviour is likely to be. (Brown and Ryan, 2004: 114)

Mindfulness Training

Brown and Ryan suggest that mindfulness is a naturally occurring characteristic, and problems only arise from the degree of our willingness to maintain awareness and attention on what is occurring in the moment. Often, they say, our mindful capacity varies because it can be 'sharpened or dulled by a variety of factors' (2003: 822). In fact some authors (for example, Fodor and Hooker, 2008) have argued that children naturally have a focused quality of experience, but that even they sometimes need help to further develop the mindfulness capacity – living as they do in a world of being told what to do. Like adults, their lack of agency may lead to them going through the motions of daily life without any conscious awareness of what they are doing. Thus it may be that our education and upbringing diminish our natural mindfulness, with the result that some form of retraining is necessary.

Spence et al. (2008) identify two types of training: attention training and mindfulness meditation, which form the basis of their research. Although it seems oxymoronic, they claim that the attentional control required to cultivate mindful states is a trainable skill and can be cultivated through dedicated mental practice. Spence et al. (2008) point out that mindfulness meditation teaches people how to direct and hold the focus of attention internally, 'whilst maintaining awareness of their unfolding internal experience (i.e. thoughts, feelings and bodily sensations) without being "captured" by any one experience' (2008: 149).

There are many meditation-based interventions which, it is claimed, increase mindfulness (Kabat-Zinn, 2003; Shapiro et al., 2005). These interventions generally involve daily practice of the principles of mindfulness, such as attention regulation, body awareness and emotion awareness. Sometimes they involve intensive meditations or retreats. Thus, the focusing trained by regular meditation practice is useful for mindfulness as it brings the mind back to the present and the object of focus. In mindfulness the mind is brought back to the environment, the body, the feelings, and the mind. As Fodor and Hooker explain: 'In practicing mindfulness, one becomes aware of the current internal and external experiences, observes them carefully, accepts them, and allows them to be let go of in order to attend to another present moment experience' (2008: 77). Unlike other forms of meditation, the goal of mindfulness is 'not to achieve a higher state of consciousness or to distance oneself from the present experience, but rather to have an increased awareness of the present moment' (Fodor and Hooker, 2008: 77).

Before moving on to discuss the relationship between mindfulness and presence, I want to discuss the related concept of 'flow', since that also has a present-moment emphasis. Flow has been described as the state in which our focus of attention is completely in the present moment, so it appears to have similarities to mindfulness. In his explanation of flow, Csikszentmihalyi argues that a problem arises 'when people are so fixated on what they want to achieve that they cease to derive pleasure from the present'; when that happens, he says, 'they forfeit their chance of contentment' (1997: 10). Thus the present moment is key in the achievement of flow – it is the place where flow occurs. However, it is important not to confuse the concept of flow with mindfulness or presence. Diaz (2010) rather equates flow with peak and other aesthetic experience, and, although mindfulness might in some way contribute to a flow experience, they are not the same, and mindfulness does not inevitably lead to flow.

To distinguish flow even further we can say that it involves timeless immersion in an activity or situation, whereas mindfulness, as a component of presence, requires awareness of the present moment as well as to the presence of others or the needs of the environment. The concepts are therefore qualitatively different. Flow has an individualistic focus involving the complete (aesthetic) absorption with a task, and so in a sense is the very opposite of mindfulness. They have in common a temporal emphasis on the now (Tolle, 2005), but whereas flow involves forgetting the concerns of the moment, mindfulness requires complete awareness of it. Topp expresses the difference well:

> Focusing my attention as I write this sentence in the Flow state, I lose awareness of everything except expressing this specific thought. Nothing else exists in my awareness: no computer, no typing, no sound, no thinking. My thinking and my fingers typing become a seamless experience, so as a thought occurs in my mind it appears on the page. In contrast, if I shift into a practice of mindfulness, my attention expands rather than narrows. I close my eyes to withdraw attention from the computer screen. As I lean back and open my eyes, I become aware of the sounds of the wind chime ringing, the leaves rustling in the wind, traffic, and a police siren in the distance. I feel my palms resting on the warm laptop while my fingertips tap the keys, making a crisp, soft snapping noise. I notice the warmth around the top of my head ... (2006: 7)

In summary, mindfulness involves bringing our awareness to the body and the environment in which it is currently situated. It involves a somatic awareness of body and mind, together with a sense of place and the environment. It is also a very individual activity, quite esoteric and meditative. Thus, mindfulness is the calling back of attention or awareness to the present moment (almost like a meditation). It does not have the focus of flow, and does not involve the same level of activity. Mindfulness requires a total awareness and acceptance of the moment, whereas flow involves focused, absorbed concentration in the moment. When coach and client are working together on client issues, it is likely that one or other may move into a flow state, that is, one where being absorbed in the content generated by the process of the coaching is paramount. But equally, flow may result from focusing or reflecting. So flow is quite different from mindfulness.

II. Presence

Like mindfulness, presence also shares a concern with the present moment. However, whereas mindfulness is a solitary concept, presence necessarily involves other people.

In this section I begin by outlining some definitions from different disciplines before considering an explanation of presence that makes sense for coaching.

One definition of presence often used in the field of leadership development is correlated with the leader's bearing and how he or she commands attention. This idea of presence is based on the quality of self-assurance and effectiveness that the person brings to situations. Often too it is seen as something that needs to be authentic. As Harper explains, it cannot be created, conjured up or manipulated. Harper argues that there is an autonomy about the human person as a presence: 'we know it immediately as someone different, because it makes itself felt; it does not wait for us to guess' (1991: 42). Marcel further confirms this view of presence as an attribute, suggesting that presence is something that 'reveals itself immediately in a look, a smile, an intonation, or a handshake' (Marcel, 1971: 25).

Another field where there is much discussion about presence is in computer mediated communications and virtual environments, where the concept is seen as relating to immersion in or transportation to an artificial environment (see Lombard and Ditton, 1997, for example). These conceptualisations suggest that presence necessarily involves a place, and that place can be distinguished from space by its sense not only of geography, but of 'identity, character, nuance, history' (Casey, 1997: xiii). Space, by contrast, is viewed as more abstract and distributed – lacking the sensory attributes of place (Rettie, 2005). In fact, IJsselsteijn and Riva (2003) also reviewed various discussions of presence, and suggested dividing presence into physical presence, the feeling of being in a place, and social presence, the feeling of being together with another person. This is interesting for our current discussion because coaches often talk of the coaching space, not of the coaching place, but it could be argued that for coaches to be present, they also need to have a sense of place. Being present, as I will argue shortly, involves that recognition of place.

Other definitions of presence, which might be relevant to coaching when using telephone, Skype or email, also come from the field of virtual environment studies. Wagner et al. (2009) describe presence as a phenomenon of human experience that has a complex, multifaceted background. They suggest that there can be no universal definition of presence, 'except for relatively simple, non-exhaustive ones such as the "feeling of being there"' (2009: 3). Wagner et al. further point out that the complexity of presence is due not only to its grounding in physical perception, but also to the fact that it has a subjective and psychological, as well as an objective and physical, component.

The field of psychology provides the other main source of understanding about presence. However, as Zahorik and Jenison (1998) explain, the notion of presence has often been perceived as resting on a rational position where there is a subject–object relationship between psychological and physical domains. Certainly, in much of the research this is the position that is taken. An example of this orientation comes from Topp (2006), who defines presence as the quality of relating to the here and now: physical presence refers to the present location of the physical body, and psychological presence refers to the present location of the focus of awareness. Thus presence becomes a quality of the helper. As Topp continues her explanation we can see how presence is conceived as 'object', something that the helper possesses that can be given to the client. I can give my physical presence and I can give my psychological presence – my attention. Furthermore, it can be deduced that it is possible to be physically present and yet psychologically not present, or vice versa, although Topp defines presence as 'when one is both physically and psychologically available and attentive to what is occurring in this immediate fragment of time' (2006: 3).

This objectivity is also evident in Harper's (1991) explanation of how the presence of the helper benefits the client: 'when somebody's presence does really make itself felt, it can refresh my inner being, it reveals me to myself, it makes me more fully myself than I should be if I were not exposed to its impact' (1991: 42). Despite the apparent benefit to the client, this description still suggests that presence is something that is controlled by helpers rather than clients, and is something that helpers can decide whether (or not) to offer to the client.

In their recent work, Maltbia, Ghosh and Marsick (2011) refer to presence as a dimension of self-awareness and self-regulation – also seeing it as a competency of the coach, albeit a 'relational competency'. They cite Bugental (1987) who suggested that the therapist first needs to experience psychological presence and exude physical presence in order for the client to respond and experience presence as well. In this conceptualisation, presence is something that each has and yet is intimately influenced by the other.

Muller (2008) discusses three papers investigating psychotherapy settings that can help us clarify the concept further. The first is a qualitative study by Pemberton (1976) aimed at arriving at a definition and identifying common factors among therapists who were recognised as having presence. Pemberton developed a model of how presence is achieved, maintained and lost. Using five humanistic therapists and their families, data collection involved observations of the therapists in clinical and personal contexts, and interviews with each therapist and their families. Pemberton suggests that presence occurs when a person has integrated and transcended the subjective and the objective while simultaneously integrating and transcending the past and the future. He claims that 'presence is knowing and being the totality of oneself in the moment' (1976: 36).

Pemberton's findings also suggested that there are three realms of 'oneness', each of which is a prerequisite to the next: 'individuational' or oneness with self; 'interpersonal' or oneness with another; and 'spiritual' or oneness with all. Pemberton claimed that the presence of the therapist exists in the individuational realm; that is, the therapist can have presence and experience oneness with him/herself, regardless of the client's state. His study therefore focused on the forces that allow presence to manifest itself in the individual, and suggested four factors that appear to increase the potential for presence (Pemberton, 1976: 93–94):

1 *Commitment* – demanding that helpers (whether therapists or coaches) must commit to be all of what they are at the moment: 'becoming in tune with what is happening within and without'. They commit to becoming available to themselves, their surroundings, and also to others;
2 *Focusing* – involving clearing the mind of extraneous 'noise';
3 *Enfolding* – requiring receiving the sensory, intellectual and feeling states of the other;
4 *Extending* – entailing actively extending one's own boundaries out to the other.

The second paper, by Fraelich (1988), explored psychotherapists' experiences of presence from a phenomenological perspective. Data were collected from six practising psychotherapists and the general description of presence that emerged was presented. In this study, presence is seen as:

> ... spontaneous occurrence, immersion in the moment, openness of being, living on the cutting edge, self-sacrifice, interest, psychotherapist as expression of self, immersed participation in the client's world, connected relationship with client, care, unconditional regard and valued acceptance of the client, completeness and definition of self, presence as trust, and genuine and authentic with self and others. (1988: 150)

The 14 'structures' outlined in this quote, suggest that the therapists were being present for the client if they were totally absorbed in the client's world, that is, if they had achieved some kind of flow!

The third study, by Stuckey (2001), looked at psychotherapists' experiences of presence from a Jungian perspective. Stuckey's data comprised interviews with six Jungian analysts. Like Fraelich, his findings emphasised the interpersonal dimensions of being present. Both Fraelich and Stuckey acknowledge that being present involves opening and surrendering to things beyond the therapist's control.

In these last two pieces of research it can be seen that helpers are doing something in order to be present: it is not a quality they have, it is something they are doing. This action is vital, as shown in Muller's own phenomenological study of eight music therapist interventions. In this research, three themes emerged that revealed tensions within the experience of being present:

1 *Reflecting/Evaluating* – Muller found that when a music therapist is present to the client their interpersonal boundaries become diffuse, and concluded that 'periodic reflection and evaluation is integral to maintaining presence' (2008: 95). This, he says, is especially important when 'the therapist lives through the client's experience and during the shared music experience when the increased rapport can blur the boundaries even further' (2008: 95). Muller identifies a problem when too much reflection and evaluation begin to encroach on the therapist's ability to be present, indicating that the therapist is having difficulty 'being with the client' (2008: 95). This finding may have implications for coaching in organisations, where the coach is an internal coach or manager, and may experience similar issues in relation to boundaries.

2 *Apprehending* – In being present, Muller reported, the music therapists worked at knowing their clients intimately:

> by being open to their own sensory experiences while near to clients they can apprehend important information about the client, the state of rapport and their own responses. Therapists who are present allow pre-reflective information to 'light the way' through important phases of work with the client. (2008: 97)

There are implications here for coaches as well, since reflecting in action will inevitably draw on such apprehending.

3 *Relating* – Muller confirmed that therapists' momentary experiences reflect an assemblage of 'thought, sensation, emotion, and ways of being in relation to the client', and that, in being present, they apprehend and relate to clients by 'adapting, living through the client, living through self, and taking action, and, periodically reflecting upon and evaluating what is experienced' (2008: 100).

Although focused on music therapists, Muller's study also reveals some general findings that uncover the relationship between intention and openness. It appears that the more open therapists are to sense experience, the more they can apprehend, but that immersion in the moment is not enough. Therapists must also reflect upon, and evaluate, what is happening. However, as Muller identifies, there is a complication here, because the more therapists reflect upon experience, the less immersed they can be in the moment. Reflection, as we saw in Chapter 6, detaches us from experience and like a life jacket buoys us away from total immersion. Presence then, according to Muller (2008) requires the music therapists to balance their immersion in the moment with reflection upon it – it requires specific, conscious action. Thus, reflexivity becomes an important aspect of presence in this formulation. Reflexivity is an ongoing process of reflecting on subjective experience as practitioners, but broadening and enhancing this source of knowing by examining contexts, challenging bias and taking action in the present. By extrapolation, in coaching it might be necessary for coaches to be continually self-reflexive about how their personal subjectivity and theoretical assumptions are each influencing the coaching.

From their earlier research, Geller and Greenberg (2002) compiled a model of therapists' experience of presence. In the second part of the model the process of reflexivity is described as:

1 preparing the ground for presence – setting the intention, clearing a space, putting aside self concerns, bracketing theories, preconceptions, etc.; adopting an attitude of openness, acceptance, interest and non-judgement;
2 the process of presence – being fully immersed in each moment as it arrives and moving attention between 'taking in the fullness of the client's experience (receptivity) to being in contact with how that experience resonates in the therapist's own body (inwardly attending) to expressing that inner resonance or directly connecting with the client (extending and contact)' (Geller and Greenberg, 2002: 78);
3 experiencing presence – including immersion, expansion, grounding and being with and for the client.

Geller and Greenberg also noted that therapeutic presence involves 'a careful balancing of contact with the therapist's own experience and contact with the client's experience, while maintaining the capacity to be responsive from that place of internal and external connection' (2002: 83). The therapists in their study described the process of 'shifting from internal to external, from self to other, from being open and receiving to being responsive' (Geller and Greenberg, 2002: 83). Presence in this context then is seen as 'the ultimate state of moment-by-moment receptivity and deep relational contact': 'It involves a being with the client rather than a doing to the client. It is a state of being open and receiving the client's experience in a gentle non-judgmental and compassionate way, rather than observing and looking at or even into the client' (2002: 85). This appears to echo Muller's later findings about the difficulty of balancing immersion in the moment with reflection on it.

In Gestalt therapy there are hints at a similar imperative that Jacobs (1989) calls 'uninvested' presence. She describes it as 'the most basic element, and the most difficult' (1989: 10). It is presence as opposed to seeming, or pretence, and we can only be present when we refrain from trying to influence the other to see us according to our own self image. While no one is free of pretence, Jacobs argues, 'presence must predominate in genuine dialogue':

For instance, a therapist must give up, among other things, the desire to be validated as a 'good therapist' by the patient. When a therapist 'heals' primarily in order to be appreciated as a healer, then the dialogic process is interrupted. The other has become an object, a means only, not an end also. Therapists' love for healing must be 'uninvested,' must not occur only to suit their needs for a certain self-image. (1989: 10)

This emphasis on the relationship with the client was also evident in Hycner and Jacobs (1995) where they described being present as the turning of the whole self towards the other, that is, not just attending to the other but moving away from preoccupation with one's self and offering one's whole being to the other. This move involves seeing the client in all of his/her uniqueness, and accepting that this is a unique and valuable person. In this moment no other concern is more important than the client. Bugental also considers that full presence means 'being truly accessible and appropriately expressive' (1987: 222).

Being Present

As suggested earlier, most theories of presence reinforce the idea that it is something that the helper has or has not, and can develop. In helping situations, therefore, presence is often used as a type of intervention. It is as though the helper has a choice – to be present or not to be present. As currently conceptualised, presence, as a noun, appears to be something that we can describe, prescribe, possess and even measure. It is an individual feeling of 'being'. By contrast, what I now identify as 'Being Present' is a verb that captures the dynamism of moment-by-moment interaction with the environment. The suggestion I want to make is that the coach cannot help but be present. The coach, unlike the therapist, has no armoury of intentional strategies, he/she can only be present: there is no such thing as absence-based coaching, there is only presence-based coaching. Thus as, Hycner and Jacobs (1995) suggest, presence is not something the person 'has', but rather it is something that they inevitably 'do'.

It can be noted that in this move towards Being Present, the focus has shifted from a pre-occupation with self to a focus on the other person (or people) in the setting. This is shown in Figure 9.1 where presence, in the individuational forms described by Brown and Ryan (2003), and others, can be seen as a precursor to a more generative form of Being Present that transcends esoteric and egoist concerns, and serves the client completely. Being Present goes beyond the personal attribute conception, which always implies some gain for the helper, and instead offers to the client a completely open, relational experience.

Figure 9.1 illustrates how our various attempts to control or unify cognitive and behavioural approaches, such as focusing, reflecting, mindfulness, and even psychological presence, are all attempts to offer something to the client, and so are all self-focused. Yet they are also necessary preparations for Being Present, a different and completely self-less concept.

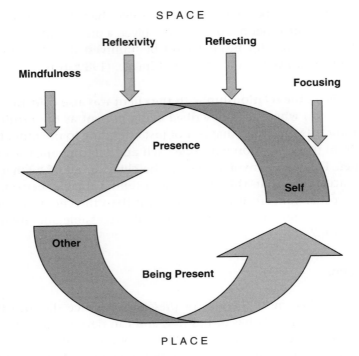

Figure 9.1   The shift from Presence to Being Present

Felgen's (2011) explanation of presence comes closest to conceptualising Being Present as I perceive it. To her, presence is a 'showing up,' in the deepest way, as in a deep commitment:

> It is being in a relationship with one or several people in this 'showing up' state, which is fully attentive in the moment not only to what is happening, but also to what might unfold. Underlying this state is a conscious intention to serve the moment and those with whom you are sharing that moment. There is an opening, if you will, that begins with what is known but has a willingness – a total commitment – to go into the unknown. Underlying it as well is the awareness of finding meaning. There is a sense of purposefulness in presence – the purposeful use of self in service to another. So, attention, intention, comfort with the unknown, and an unfolding. What does it look like? A person who is calm, confident, and joyful in being in service. It feels as if there is safety – an emotional safety because there's a connection and a commitment that are palpable. (2011: 5)

In order then to be useful to our coaching clients, our presence needs to be transformed into action, so that not only does it encompass our mindfulness, but it also involves interaction with the client, the coaching alliance and the setting of the coaching. So it also takes account of place as well as space, and is a way of being for the client in the moment – a dynamic interaction between coach, client and environment.

This alternative position, as Zahorik and Jenison (1998) argue, is a more ecological one, and is influenced by Heidegger's notion of *Dasein*, which holds that existence is bound up with our everyday physical interaction in the world. Heidegger's claim that we are 'thrown' into the world, and must continually interact and interpret that world, has implications for our definition of Being Present. Being, according to Heidegger, is defined in terms of action in the world. The definition of presence proposed by Senge, Scharmer, Jaworski and Flowers is close to this position. They argue that the nature of presence is 'by definition experiential – something we feel and know in certain moments of insight, inspiration, and power' (2004: 11). Senge et al. also understand presence as more than merely being in the moment; they explain how it is also a 'deeper way of listening that allows us to let go not only of habitual ways of understanding the external world but also of our own fixed sense of identity. It loosens our desire for personal confirmation and control in favour of "making choices to serve the evolution of life"' (2004: 11). Presence for them is defined as a process of 'letting come', a way of 'participating in a larger field of change' by which 'the forces shaping a situation can shift from recreating the past to manifesting or realizing an emerging future' (2004: 13). The sense of 'place' within this conceptualisation is central.

It is also useful for the coach to recognise how being present could help clients in their daily lives, and the use of 'immediacy' in the coaching session could be helpful here. Immediacy is a reflexive response to events in the moment. It involves action and could be seen as a demonstration of Being Present. The use of immediacy helps encourage a sense of place for clients, and helps them understand where they are in the moment. In its most general meaning, as Kondratyuk and Peräkylä (2011) note, immediacy denotes discussions about the here-and-now in relation to the relationship. In this sense, they argue, it works as a device for directing talk to the present-moment perspective, as the following exchange with Jasmine reveals:

Coach: I noticed when you were explaining how you had to leave before your agenda item that you seemed impatient and I felt you were impatient with me at that moment too.

Jasmine: Well yes, I suppose I was impatient and I still am a bit. I find it hard to believe that he really has my interests at heart.

Coach: What would make you less impatient?

Thus it can be seen that immediacy questions perform 'a temporal shift into the present', inviting clients to view their reasoning in the now. Immediacy helps clients to 'listen' to the current experience, the coaching session, as a separate activity from thinking rationally about the coaching problem. In this sense it is similar to Bugental's existential process, described earlier. Although Kondratyuk and Peräkylä (2011) also claim that immediacy brings clients closer to their authentic self, it could better be seen as making them aware of their 'thrownness', their Being in the World, and that this allows them the freedom to be authentic in the somewhat different, Heideggarian, sense of the word. For Heidegger (2010) people are not individual subjects, but are manifestations of *Dasein*, thrown like a piece of potter's clay into a world of contexts and possibilities. The following points that follow Winograd and Flores (1986: 34) may help to explain how this 'thrownness' affects Being Present in the coaching context:

1   Coaching is an action. As a coaching session progresses, the coach is continually listening, questioning and being present for the client. These actions are part of the coaching action – often referred to as coaching 'practice'. As Winograd and Flores suggest 'if you just sit there for a time, letting things go on in the direction they are going, that in itself constitutes an action' (1986: 34). So, even if there are long silences during the coaching, the coach is still in action, since that very silence is inviting the client to do something – think, reflect or be silent too. A logical extension of this suggests that the whole ecology of the coaching session is part of the action, and being present is tied to action in the environment.

2   It follows that reflection on coaching action or practice becomes possible only after the action. It is not possible for the coach to stop and reflect during the act of coaching, since that too becomes an action that forms part of the coaching.

3   Even if it were possible for the coach to step back from the coaching practice and analyse the outcomes of actions, the effects of the actions could not be accurately anticipated. Like any form of plan, the map can never be the territory! The coach may ask one question or another, or may introduce some activity to move the client forward, but the results, the impact, cannot be known. As Winograd and Flores suggest, the coach has to 'flow with the situation' (1986: 35) – and all the coach can ever do is improvise.

4   Additionally, and quite disconcertingly for some, the coach can never have a stable representation of the situation. After the session, or in supervision, the coach may be able to reflect on practice, study a transcript of a recording of the session, or pull out critical moments, but despite such efforts, a complete analysis is elusive. It is always a relativistic interpretation. If the coach was to ask the client for an interpretation of the session it would be different again. Every party has the potential to interpret the coaching differently.

Summary

In this chapter I have discussed the nature of mindfulness and how it can be developed. I pointed out some of its benefits for the coach (and by extension, the client) and discussed how mindfulness is different from flow.

I also explored presence as a state of being in which the coach is sensitive to the flow of events. Mindfulness and other activities designed to develop awareness can all be seen as contributors to the concept, so that presence is an amalgamation of a complex mixture of awareness, mindfulness, reflexivity and contextual awareness (shown in Figure 9.1). In addition, I reported how in recent conceptions of therapeutic presence there appears be a reduced sense of self, where the helper works for the other in service of the other. In order to distinguish this type of presence from a more rational, attribute model of presence, I introduced the term 'Being Present' and highlighted how it is a dynamic way of existing solely for the client.

I also noted the role of place in Being Present and how immediacy can be used to encourage awareness of what is happening now for the client. It was suggested that one of the tasks for the coach is to encourage the client to be present too. A way of doing this is for clients to experience their coach being open to the present moment so that this can be modelled in their work settings.

Tolle described space consciousness as sensing 'an alert inner stillness in the background while things happen in the foreground' (2008: 77). According to Tolle, we are the space from which all experiences unfold; we are timeless transcendent presence. It is that transcendent presence that we bring to coaching when we are being present. In some senses it does not require mindfulness training or reflective practice. Indeed, it could be argued that just being present for the client is enough to bring about feelings of rapport and well-being.

In closing this chapter, I should also point out how being present for the other does not necessarily have benefits for the coach in the way that mindfulness does. In fact, it may be that coaches have to take steps to protect themselves from the feelings of depletion that can arise through being present entirely for the client. This is an area of self-care that needs further research.

10

Integrating Experience

Chapter Aims:

- To examine the complexity of integrating the learning experience undertaken during coaching with existing or new life events
- To discuss the process of transfer of learning and how it can be enhanced

One of the unwritten goals of coaching is to ensure enduring learning and development for the client that can be sustained long beyond the end of the coaching intervention. Such sustainability would guarantee a return on investment for both the client and any sponsoring organisation. In this chapter therefore, I discuss the potential for transfer to the workplace and other areas of life, of the learning achieved through coaching. Through this discussion, I hope to assure stakeholders in the coaching enterprise that what is ultimately achieved through any coaching intervention is valuable, transferable and ultimately sustainable.

In some ways the process of transfer is the reverse of what is attempted when clients try to make explicit their tacit experience as described in Chapter 2. Whereas at that early stage clients were trying to articulate their experience in order to explore it rationally, at this final stage clients need to make tacit the understanding that has been made explicit during the coaching process – to 'unarticulate' it and embed it in their lives. This chapter identifies how, just as it was difficult to get a cognitive grasp of experience, so it is difficult to make the return journey from cognitive understanding and intention to integration into the experiential domain. This transition between the post-reflective thinking discussed in Chapter 7, and its transmission to pre-reflective experience (i.e. the transition that brings us full circle in the model outlined in Chapter 1) appears to be a most complex and under-researched area. One of the aims of the chapter, therefore, is to look at theories of transfer of learning and relate these to what happens in the coaching process.

This chapter also examines the challenge of transferring learning to day-to-day contexts. Having come this far in relation to self-understanding and developing skills such as mindfulness, reflection and critical thinking, it is eventually necessary for the coaching alliance to consider how to actually implement changes and decisions relating to the coaching issue. The chapter therefore considers how transfer can be achieved, looking at issues affecting the practical transfer of learning, and at a range of intention and intervention strategies, such as role play, anchoring and using future scenarios.

The chapter is divided into three main sections. In section I, I look at extant literature relating to transfer of learning, and in particular the definition of transfer of learning as it might apply in coaching. In section II, I explain how transfer is visible in the workplace through what I call the 'manifestations of transfer', comprising, for example, expertise, intuition or sense-making ability. So the manifestations of transfer could be a new enhanced understanding of a particular situation, the ability to look at wider perspectives as a result of that understanding, or the implementation of a well formed action plan. I explain the differences between these phenomena and their situational nature. In section III, I consider some possible strategies that could be used to enhance transfer. These are gathered from a number of theoretical and practical settings: business, the military, Neuro-Linguistic Programming (NLP), theatre, goal setting.

I. Transfer of Learning

Many commentators in the coaching field, for example Stewart et al. (2008), refer to coaching transfer as the sustained application of the knowledge, skills, attitudes and other qualities gained during coaching, into the workplace. Transfer of learning has also been defined as 'the influence of prior learning on new contexts of learning or performance' (Súilleabháin and Sime, 2010: 113), or as information learned at one point in time that influences 'performance on information encountered at a later point in time' (Royer, Mestre and Dufresne, 2005: 83). There are various classifications of this process. Foxon (1994), for example, distinguishes between two types of transfer: specific point transfer where the emphasis is on whether learners are transferring what they learned in the workplace, and process transfer, which is more diffuse and ongoing. Similarly, Perkins and Saloman (1994) highlight the difference between near transfer and far transfer. Far transfer relates to transfer between contexts. In coaching, an example of far transfer would be the analysis of impediments or forces for implementation of a specific project, where the strategic principles of the analysis are later used in other completely unrelated situations. An example of near transfer would be the rehearsal in a coaching session for an upcoming interview, where this is a specific rehearsal of a situation that is likely to occur in the near future.

According to Gass (1991), there are three levels of transfer: specific, non-specific and metaphoric. Specific transfer is similar to near transfer and occurs when skills are learned within the activity or training room and then applied to other situations. These are usually concrete skills. Non-specific transfer, on the other hand, happens when generalisable or abstract principles are learned though an activity and are then applied in different situations in the future. Metaphoric or cognitive transfer occurs when the experience in the training programme is close to the situation to be experienced by the participant. An example would be where a client adopted an increased risk-taking approach following role play of events with a perceived high-risk factor.

The term 'transfer' is not always useful since it suggests that something is being carried from the learning context into the new situation, and that transfer occurs if 'they overlap, or if a mapping can be constructed' (Lobato, 2006: 433). Lobato considers that this denies the possibility of construction of new knowledge from previous learning. He thus introduces two contrasting transfer approaches:

1   the classical approach involving improved performance of a pre-determined set of knowledge or skills from training to workplace;
2   the actor-oriented approach, involving an analysis of the learner's knowledge as well as performance; the extent to which participation in an activity influences the ability to participate in another activity in a different situation.

In my view, the second approach appears to be more congruent with coaching. Transfer in this definition is not the reproduction of something that has been acquired elsewhere, but is a transition involving the transformation of knowledge, skills and identity across multiple forms of social organisation: 'What transfers is not knowledge from task to task, but patterns of participation across situations' (Lobato, 2006: 437). Kolb (1984) similarly describes knowledge as a transformation process that is created and recreated continuously, 'not an independent entity to be acquired or transmitted' (1984: 38) – or transferred; and Bennet and Bennet, confirm the process, arguing that:

> As we move through life, our unconscious is exposed to and learns more than we are consciously aware, that is, the unconscious mind does more associating and learning than the conscious mind. This learning supports the needs and wants of the living organism through the creation and application of tacit knowledge. (2009: 206)

The generalisation of learning that occurs when transfer is made across contexts appears, according to Lobato, to be a dynamic process that cannot be entirely captured by the transfer metaphor. The process involves taking account of changes in environment and the construction of relationships, rather than reproduction of unchanging knowledge or skills. Transfer is thus determined, as Judd documented, by the extent to which the learner is 'aware of underlying shared causal principles or deep structure' (1908, quoted in Lobato, 2006: 433). Lave (1988) also recognised this interaction as an ongoing dialectic between learners and the settings in which their activity is constituted. So what appears to be important is the fact that the learning, particularly actor-oriented learning, is ongoing; and so, transfer is an ongoing process of integration with potentially massive implications for return on investment! This point is not often recognised by evaluators of learning, and only rarely acknowledged by organisations.

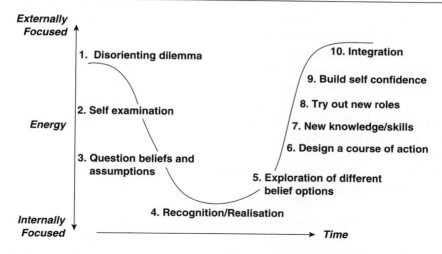

Figure 10.1   Ten-step process of transfer of learning through coaching, based on Mezirow's 10 Steps of Transformative Learning

Mezirow (1991) also recognises the importance of integration and step 10 of his transformative learning process is so named. This transformative learning model is concerned with the reintegration of enhanced perspectives into the learner's cognitive schema. However, it is also of interest in our discussion of the process of transferring learning to the workplace through coaching. In Figure 10.1 I have plotted Mezirow's steps against axes of time and energy. It can be seen that the dilemma has its origin in the external world, but as self-exploration deepens, energy becomes more internally focused. The process of integration begins after a point of recognition or realisation that comes at a low point in terms of external energy. Some significant thinking has to occur, and the result could be seen as similar to crossing the Rubicon, as discussed later in this chapter. The integration stage itself is preceded by a process of exploration of options, planning a course of action, acquiring new knowledge and skills for implementing such plans, and the provisional trying out of new roles and opportunities to build self confidence in the new roles.

Mezirow's process is important because, unlike Kolb's learning cycle, it recognises a learning need at the outset (the disorienting dilemma), and the importance of self-examination and exploration of beliefs and assumptions throughout the process.

II. Manifestations of Transfer in Coaching

In this section, I introduce the term 'manifestations of transfer' to describe the indicators of how knowledge, understanding and skill be discerned in the workplace. They can be seen as the cognitive and physical manifestations of tacit knowing that have the capacity to enhance effectiveness, and are what coaching needs to initiate in order to effect transfer of learning and complete the cycle of coaching for the client.

In Figure 10.2, I present what I consider to be the four main manifestations of transfer: role application, intuitions or hunches, skill or expertise and sense making. Each of these manifestations of learning has a part to play in our inter-action with our environment, but some conventionally have much more value than others. I have then mapped each of the manifestations against three axes: level of experience, level of environmental uncertainty and level of cognitive awareness.

The horizontal axis relates to the level of experience of the learner, with rote applications requiring less experience, and the more skilled or expert applica-tions requiring more. The left vertical axis moves from low to high environ-mental uncertainty, capturing the idea that in times of organisational instability it is difficult to apply learning in a predictable manner, and that rather than rote or repetitious applications being displayed in the setting, a more intuitive approach is at play. In situations where there is high uncer-tainty, and yet high levels of awareness and reasoning are appropriate, learners would have to rely on sense making and improvisation. It is interesting to note that skill and expertise only thrive in stable environments where there is rec-ognition of situations and pattern matching: 'skilled intuitions will only develop in an environment of sufficient regularity, which provides valid cues to the situation' (Kahneman and Klein, 2009: 520). So, where situations are uncertain or complex, other more tacit forms of knowledge are essential.

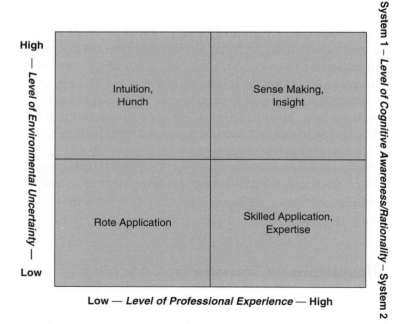

Figure 10.2   Manifestations of transfer in relation to levels of experience, cognitive awareness and situational uncertainty

The right vertical axis moves from System 1 (at the top) to System 2 (at the bottom) to describe differences in cognitive awareness, that is, it shows the amount of conscious awareness needed to effect the transfer. Theories of thinking have traditionally been associated with two distinct modes: the cognitive rational activity that aspires towards pure reason, and the seemingly more irrational forms of thought, such as intuition – the former having always attracted more credence than the latter. However, recently, Evans has confirmed that in Dual Process Theory there are in fact two equally vital systems. He suggests that they are interlinked, but that effectively there are 'two minds in one brain' (Evans, 2003: 454), and each has a different, but important function. System 1, he describes as the associative form of cognition that humans share with other animals. This process is considered rapid, parallel and automatic, with only the final product being 'posted in consciousness' (2003: 454). System 2 is considered to be unique to humans. It is slower and more sequential in nature, and utilises the central working memory system. However, despite a limited capacity and slower speed of operation, System 2 allows 'abstract hypothetical thinking that cannot be achieved by System 1' (2003: 454). We often make decisions using intuition, based on our past experiences and tacit knowledge, but, as Evans explains, we can also use models and simulations to aid our decision making in a slower, more 'rational' System 2 process. The result of this is that System 2 thinking appears more far reaching than System 1, which Evans describes as including 'instinctive behaviours that are innately programmed' (2003: 454). In System 2 there is an emphasis on evidence-based deduction, based in logic. These dual process theories of thinking uphold the notion that two types of thinking operate in our brains (one rational and one automatic). In this model, intuition and reflection in action as described by Yanow and Tsoukas (2009) would belong in System 1, while reflection on action (Schön, 1995) and critical thinking (Brookfield, 1987) both belong to System 2.

The four manifestations of transfer are now discussed in turn.

(1) Rote Application

Rote application is the expected product of some forms of training, and does of course have value in many settings. However, as Reiter-Palmon, Herman and Yammarino have argued: 'Rote application of problem representations typically results in less creative solutions, whereas a more deliberate and effortful application of the process results in more creative solutions' (2007: 211). Rote application is not seen as useful for generating creativity or maximum human performance, mainly because it leaves learners with a shallow understanding of underlying conceptual meanings and processes. Rote application is traditionally viewed as an impoverished form of action that requires little cognitive input.

(2) Expertise and the Application of Skill

Expertise and skill are also expected manifestations of training and education. Both involve the recognition of situations and pattern matching to the extent that learned skills or crafts can be used to produce predictable solutions. Schemas can generate accurate intuitive judgements since they enable clients to chunk information for easy retrieval and to be used in a recognition and pattern matching process (Hayashi, 2001).

In the dual process model, it is claimed that experience affects the organisation of knowledge, and that expert knowledge 'is organised according to highly sophisticated schemas, whereas novices lack this deep structure, organising their knowledge on more surface features' (Pretz, 2008: 555). This lack of schemas is said to force novices to rely on other strategies for their problem solving. Individuals with more experience have more tacit knowledge, which, as Pretz argues, makes them 'more likely to be able to articulate that knowledge' (2008: 555). They respond to problems by tacitly matching them to a similar pattern in their memory.

(3) Intuition

Mavor, Sadler-Smith and Gray explain how intuitions are 'involuntary and pervasive in work and personal life and are used (skilfully or unskilfully) by employees in organizational decision processes' (2010: 824). Intuition is located in Figure 10.2 as involving less thinking, but also as a manifestation that tends to operate in new situations or situations of high uncertainty.

As mentioned in Chapter 2, Miller and Ireland's (2005: 21) conceptualisation of intuition suggested that it can be thought of either as holistic hunch or as automated expertise (a form of heuristic). Pretz similarly differentiates between the two types of intuition – the classical and the inferential. Intuitive thinking of the classical kind is a holistic perspective that 'integrates all information without the potentially biasing influence of prior expectations' (2008: 555). In this model, unconscious thought is deemed to be superior to conscious thought. The second type is inferential and defines intuition as a heuristic, in which the intermediate steps have been hidden. Pretz explains how the inferential type has its roots in an analytical process that has become automatised. The implication is that inferential intuitions take shortcuts, and therefore can introduce bias, based on the environment where the intuition was acquired. This implies that critical analysis of intuitions is important, as they may often be of the inferential kind. One critique of this second type, the more analytical inferential variety of intuition, is that it can lead to the neglect of relevant information, since it cannot take account of all information. Pretz provides an example that explains the difference:

> An experienced individual sees the relevant information in a problem and knows how to analyze it in an explicit, logical manner. Relying on intuition may distract the expert from this critical information. In contrast, an inexperienced individual does not recognize the critical information in the problem and, thus, performs worse when relying on analysis. Instead, an intuitive, holistic approach may facilitate the solution of the problem for the novice by bringing to mind as much relevant information as possible. (2008: 563)

However, despite concerns, Pretz also argues that the holistic nature of intuition 'has strong advantages over analytical processing, especially when tasks are so complex that analysis leads to neglect of important information, where the whole is greater than the sum of its parts' (Pretz, 2008: 564).

Literature on intuition also emphasises that intuition is often accompanied by a sense of self confidence (see for example, Hodgkinson et al., 2008). Mavor et al. (2010) suggest that coaches refer to the existence of self belief or self confidence as being vital for accessing and applying intuition. It follows then that for the client there is a similar imperative. However, whilst intuition may be accompanied by feelings of self assurance, Mavor et al. suggest 'it is important for intuitors, especially novices, to avoid "trusting their gut" come what may'. They suggest that 'the certitude which many experienced intuitors display is illusory' (2010: 828). Inexperience leads to ineffective use of intuition, whereas experience leads to more effective use. In their research Mavor et al. reported how the coaches talked of the 'interplay between experience and reflection being crucial, and of trusting and "playing with" intuition and seeing its effect and thereby building one's confidence in using it more' (2010: 832). Kahneman and Klein (2009) similarly note how intuition is seen as a judgement for a particular course of action and comes into the mind with 'an aura or conviction of rightness or plausibility, but without clearly articulated reasons or justifications – essentially "knowing" but without knowing why' (2009: 519). They use the term 'illusion of validity' to describe the unjustified sense of confidence that invariably comes with intuitions and hunches. However, Kahneman and Klein explain how expert intuitions are just as likely to be 'off the mark' (2009: 515) as they are to be accurate, because they arise from the operations of memory. A problem arises then as to whether there is inaccuracy in those memories. Kahneman and Klein thus tend to support the skill-based intuition model, but caution that skilled intuitions can only develop in an 'environment of sufficient regularity, which provides valid cues to the situation' (2009: 520).

Similarly, Jackson questions the reliability of hunches, asking 'what is the dividing line between the wisdom of the experience and an unwarranted belief based on an unfortunate incident? When we feel a hunch do we know how many experiences it is based on?' (2008: 86). Jackson suggests it may be difficult to differentiate, without the conscious effort of self-examination and argues for coaches to consider explicit self-examination. They might also consider if it is their responsibility to encourage clients to undertake such reflection, to, in a sense, verify their hunches. So although hunches have a truth value for the individual, this is in effect a call by Jackson for coaches to move clients away from 'pure' reflection towards a more critical thinking approach, in order to examine and possibly challenge the strength of the hunch.

Interestingly Baylor (2001) proposes that intuition is used by both novices and experts, but that 'intermediate' experts use a more analytical strategy. So, as novices gain knowledge, they become better able to articulate their knowledge, and as they become intermediate experts who see the structure and logic of problems, they benefit from an analytical strategy. However, as the knowledge becomes part of an 'automatized expert schema, they become true experts who can rely on inferential intuition to make decisions and solve problems' (Pretz, 2008: 564).

This formulation has resonances with the Dreyfus and Dreyfus (1980) model of skill acquisition where unconscious competence is preceded by a period of conscious competence.

It is worth noting Hodgkinson et al.'s explanation of the difference between intuition and insight: insight, is defined as:

> a sudden and unexpected solution to a problem, arrived at after an impasse has been reached and an incubation period has elapsed ... An incubation period is often necessary for insight to occur because it enables non-conscious processes to operate more freely by relaxing constraints imposed by rational analysis. (2009: 279)

These authors suggest that insight and intuition cannot happen in a cognitive vacuum or in an 'unprepared mind'. They suggest these associative processes necessarily rely on learning and experience for their expression. The challenge for managers, leaders and organisations, they say is to be able to create the conditions that enable these processes to thrive.

(4) Sensemaking and Improvisation

(i) Sensemaking
According to Ntuen and Leedom (2007), the concept of sensemaking is a gathering of all available information. It involves both a retrospective process of interpretation (sense), and a prospective process of enacting a new configuration of the environment (making). It also appears to combine both the skill of rational expert deduction with more hunch-like intuitions. Thus, since it relies on both expertise and intuition it can be seen to be vital in chaotic, changing organisational settings. Ntuen and Leedom give the example of military environments, where officers must be trained to 'recognise critical issues in a battle scenario – analysing situational information and cues, interpreting events, and forming an understanding of the situation that will lead to action' (2007: 1). They also argue that sensemaking is the ongoing process of finding out how to act in order to reach certain goals. They suggest that it provides a foundation for 'enacting actionable knowledge' and utilising, for example, 'tacit knowledge versus explicit knowledge; linear predictive processes versus nonlinear processes; and simple tasks versus wicked (unstructured) tasks' (2007: 1).

Ideas such as rapid thinking and intuitive decision making have also garnered a lot of interest in recent years in relation to sensemaking (for example, Gladwell, 2005; McCown, 2010). In the armed forces, this ability to make intuitive, rapid decisions is important, and in military leadership the term *coup d'oeil*, literally a quick glance, is used to refer to the ability to at once visualise and comprehend the battlefield and decide on a course of action (McCown, 2010).

In order to accumulate enough experience to become intuitive thinkers and make such rapid decisions, leaders in the armed services accumulate vicarious experience through the critical analysis of historic military events. The fact that these leaders have no time to think implies reliance on a fast, parallel, automatic thinking process, coming straight from the basic regulation processes described by Damasio and akin to Schön's reflection in action, rather than being routed through the reasoning system which is controlled, effortful and flexible. Returning to the example of military experience, defence training does not have long to train novices. Time is particularly important where the novice is not experienced in a particular area, may have little intuitive judgement upon which to draw, and yet needs to be in the field of action within a very short time. Scenarios and role plays are vital in this training context.

So far we have seen how people engage in sensemaking when they are under conditions of equivocality and uncertainty: such situations involve a lack of information that makes the construction of a 'plausible interpretation about a situation difficult' (Sonenshein, 2007: 1024). Sonenshein further suggests that individuals in situations involving unclear problems use intuitions first and then use *post hoc* reasoning. However, as Storch (2004) notes, not even the best preparation for a chaotic situation can anticipate every aspect of unpredictability.

Further research is needed in this area, but it may be that increased perspective taking encouraged through coaching, together with other scenario and role-play based exercises, could enhance the ability to deal with stressful or chaotic situations.

(ii) Improvisation

In the theatre, improvisation (discussed by Yanow and Tsoukas, 2009) is overtly practised. But it is interesting to note that in both of these professions, the military and the theatre, there is little reliance purely on the happenstance of intuitive learning for the development of their experts.

Definitions of improvisation have tended to emphasise its spontaneous, intuitive nature, but as Berliner points out:

> this belies the discipline and experience on which improvisers depend, and it obscures the actual practices and processes that engage them. Improvisation depends on thinkers having absorbed a broad base of knowledge, including myriad conventions that contribute to formulating ideas logically, cogently, and expressively. (1994: 492)

The root of the term improvisation comes from the Latin *proviso* which means to stipulate beforehand or to foresee. The 'Im' part means 'not'. Hence it means *not* to see beforehand. In that sense it is the opposite of intuition where there is much more a sense of anticipation and prediction.

From this discussion, I would argue that it is essential for both coaches and clients to develop broad bases of knowledge in order to facilitate improvisation as a further manifestation of transfer, especially in high risk, complex environments.

Stein explains how 'in order to be able to respond effectively in context, the improviser must have at his or her disposal sets of routines and packets of knowledge that roughly match that context' (2011: 18). In other words, 'you can't improvise on nothing; you got to improvise on something' (Kernfield, 1995: 119, cited in Weick, 1998). Once new routines are established, they can then be modified to fit the novel conditions that exist in the new situation.

As suggested in Chapter 7, learning to be critical can be seen as the main preparation for improvisation, the development of expertise and the subsequent transfer of these skills into the workplace. Being critical endeavours to make tacit knowledge less tacit, works with portability and so increases transfer potential. So, a part of the coach's task is to facilitate expansion of client's stores of tacit knowledge in order to increase expert understanding:

> Tacit knowledge is largely learned through experience. The way experts become experts is by effortful study that involves the chunking of ideas and concepts and creating understanding through the development of significant patterns useful for solving problems and anticipating future behaviour within their area of focus. (Ross, 2006: 65)

In other words, experts use long-term working memory, pattern recognition and chunking, rather than logic, as a means of understanding and decision making. This indicates that by exerting mental effort and emotion while exploring complex situations, knowledge becomes embedded in the unconscious mind. Expertise is not just knowledge, it is knowledge in action.

It has been suggested that the most reliable method of ensuring transfer from past experience to new situations is through 'varied and extensive experience in the relevant domain of knowledge and skill' (Molesworth et al., 2011: 933). However, Molesworth et al. also suggest that no matter how extensive the experience, it may still be inadequate in building high levels of expertise. The issue is, as they also say, that 'learning depends on engagement by the learner in active processing of each episode of experience so that potential additions, corrections and refinements to one's existing knowledge and skill are incorporated into long-term memory structures' (2011: 933). Reflection and techniques such as self-explanation maximise the benefits of limited rehearsal. Thus, the two higher level manifestations of transfer – expert intuition and sense-making, as shown in Figure 10.2 – require a particular kind of support and development. Many would argue that coaching is that support, since it is the most efficient method of ensuring that individuals are guided through the reflective and analytical processes necessary to enable swifter, possibly more effective transfer from rote, and expert applications of skill to the higher levels of cognitive processing that complex situations demand.

So, we can see how coaching is a form of sensemaking that can increase the impact of clients' intuitions and expertise, making them more informed and less perplexed as a result. As a result of coaching they have more certainty about them, more confidence and are enabled to cope with surprise (malfunction) and temporary breakdown (Yanow and Tsoukas, 2009). Coaching encourages clients to examine their intuitions and hunches, and develop the necessary criticality for becoming skilled in sensemaking and improvisation. Ways to do this during the coaching and afterwards, as maintenance activities that give support whilst confidence is developed, are discussed in the next section.

III. Coaching Strategies to Encourage Transfer of Learning and Sensemaking

This section discusses two types of strategy: intention and implementation. Intention strategies prepare clients for eventualities that may occur in the workplace, whilst implementation strategies support them as they are actually putting their plans into action.

(1) Intention Strategies

Perkins and Salomon (1994) mention two types of learning that foster their notions of near and far transfer, namely hugging and bridging. Hugging involves learning in concrete role-play activities, which 'hug' the target performance. In the process the content of the learning activity is deliberately chosen because it is germane to the transfer context. Such activities are thus connected temporally with the setting in which the learning experiences will be relevant. Bridging is more abstract, and involves searching for connections between the learning and potential future scenarios. These have been described elsewhere as specific and non-specific transfer techniques (Royer et al., 2005: ix). Both can be used in coaching to plan, and prepare for implementation and strengthen the manifestations of transfer.

In this section, therefore, I identify some of the strategies that can promote both specific and tacit understanding in preparation for implementation. They are designed to increase the expertise driven sensemaking that is most desirable in work settings. As mentioned in Chapter 6, most reflective practice models include a final process of identifying learning which can help bolster intention. In addition, as we saw in Chapter 7, critical thinking strategies that facilitate clients in examining their experiences are in fact instrumental in achieving transfer of learning to other contexts, since they provide the opportunity for clients, with the support of the coach, to consider other perspectives and begin to engage in preparing for the future. In learning terms, such expansion builds tacit knowledge and leads more quickly to unconscious competence. However, whether such competence gets the opportunity to be displayed as intuition, expertise or indeed sensemaking is dependent, as mentioned earlier, on the stability and complexity of the working environment.

So in addition to the generic skills developed during the earlier stages of coaching, such as reflection on practice, critical thinking, even mindfulness, there are a number of specific strategies that coaches use to bolster sensemaking capability:

(i) Action planning and goal setting

With a historical reference to Julius Caesar's military endeavours in 49 BC, Storch (2004) explains how there is a metaphorical river Rubicon to cross between the process of becoming motivated to act and the forming of actual intentions to act, that is, between the pre-decisional phase and the implementation or action phase. Storch depicts how a five-stage Rubicon process moves clients from accessing and understanding their needs and motives, through to crossing the Rubicon in order to set real intentions and make preparations for action. If the needs and motives are not fully explored and understood, the coach may find that clients are following a number of intentions simultaneously and that these are not concordant (Storch, 2004). They may, in fact, be the intentions of our various mini-selves (Bachkirova, 2011), with the result that there is stagnation and lack of realisation of any of them. Thus, working on needs and motives early in the coaching process, as described in earlier chapters, is an important precursor to the implementation and transfer work outlined here. In Ives and Cox (2012), these needs and motives are mapped as higher-level goals. Examples of these are 'I want to feel happy and secure' or 'I want to be a good father and husband'. Examining these higher-level attitude goals, and making them available to consciousness, is an important first step for the transfer process and speeds the adoption of realistic, attainable goal intentions, and ultimately the implementation of specific concrete actions that demonstrate that goal intentions have transferred. In particular, apparent external goals have to be examined in this way, in order to assess their congruence and ensure they have a chance of implementation. Similarly, intrinsic goals need exploration, because they may just replicate the status quo; they may need to be challenged in order for clients to develop and achieve their potential.

Storch (2004) also points out that clients should be encouraged to acknowledge the signals of the self system, comprising attitudes, abilities, and cognitive skills, in relation to goal concordance. She talks about a positive affect that is experienced at the point when a decision and commitment have been made and action can begin. Most coaches are familiar with the somatic markers demonstrated by clients when this point is reached. They talk about a weight being lifted, or how they can see the way forward quite clearly now. The coach often thinks the work is done at this point, but unfortunately even crossing the Rubicon is still not enough to support successful action. The transfer is still challenging; making changes is still difficult.

Another useful distinction, also made by Storch, is between goal intentions and implementation intentions. Goal intentions specify what is intended (for example, 'I intend to call an extra meeting'), whereas an implementation intention focuses on how something will be tackled should such a situation occur (for example: 'If there is a need, I will be able to call an extra meeting'). Research suggests that implementation intentions 'because they are coupled with situational conditions, have sustained impact. They continue to be effective for long periods after the intention was formed, whenever the specific situation occurs' (Storch, 2004: 49). It is thought that forming implementation intentions begins to automate in some way the start of goal-realising actions. Action planning then is a recognised and important mechanism for transfer and goal attainment, particularly in relation to longer-term performance (Cowan et al., 2010).

Planning the transfer also needs to be an active part of coaching. Greif (2011) explains a useful four-part process that extends the Rubicon model. It begins with the transition from need to motive. I would argue that this is often the longest phase in coaching and incorporates all the work that we have discussed so far in this book. The next stage involves forming implementation intentions and planning resources to support the transfer process, one of which might be planning the availability of the coach to shadow the process. The third stage is the transfer process itself, which may be supported through shadowing (Greif, 2011), post-transfer evaluations and feedback. It can include analysis of failure and goal redefinition if necessary. Coaches who accompany their clients on this stage of their learning journey frequently have to help them address complex situations that get in the way of achieving their original outcomes. The final stage is what Greif describes as 'lessons learned for my future', a recursive exercise to ensure ongoing transfer.

(ii) Resources

Storch (2004) describes how in training her participants built up personally meaningful reminders and triggers, as well as important resources to facilitate goal achievement, and that this was done at the intention phase, rather than at the later preparation for action phase. Focus on physical resources, such as finding mentors, joining networks, and locating other forms of help, are all important parts of the resourcing of learning transfer.

In coaching an additional way in which inner resources are often built is by considering strengths. Linley and Harrison (2006) believe that strengths are an inner capacity that can be both facilitated and harnessed through coaching, and that clients' resources and strengths are crucial to successful coaching outcomes.

There are a number of exercises that the coach can introduce to help the client understand his/her strengths. One way to begin would be to differentiate between natural talents or attributes and things that can be learnt. A second approach is to explore which talents are dominant and then explore likely areas of potential. The StrengthsFinder Profile, which is popular with some coaches, is useful for this (Buckingham and Clifton, 2004). The third approach, also suggested by Buckingham and Clifton, is to develop a strengths language, so that the client has a vocabulary for talking about their strongest points. Thus, the focus on coaching approaches that connect with clients' inner strengths are likely to be very effective as a form of resource building.

(iii) Role plays and rehearsal

From a neurological perspective it is recognised that new activation patterns do not exist in the brain when we first go into a new situation. A client starting a new job role, for instance, relies on existing patterns, and the new way of doing things, the new route, still needs to be established. There are a number of ways in which this journey can be made easier through practice and priming. Fantasies, role plays and scenarios that many coaches use to help clients in their preparation for future events fall into this category. They can all begin the building of new neural pathways. In effect they 'blaze a trail' that can then be completed when the client is actually in the new situation.

Role play has been defined as 'participation in simulated social situations that are intended to throw light upon the role/rule contexts governing "real" life social episodes' (Cohen and Manion, 1994: 252). Carefully orchestrated, role play can help clients to experience a problem with an unfamiliar set of constraints in order that ideas may emerge and understanding increase (van Ments, 1983). Such parallel or analogous experiences also help clients to 'identity key patterns and processes embedded in their behaviour, then practice new behaviour' (Kemp, 2006: 287).

Another important aspect is the safety of the role-play setting. Role plays that emphasise strategy and organisation, rather than personal roles, give clients an opportunity to 'try on' aspects of the role in a safe coaching environment, where mistakes do not matter.

(iv) Scenarios and vicarious experience

Scenario planning similarly offers clients an opportunity to rehearse options or decision-making outcomes. The hypothetical preparation involved in creating potential scenarios alerts them to critical information that they might otherwise have missed. Helsdingen, van Gog and van Merriënboer (2011) explain how training programmes for professional decision makers, such as military commanders, often involve scenario exercises. They also discuss how these are often preceded by theory classes where the rules of the domain are explained. 'Theory' sessions in coaching could similarly be useful and provide insights through an enhanced understanding of other people's experiences. They might include reading a biography of a revered person in order to gain inspiration, or finding a mentor in the area where expertise is sought.

The combination of metacognitive understanding and analysis of practical application in scenario planning is powerful and leads to a deeper understanding of how to approach problems and/or identify cues in the environment.

(v) Visioning and self-efficacy through remembered success

One of the ways in which coaches often increase awareness of tacit understanding is by asking clients to think of a time when a similar situation occurred, and to remember their success in dealing with that event. The aim of this exercise is not only to raise self-efficacy (Bandura, 1997) in order to take the success from a recent situation into a future scenario, but also to raise awareness of *how* that success was achieved. This can be done in an exploratory way so that clients are aware of environmental factors that may have impacted the event, and might usefully include discussion of systemic issues, cultural influences and interpersonal aspects. So, through re-visiting positive experiences, the feeling of success not only becomes embedded, but clients see how the success was based on their own situated expertise. This emphasis on an understanding of previous events as pertinent to potential future events may then be transferred into new situations via the new knowledge created in the coaching analysis.

(2) Implementation Strategies

The transfer of new understanding and enhanced expertise into practice and workplace situations can involve the resolution of a number of interrelated external and internal barriers (Greif, 2011):

- External barriers are the organisational climate stressors that disrupt implementation intentions through unpredicted problems and tasks and reactions in the environment;
- Internal barriers can be related to energy and motivation, difficultly in changing entrenched habits, in changing priorities and in persistence of distractive thoughts or emotions.

Specifically, the barriers that can hinder transfer include: lack of trust; different cultures, vocabularies and frames of reference; lack of time and meeting places; the belief that knowledge is the prerogative of particular groups; and intolerance for mistakes or appeals for help (Davenport and Prusak, 1998). There are also two types of workplace stress that can become barriers to the transfer of learning and achievement of goals: threat-related stress, which limits self-congruent choice of specific goals; and demand-related stress, which limits the pursuit of specific goals. Such stress or unpleasant affect, according to Kuhl and Quirin can also reduce the degree to which higher levels of processing can be involved in action planning, and thus they 'reduce the amount of volitional freedom' (2011: 74). The coach can help with the first of these stressors through discussions in the coaching sessions, but the second stressor has to be addressed through shadowing or follow-up.

It can be seen then that the coach's role does not end once an action plan has been commissioned, but needs to continue as a resource to help the client understand and overcome these various implementation barriers, whether they be self-imposed or imposed in the environment itself. Coaches can do this in a number of ways in order to provide reassurance and feedback, creative and adaptive solutions, and to encourage a results orientation. Below I identify some of the most effective approaches.

(i) Shadowing and accountability

Shadowing, either through attendance and observation, or more often by telephone, is an important transfer method that is used by some coaches (Greif, 2011). It is good if the coach is there to unpick the 'tales of the unexpected'. If the coach is present for the client when he/she is attempting to make the changes set out in the action plan it means that negative responses to unsuccessful attempts can be transformed, and that the client can be re-motivated and supported to make adjustments to the implementation plan. Greif also suggests that shadowing allows a coach to support the client in learning how to 'monitor and reflect on their transfer trials in a result-oriented and autonomous way and use self-motivation techniques without assistance' (Greif, 2011: section 3.3).

Shadowing in coaching helps clients to explore and reflect on what has happened and what is likely to happen, and to have contingencies available for unpredictable circumstances. In recent research Cook explained how her clients referred to having 'Janice on my shoulder' – they could 'hear' the words of the coach as they encountered situations (Cook, 2012). Shadowing thus keeps nudging a client's short-term memory and providing a point of accountability. Accountability explains why it is easier to go to the gym if we are meeting a friend there. Thus the client is prompted by the ongoing presence of the coach to continue with new actions until they become habits. Accountability can be built into action plans and becomes a kind of resource in itself. It can be encouraged using the telephone, and is one part of the telephone shadowing process that Greif describes. The question then becomes how to generate self-accountability.

(ii) Memory aids and cues

Distractions and competing intentions that emanate from the memory can compete for the client's attention once they are back in the workplace. Greif (2011) talks about external intention reminders such as electronic calendars and lists, and recognises the value of cues in the transfer situation. These are the reminders that reactivate the short-term memory. Other mechanisms include memory aids, such as daily reminders, or anchors and triggers, such as music, colours or pictures.

Body work is also sometimes used to promote new neural connections, since remembering can be viewed as having an embodied, emotional component. In fact, Storch suggests that a new goal always needs to be encoded bodily, and that the anchors used in Neuro-Linguistic Programming, such as pinching fingers together or standing in a particular way can be useful: often imagining bodily movement 'is sufficient to stimulate plastic changes in corresponding motor areas of the brain' (Storch, 2004: 45).

Research in learning transfer, as mentioned earlier, has suggested that for transfer to occur learning must be accompanied by some form of emotional hook. In coaching, memory aids can remind clients about that hook. In addition, daily ongoing reflection can be used as a reminder. It helps clients to focus on whether their needs and goals are actually being addressed through daily action. At this point it is useful to note that internal (high-level) goals may need fewer memory aids. These are more likely to have an emotional content and so already be linked to long-term memory. For example, if we have to pick our children up from school each afternoon, we are very unlikely to forget or to decide to procrastinate and go later instead. This is for two reasons: the emotional attachment and the accountability – we love them and they are expecting us to be there.

There is not space in this book to look in detail at how the motivation to transfer learning is affected by emotions, but since emotions provide clients with important evaluative information about what is relevant to them, it would be logical to assume that the link is substantial. Emotions have an arousing function that creates a state of 'action readiness' (Frijda, 1988: 351), but I would also suggest that they play a role in coaching for sustainable transfer of learning. This is another area for further research.

Summary

In this chapter I have been concerned with the final crossing point between thinking and planning and actual experience. This involves making plans for change, and testing and implementing new knowledge so that it becomes embedded and integrated in experience. This final and most important transition, this integration, completes the Experiential Coaching Cycle introduced in Chapter 1.

In this chapter I discussed theories of transfer of learning and explored what I call the 'manifestations of transfer', such as expertise, intuition and sensemaking. Then, because integration of learning is key, I introduce two types of integration strategy: intention strategies and implementation strategies. These strategies are inherent in many of the tools and techniques that coaches already use, but it is useful to consider their impact specifically in relation to transfer. The reflective practice models discussed in Chapter 6 have application in this integration stage, and, in addition, most incorporate both an intention and an implementation element. As clients leave the relative security of the coaching they can continue to self-coach using a reflective practice journal/log of some kind to continue the reflection and critical work begun during the coaching. They may even find ways of securing self-accountability.

I have also suggested here that there is a significant role for the coach in helping the client to focus on implementation. As we have seen, the increased understanding developed during coaching can take two forms: (i) a greater self-awareness and understanding of own values and motivation; and (ii) a greater acceptance of others, enhanced perspectives and appreciation of systems. The learning that is transferred and integrated is therefore complex and multi-faceted. It may involve things the client needs to do differently, or it may involve things the client just needs to understand differently in order to develop and/or improve performance. In any event, the role of the coach was offered as vital to this process, even to the extent of providing shadowing and accountability following the coaching assignment.

11
Conclusion

Chapter Aims:

- To draw together main findings from previous chapters in relation to different stakeholders
- To highlight areas for ongoing research

The Experiential Coaching Cycle introduced in this book illustrates how clients' experiences create dilemmas for them that lead them initially to seek coaching. These coaching problems then need to be articulated, reflected on and thought about critically before the learning, the new perspectives and the potential solutions can become integrated or transferred into later experience. This, I would argue, is the sequence that underpins all forms of coaching.

The cycle of how experience regenerates is analogous to how the ocean becomes rain and then the rain falls to become part of the ocean again. In Figure 11.1 the Experiential Coaching model is depicted again with arrows to indicate this ongoing dynamic. The spokes in the model (Touching Experience; Becoming Critical and Integrating) each involve varying amounts of emotional, cognitive and physical effort, and so drive the coaching process. The spaces provide time for events to occur or for deeper reflection and thinking to take place. Although depicted as linear, in practice these activities may occur iteratively and concurrently, and are only separated for the purposes of explaining the progression.

Throughout this book I have taken a pragmatic approach to understanding coaching. However, I have only undertaken one part of the pragmatic process. I have looked at theories, and although I have tried to suggest applications to practice through examples, I have not tested them through research. I have created here an initial evidence base founded on existing literature, but would invite practitioners and researchers to continue my exploration and extend the findings. This book opens up a raft of theoretical ideas for testing in the coaching context. The next phase is for coaches to become pragmatic constructivists, undertaking research into their own practice and contributing to the body of knowledge in the form of 'practice-based evidence'. The book is meant to be a springboard for further research into how coaching really works, so that we can continue to explore coaching and understand it in all its richness.

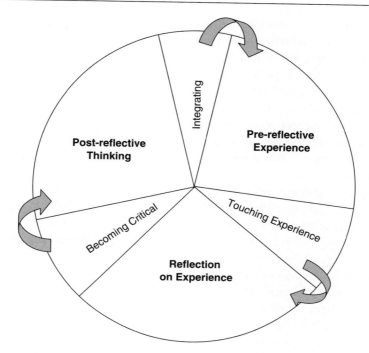

Figure 11.1   The three drivers of the Experiential Coaching Cycle

I began this book by considering how pre-reflective experience begins its journey into conscious awareness and how this involves a real struggle. I looked at ways in which clients can be facilitated to understand the fullness of their experience. Chapter 2 described how often problems are first felt through intuitions or uneasy feelings and that it is some feeling of confusion or 'lack' that brings clients to coaching in the first place. In that chapter some strategies for facilitating awareness around this confusion were discussed, together with the possibility that such awareness begins a process of development for the client. So it could be argued that all coaching is ultimately developmental, even if not intended by the coach at the outset and not explicitly stated in the client agenda. In fact, it may be that the longer the coach spends helping clients to focus on understanding the incongruities of their experience, increasing their awareness and helping them create coherence, the more development will occur. The implications of this for organisations are immense. They may find that as a result of coaching there are unexpected benefits: apart from improved performance in desired areas, employees in receipt of coaching may achieve benefits far beyond those expected at the outset.

I also explained in Chapter 3 how clients position themselves in relation to the coach and their world, and that this is discernable through the narratives they use in the coaching session. It was suggested that awareness of such positions provides information for the coach on how best to support the client. It was also noted that coaching is not an everyday two-way communication, and that in fact there is an element of soliloquy in the response from the client.

Coaching generates a dialogue by the client with him/herself. This is one of the significant ways in which coaching differs from mentoring or counselling. The client-centred approach in coaching can also be seen as different from Rogers' (1980) client-centred approach, in that it is not adopted for any other purpose than to allow clients to think for themselves – there is no underlying therapeutic model to be used to shift the client's thinking in a particular (better) way, nor any helper agenda regarding aspects of career development or advancement, as in mentoring. Research into the nature of coaching dialogue in comparison with other helping strategies is long overdue and would help with demarcation.

In Chapter 4, theories of listening were examined and an integrative model of listening for coaching suggested. In the chapter, I presented a comparison of empathic and authentic listening, suggesting that for coaching a model of integrated active and authentic listening with its emphasis on reflexivity, openness and generativity is more appropriate that a purely empathic approach. Again, the introduction of this approach points up differences between coaching and counselling, since the empathic relationship belongs to a scientific/ medical paradigm. Further exploration is needed into whether empathic or generative listening approaches best achieve coaching aims.

Clarifying techniques were explored in Chapter 5 and culminated in the presentation of a continuum of clarification approaches, some involving little or no interpretation by the coach, and others, like summarising, involving much more interpretation. The chapter also pointed out a difference between the use of these techniques in coaching and their use in counselling and therapy. In coaching, clients are provided with an opportunity to order and reorder their thoughts. Through reflecting back, they are presented with their own words, either for validation or repudiation, or through paraphrase they hear themselves differently, which leads to an understanding that there are different perspectives than the ones they currently hold. This chapter further highlighted how some strategies and tools used by coaches, such as reflecting back, are also used by counsellors or therapists working with a medical model (i.e. they have an hypothesis that after assessment a certain model of helping will assist the client), but equally I showed that they can be useful for coaches to use in order to help clients come to their own assessment and decide what they think will help. So again we see an example of the power of coaching, where the client has total ownership of the content and agenda.

In Chapters 6 and 7, I made clear the difference between phenomenological reflecting and critical thinking as separate cognitive activities of the Experiential Coaching Cycle. The reflecting process examined in Chapter 6 extends beyond merely focusing on experience as described in Chapter 2, and brings it instead into stark relief by objectifying it through phenomenological reflection. The purpose is to enable clients to stand away from their experience and separate themselves from it – to see it for what it is. In doing this they are able to separate the experience of the whole 'me' (the one immersed in the action) from the understanding of the cognitive 'me' (the one who observes the action).

Once isolated in this way, the experience can be observed through critical examination, without the pain of subjective attachment.

In Chapter 7, therefore, I presented a quadrant model showing how the transformative shift that occurs when values and beliefs are actively challenged differs from validation, which involves confirmation of needs, values and beliefs through a focus on self-awareness. I also examined Brookfield's (1987) four components of critical thinking in relation to coaching practice, making some important links between adult learning theories and coaching practice. The emphasis on the critical element in coaching could be seen as one of its most important and distinguishing features, and yet it is one that has received very little attention in the coaching literature. The implications of these findings for organisations are immense. Buyers of coaching, for example, will want to ensure that coaches are learning specialists, willing and able to encourage self-direction and criticality.

I would want to argue that a more overt reflective and critical exploration of experience as proposed throughout this book, not only helps us to make sense of experience, but also strengthens our intuitive repertoire. When experience becomes articulated it acquires meaning, it becomes joined up with other experiences and a number of benefits are achieved: we can compare what we are doing with what we intended to do (i.e. achievement of goals); or with what is best for our organisation, our client or our profession.

A focus on the use of questions in Chapter 8 suggested that as the construction of the client's story becomes a reference point, questions are formulated in the alliance in order to provide focus for the client, rather than to satisfy some need of the coach. This chapter also presented a model that demonstrates how knowledge is constructed from a position of ignorance within the alliance, the alliance being an empty space within coaching, free from hypotheses. The aim is for clients to generate answers that satisfy themselves and the alliance, rather than providing information for the coach. Again this emphasises the difference between coaching and other helping approaches, since in both mentoring and therapy, questions are used to provide the helper with information, either about what the client doesn't know yet (mentoring), or about the client's state of mind (therapy). I also suggested that Socratic questioning is not an appropriate approach for coaching, and gave a number of reasons for this. Further research into the nature of questioning in the coaching alliance is urgently needed.

Chapter 9 focused on the contributory role of mindfulness and presence to a more all-embracing concept of 'Being Present'. Again, this concept moves us outside of traditional psychotherapeutic paradigms where the focus is on using particular designed approaches to help the client. As we have seen, the coach has no agenda; the coach can only ever be present for the benefit of the client and the coaching task that has been presented in the coaching space. It was also noted that being present in the ways described in this chapter demands a special kind of commitment from coaches. As well as requiring more research, this more ecological interpretation of being present has considerable implications for the coaching profession. For example, it seems to me that it would be quite impossible to create competences that measure these attitudes and attributes, because they are so dependent on context.

Chapter 10 brought us full circle, to the close of one revolution of the Experiential Coaching Cycle. I examined manifestations of coaching transfer to the workplace and related them to levels of experience, cognitive awareness and situational uncertainty. I then looked at how clients can be helped to take their perspectives and new learning forward into future experiences. This help takes two forms. Intentions are supported through familiar action planning and goal setting strategies, ensuring resources are in place and making time to rehearse upcoming situations, while the support for implementation suggests that coaching may often need to continue in some form beyond the normal six or 12 coaching sessions, in order to guarantee sustainability.

This book has shown how the coach can help clients meet the fullness of their experiential dilemmas, stand back and observe that experience through the use of a reflective space, and then work in a critical, rational way with reflective material in order to transform it into learning. From there the coach and client can work together to identify plans and opportunities for integration into everyday life.

The theoretical discussions and arguments in the book are created from literature from across disciplines. However, these theories are my choices, based upon my professional background and preferences. Most, if not all of them have never been examined empirically in a coaching context. This indicates that there are rich areas for research for other evidence-based practitioners and researchers. It is still early days in our understanding of coaching, and hopefully this book has prepared some useful ground. Researchers and practitioners are urged to take up the challenge and test these ideas, reporting back to the profession through appropriate articles and papers. I look forward to reading them.

References

Adler, R.B. and Towne, N. (1990). *Looking out, looking in*. Fort Worth: Holt, Rinehart and Winston.

Afford, P. (2008). Why focusing makes the human brain work properly, revised version of a paper written for the 2008 Montreal international. Retrieved 18/7/11 from http://www.focusing.co.uk/PDFfiles/whyfocusingarticle.pdf

Aldao, M., Nolen-Hoeksema, S. and Schweizer, S. (2010). Emotion-regulation strategies across psychopathology: A meta-analytic review, *Clinical Psychology Review*, 30: 217–237.

Alexander, G. (2006). GROW coaching. In J. Passmore (ed.), *Excellence in coaching: The industry guide* (pp. 61–71). London: Kogan Page.

Allen, R.E. (1959). Anamnesis in Plato's *Meno* and *Phaedo*, *The Review of Metaphysics*, 13(1): 165–174, Philosophy Education Society Inc. Retrieved 18/8/10 from http://www.jstor.org/stable/20123748

Argyris, C. (1982) *Reasoning, learning, and action: Individual and organizational*. San Francisco: Jossey-Bass.

Argyris, C. and Schön, D. (1978). *Organizational learning: A theory of action perspective*. Reading, MA: Addison Wesley.

Atkinson, T. and Claxton, G. (2000). *The intuitive practitioner*. Buckingham, UK: Open University Press.

Bachkirova, T. (2010). The cognitive-developmental approach to coaching. In E. Cox, T. Bachkirova and D. Clutterbuck (eds), *The complete handbook of coaching* (pp.132–145). London: Sage.

Bachkirova, T. (2011) *'Developmental Coaching: Working with the Self'*. Maidenhead, UK: Open University.

Bachkirova, T. and Cox, E. (2005). A bridge over troubled water: Bringing together coaching and counselling, *Counselling at Work*, 48, Spring: 2–9.

Bachkirova, T. and Cox, E. (2007). Coaching with emotion in organisations: Investigation of personal theories, *Leadership and Organization Development*, 28(7): 600–612.

Bachkirova, T. and Cox, E. (2008). Cognitive-developmental approach to the development of coaches. In S. Palmer and A. Whybrow (eds), *Handbook of coaching psychology* (pp. 351–366). London: Routledge.

Bachkirova, T., Cox, E. and Clutterbuck, D. (2010). Introduction. In E. Cox, T. Bachkirova and D. Clutterbuck (eds), *The complete handbook of coaching* (pp. 1–19). London: Sage.

Badiee, M. (2008). On the road to being, *Journal of Humanistic Psychology*, 48(4): 477–488.

Bakhtin, M.M. (1986) *Speech Genres and Other Late Essays*. Trans. by Vern W. McGee. Austin, Tx: University of Texas Press.

Balbi, J. (2008). Epistemological and theoretical foundations of constructivist cognitive therapies: Post-rationalist developments, *Dialogues in Philosophy, Mental and Neuro Sciences*, 1(1): 15–27.

Bandura, A. (1997). *Self-efficacy: The exercise of control*. New York: Freeman.

Baylor, A.L. (2001). A U-Shaped model for the development of intuition by expertise, *New Ideas in Psychology*, 19(3), 237–244.

Beck, A.T., Rush, A., Shaw, B.F. and Emery, G. (1979). *Cognitive therapy of depression*. New York: Guilford Press.

Bennet, D. and Bennet, A. (2009). Associative patterning: The unconscious life of an organization. In J.P. Girard (ed.), *Building organizational memories: Will you know what you knew?* (pp. 201–224). Hershey, PA: ICI Global.

Berliner, P.F. (1994). *Thinking in jazz: The infinite art of improvisation*. Chicago: University of Chicago Press.

Bitbol, M. and Petitmengin, C. (2011). On pure reflection: A reply to Dan Zahavi, *Journal of Consciousness Studies*, 18(2): 24–37.

Black, D.S. (2010). Defining mindfulness. *Mindfulness research guide*. Retrieved 7/4/12 from http://www.mindfulexperience.org/resources/files/defining_mindfulness.pdf

Blenkinsopp, J. (2009). Careers, emotion and narrative: How stories become scripts and scripts become lives. In D. Robinson, P. Fisher, T. Yeadon-Lee, S.J. Robinson and P. Woodcock (eds), *Narrative, memory and ordinary lives* (pp.1–10), Huddersfield, UK: University of Huddersfield Press.

Block Lewis, H. (1944). An experimental study of the role of the ego in work, *Journal of Experimental Psychology*, 34(2): 113–126.

Bloom, B. (ed.) (1956). *Taxonomy of Educational Objectives, the classification of educational goals – Handbook I: Cognitive Domain*. New York: McKay.

Borton, T. (1970). *Reach, touch and teach*. London: Hutchinson.

Boud, D., Keogh, R. and Walker, D. (eds) (1985). *Reflection: Turning experience into learning*. London: Kogan Page.

Bowers, K.S., Regehr, G., Balthazard, C. and Parker, K. (1990) Intuition in the context of discovery, *Cognitive Psychology*, 22, 72–110.

Boyd, E.M. and Fales, A.W. (1983). Reflective learning: Key to learning from experience. *Journal of Humanistic Psychology*, 23(2), 99–117.

Bresser, F. and Wilson, C. (2006). What is coaching? In J. Passmore (ed.), *Excellence in coaching* (pp. 9–15). London: Kogan Page.

Brockbank, A. and McGill, I. (2006). *Facilitating reflective learning through mentoring and coaching*. London: Kogan Page.

Brockbank, A., McGill, I. and Beech, N. (2002). *Reflective learning in practice*. Aldershot: Gower.

Bromberger, S. *(1992). On what we know we don't know: Explanation, theory, linguistics, and how questions shape them*. Chicago: The University of Chicago Press.

Brookfield, S. (1987). *Developing critical thinkers: Challenging adults to explore alternative ways of thinking and acting*. San Francisco: Jossey-Bass.

Brookfield, S. (2005). *The power of critical theory for adult learning and teaching*. Maidenhead: Open University Press.

Brothers, D. (2008). *Towards a psychology of uncertainty*. New York: Analytic Press.

Brown, K.W. and Ryan, R.M. (2003) The benefits of being present: Mindfulness and its role in psychological well-being, *Journal of Personality and Social Psychology*, 84(4): 822–848.

Brown, K.W. and Ryan, R.M. (2004). Fostering healthy self-regulation from within and without: A self-determination theory perspective. In P.A. Linley and S. Joseph (eds), *Positive psychology in practice* (pp. 105–124). New York: Wiley.

Brown, K.W., Ryan, R. and Creswell, J.D. (2007). Addressing fundamental questions about mindfulness, *Psychological Inquiry*, 18(4), 272–281.

Brune, J.P., Gronke, H. and Krohn, D. (eds) (2010). *The Challenge of Dialogue: Socratic Dialogue and Other Forms of Dialogue*. Munich: LIT-Verlag.

Bruner, J. (1991). The narrative construction of reality, *Critical Inquiry*, 18: 1–21.

Buckingham, M. and Clifton, D.O. (2004). *Now discover your strengths*. London: Simon and Schuster.

Bugental, J.F.T. (1987). *The art of the psychotherapist*. New York: Norton.

Burgess, R. (2005). A model for enhancing individual and organisational learning of 'emotional intelligence': The drama and winner's triangles, *Social Work Education*, 24(1): 97–112.

Campone, F. (2011). The reflective coaching practitioner model. In J. Passmore (ed.), *Supervision in coaching: Supervision, ethics and continuous professional development*. London: Kogan Page.

Casey, E.S. (1997). *The fate of place: A philosophical history*. Berkeley: University of California Press.

Cavanagh, M. (2006). Coaching from a systemic perspective: A complex adaptive conversation. In D. Stober and A.M. Grant (eds), *Evidence based coaching handbook* (pp. 313–354). New York: Wiley.

Chemero, A. and Silberstein, M. (2007). Defending extended cognition. In F. Love, K. McRae and V. Sloutsky (eds), *Proceedings of the 30th Annual Meeting of the Cognitive Science Society* (pp. 129–134). Retrieved 21/8/10 from http://philsci-archive.pitt.edu/archive/00003204/

Clark, A. and Chalmers, D. (1998). The extended mind, *Analysis*, 58: 7–19.

Claxton, G. (1999). *Wise-up: The challenge of lifelong learning*. London: Bloomsbury Publishing.

Clutterbuck, D. (1998) *Learning alliances: Tapping into talent*. London: Chartered Institute of Personnel Management.

Cohen, L. and Manion, L. (1994) *Research Methods in Education*. London: Routledge.

Coleman, D. (2002). The coach's lessons learned. In C. Fitzgerald and J. Garvey Berger (eds), *Executive coaching practices and perspectives* (pp. 3–26). Mountain View, CA: Davies Black.

Collard, P. and Walsh, J. (2008). Sensory awareness mindfulness training in coaching: Accepting life's challenges, *Journal of Rational-Emotional Cognitive Behavioral Therapy*, 26: 30–37.

Collins, S.D. and O'Rourke, J. (2008). *Interpersonal communication: Listening and responding*. Mason, OH: Cengage Learning.

Collins, S.D. and O'Rourke, J.S. (2009). *Managing conflict and workplace relationships*. Mason, OH: Cengage Learning.

Conoley, C. and Conoley, J. (2009). *Positive psychology and family therapy: Creative techniques and practical tools for guiding change and enhancing growth*. Hoboken, NJ: Wiley.

Conway, M.A. (2001). Sensory-perceptual episodic memory and its context: autobiographical memory, *Philosophical Transactions of the Royal Society*, B356 (1413): 1375–1384.

Cook, J. (2012). The effect of coaching on the transfer and sustainability of learning: Coaching for leaders, a collaborative action research study. Unpublished doctoral thesis, Oxford Brookes University.

Cope, M. (2004). *The seven Cs of coaching: The definitive guide to collaborative coaching*. Harlow: Prentice-Hall Business.

Cormier, S. and Cormier, B. (1998). *Interviewing strategies for helpers: Fundamental skills and cognitive behavioural interventions* (4th edn). Pacific Grove, CA: Brooks/Coles.

Cormier, S. and Nurius, P. (2003). *Interviewing and change strategies for helpers: Fundamental skills and cognitive behavioural interventions* (5th edn). Pacific Grove, CA: Brooks/Coles.

Cornell, A.W. (1993). *The focusing guide's manual* (3rd edn). Berkeley, CA: Focusing Resources.

Corradi Fiumara, G. (1990). *The other side of language: A philosophy of listening*. London and New York: Routledge.

Corrie, S. and Lane, D.A. (2010). *Constructing stories, telling tales: A guide to formulation in applied psychology*. London: Karnac Books.

Cowan, C.A., Goldman, E.F. and Hook, M. (2010). Flexible and inexpensive: Improving learning transfer and program evaluation through participant action plans, *Performance Improvement*, 49(5): 18–25.

Cox, E. (2003). The contextual imperative: Implications for coaching and mentoring, *International Journal of Evidence Based Coaching and Mentoring*, 1(1): 9–22.

Cox, E. (2005). Adult learners learning from experience: Using a reflective practice model to support work-based learning, *Reflective Practice*, 6(4), 459–472.

Cox, E. (2006). An adult learning approach to coaching. In D. Stober and A. Grant (eds), *Evidence based coaching handbook* (pp. 193–218). San Francisco, CA: John Wiley.

Cox, E. (2011). Coaching philosophy, eclecticism and positivism: A commentary, *Annual Review of High Performance Coaching and Consulting*, 91–4.

Cox, E. and Jackson, P. (2010). Developmental coaching. In E. Cox, T. Bachkirova and D. Clutterbuck (eds), *The complete handbook of coaching* (pp. 217–230). London: Sage.

Cox, E., Bachkirova, T. and Clutterbuck, D. (2010) *The complete handbook of coaching*. London: Sage.

Cranton, P. (2006). *Understanding and promoting transformative learning: A guide for educators of adults* (2nd edn). San Francisco, CA: John Wiley.

Csikszentmihalyi, M. (1997). *Finding flow: The psychology of engagement with everyday*. New York: Basic Books/HarperCollins.

Damasio, A. (2000). *The feeling of what happens: Body and emotion in the making of consciousness*. London: Random House.

Dane, E. and Pratt, M.G. (2007). Exploring intuition and its role in managerial decision making. *Academy of Management Review*, 32: 33–54.

Davenport, T.H. and Prusak, L. (1998). *Working knowledge*. Boston MA: Harvard Business School Press.

Davey Chesters, S. (2010). Engagement through dialogue: An exploration of collaborative inquiry and dimensions of thinking. In J.P. Brune, H. Gronke and D. Krohn (eds), *The challenge of dialogue: Socratic dialogue and other forms of dialogue in different political systems and cultures* (pp. 73–96). Munster: LIT-Verlag.

Denham-Vaughan, J. and Edmond, V. (2010). The value of silence, *Gestalt Journal of Australia and New Zealand*, 6(2): 5–19.

Depraz, N., Varela, F. and Vermersch, P. (2003). *On becoming aware*. Amsterdam: John Benjamins Publishing.

Dewey, J. (1910). *How we think*. Lexington, MA: D.C. Heath.

Dewey, J. (1916). *Democracy and education*. New York: Macmillan.

Dewey, J. (1934). *Art as experience*. New York: The Berkeley Publishing Group.

Dewey, J. (1938). *Logic: The theory of inquiry*. Troy, MN: Rinehart and Winston.

Diaz, F. (2010). A preliminary investigation into the effects of a brief mindfulness induction on perceptions of attention, aesthetic response, and flow during music listening. Unpublished doctoral thesis. Retrieved 29/1/12 from http://etd.lib.fsu.edu/theses/available/etd-05072010-130110/unrestricted/Diaz_F_Dissertation_2010.pdf

Doddington, C. (2007). Critical thinking as a source of respect for persons: A critique, *Educational Philosophy and Theory*, 39: 449–459.

Dilts, R. (1996). *Visionary leadership skill*. Capitola: Meta Publication.

Downey, G. (2008). Coaches as phenomenololgists: Para-ethnographic work in sports, *Proceedings of the 2006 Annual Conference of the Australasian Association for Drama, Theatre and Performance Studies*. Retrieved 10/11/11 from http://ses.library.usyd.edu.au/bitstream/2123/2490/1/ADSA2006_Downey.pdf

Drake, D. (2010a). Narrative coaching. In E. Cox, T. Bachkirova and D. Clutterbuck (eds), *The complete handbook of coaching* (pp. 120–131). London: Sage.

Drake, D. (2010b). What story are you in? Four elements of a narrative approach to formulation in coaching. In D. Lane and S. Corrie (eds), *Constructing stories, telling tales: A guide to formulation in applied psychology* (pp. 239–258). London: Karnac Books.

Drake, D., Brennan, D. and Gørtz, K. (2009). *The philosophy and practice of coaching*. San Francisco, CA: Jossey Bass.

Dreyfus, H.L. (1991). *Being in the world: A commentary on Heidegger's Being and Time, Division 1*. Cambridge, MA: MIT Press.

Dreyfus, S.E. and Dreyfus, H.L. (1980). *A five-stage model of the mental activities involved in directed skill acquisition*. Berkeley, CA: University of California Press.

Dryden, W. (2010). *Dealing with clients' emotional problems in life coaching: A rational-emotive and cognitive behavioural therapy (RECBT) approach*, London: Routledge.

Dye, D. (2006). Enhancing critical reflection of students during a clinical internship using the self-SOAP note, *The Internet Journal of Allied Health Sciences and Practice*, 3(4). Retrieved 15/11/11 from http://ijahsp.nova.edu

Egan, G. (2007). *The skilled helper: A problem-management and opportunity development approach to helping*. London: Thomson Brooks/Cole.

Elkjaer, D.B. (2009). Pragmatism: A learning theory for the future. In K. Illeris (ed.) *Contemporary theories of learning: Learning theorists ... in their own words*. Abingdon, UK: Routledge.

Ellis, A. (1957). Rational psychotherapy and individual psychology. *Journal of Individual Psychology*, 13: 38–44.

Ellis, A. (2003). Early theories and practices of rational emotive behavior theory and how they have been augmented and revised during the last three decades, *Journal of Rational Emotive and Cognitive-Behavior Therapy*, 21(3/4): 219–243.

English, A. (2007). Interrupted experiences: Reflection, listening and negativity in the practice of teaching, *Learning Inquiry*, 1: 133–142.

Evans, J. St. B.T. (2003). In two minds: Dual-process accounts of reasoning, *Trends in Cognitive Sciences*, 7(10): 454–459.

Evans, J. St. B.T. (2008). Dual-processing accounts of reasoning, judgment, and social cognition, *Annual Review of Psychology*, 59: 255–278.

Feigl, H. (1958). Critique of intuition according to scientific empiricism, *Philosophy East and West*, 8(1/2): 1–16.

Felgen, J. (2011). The making and meaning of presence: A conversation with Jayne Felgen, interviewed by Marty Lewis-Hunstiger, *Creative Nursing*, 17(1): 5–11.

Feltham, C. (2010). *Critical thinking in counselling and psychotherapy*. London: Sage.

Flaherty, J. (2010). *Coaching: Evoking excellence in others*. Oxford: Butterworth-Heinemann.

Fleischman, P.R. (1989). *The healing zone: Religious issues in psychotherapy*. New York: Paragon House.

Fodor, I. and Hooker, K. (2008). Teaching mindfulness to children, *Gestalt Review*, 12(1): 75–91.

Forneris, S.G. and Peden-McAlpine, C. (2009). Creating context for critical thinking in practice: The role of the preceptor, *Journal of Advanced Nursing*, 65(8): 1715–1724.

Foxon, M. (1994). A process approach to the transfer of training, *Australian Journal of Educational Technology*, 10(1): 1–18.

Fraelich, C. (1988). A phenomenological investigation of the psychotherapist's experience of presence. Doctoral dissertation, The Union Institute, Dissertation Abstracts International, 50–04B, 1643.

Frankl, V. (1984). *Man's search for meaning.* New York: Simon and Shuster.

Frijda, N. (1988). The laws of emotion, *American Psychologist*, 43: 349–358.

Gabbard, G. (2009). *Textbook of therapeutic treatments.* Arlington, VA: American Psychiatric Publishing.

Gadamer, H.G. (2004). *Truth and method* (translated by J. Weinsheimer and D. Marshall). New York: Continuum. (Original work published 1975.)

Gallagher, S. and Zahavi, D. (2008). *The phenomenological mind.* Abingdon: Routledge.

Gallese, V. (2003). The roots of empathy: The shared manifold hypothesis and the neural basis of intersubjectivity, *Psychopathology*, 36(4): 171–180.

Gass, M.A. (1991). Enhancing metaphor development in adventure therapy programs, *The Journal of Experiential Education*, 14(2): 6–13.

Gavin, J. (2005). *Lifestyle fitness coaching.* Champaign, IL: Human Kinetics Publishers.

Geertz, C. (1995). *After the fact.* Cambridge, MA: Harvard University Press.

Geller, S.M. and Greenberg, L.S. (2002). Therapeutic presence: Therapists' experience of presence in the psychotherapy encounter, *Person-Centered and Experiential Psychotherapies*, 1(1/2): 71–85.

Gendlin, E.T. (1962). *Experiencing and the creation of meaning.* New York: The Free Press of Glencoe.

Gendlin, E.T. (2003). *Focusing: How to gain direct access to your body's knowledge.* London: Rider.

Gendlin, E.T. (2009). We can think with the implicit, as well as with fully-formed concepts. In K. Leidlmair (ed.), *After cognitivism* (pp. 147–162). New York: Springer Science.

Gergen, K.J. and Gergen, M.M. (1988). Narrative and the self as relationship. In L. Berkowitz (ed.), *Advances in experimental social psychology* (pp.17–56). San Diego: Academic.

Gibbs, G. (1988). *Learning by doing: A guide to teaching and learning methods.* Oxford Centre for Staff and Learning Development, Oxford Polytechnic. London: Further Education Unit.

Gladwell, M. (2005) *Blink: The power of thinking without thinking*, 1st edn. New York: Little, Brown and Co.

Gordon, T. (1970). *PET: Parent Effectiveness Training.* New York: Plume Books.

Graesser, A.C., Person, N.K. and Magliano, J.P. (1995). Collaborative dialogue patterns in naturalistic one-to-one tutoring, *Applied Cognitive Psychology*, 9(6): 495–522.

Grant, A.M. (2005). What is evidence-based executive, workplace and life coaching? In A.M. Grant, M. Cavanagh and T. Kemp (eds), *Evidence-based coaching Vol. 1: Theory, research and practice from the behavioural sciences* (pp. 1–12). Bowen Hills QLD: Australian Academic Press.

Greenberg, L.S. and Geller, S. (2001). Congruence and therapeutic presence. In G. Wyatt (ed.), *Rogers' therapeutic conditions: Evolution, theory, and practice, Volume 1: Congruence* (pp. 131–149). Ross-on-Wye: PCCS Books.

Greenfield, B.H. and Jensen, G.M. (2010). Understanding the lived experiences of patients: Application of a phenomenological approach to ethics, *Physical Therapy*, 90: 1185–1197.

Greeson, J.M. (2009). Mindfulness research update: 2008, *Complementary Health Practitioner Review*, 14(1), 10–18.

Greif, S. (2011). Goal and implementation intentions and their complex transfer into practice. In D. Megginson and D. Clutterbuck (eds) (in prep.), *Goalbreak: The coach's or mentor's antidote to the tyranny of goal-setting*. Retrieved 10/4/12 from http://www.home.uni-osnabrueck.de/sgreif/downloads/Implementation_intentions.pdf

Griffiths, M. and Tann, S. (1991). Ripples in the reflection. In P. Lomax (ed.), *BERA dialogues No. 5* (pp. 82–101). Clevedon: Multilingual Matters.

Gronke, H. (2010). The different use of Socratic Method in therapeutical and philosophical dialogue. In J.P. Brune, H. Gronke and D. Krohn (eds), *The challenge of dialogue: Socratic dialogue and other forms of dialogue in different political systems and cultures*. Munster/London: LIT-Verlag.

Grove, D.J. and Panzer, B.I. (1991) *Resolving traumatic memories: metaphors and symbols in psychotherapy*. New York: Irvington Publishers.

Hardingham, A. (2004). *The coach's coach: Personal development for personal developers*. London: CIPD.

Hardy, B. (1968). Towards a poetics of fiction: An approach through narrative, *Novel*, 2: 5–14.

Harper, R. (1991). *On presence: Variations and reflections*. Philadelphia, PA: Trinity Press.

Harré, R. and van Langenhove, L. (1999). *Positioning theory*. Oxford: Blackwell Publishers.

Hart, T. (2009). *From information to transformation*. Oxford: Peter Lang.

Hassabis, D. and Maguire, E.A. (2007). Deconstructing episodic memory with construction, *Trends in Cognitive Science*, 11(7): 299–306. Retrieved 29/2/12 from http://www.gatsby.ucl.ac.uk/~demis/SceneConstruction(TICS07).pdf

Hawkins, P. and Schwenk, G. (2006). Coaching Supervision: Maximising the potential of coaching. London: CIPD.

Hawkins, P. and Schwenk, G. (2010). The interpersonal relationship in the training and supervision of coaches. In S. Palmer and A. McDowall (eds), *The coaching relationship: Putting people first* (pp. 203–221). London: Routledge.

Hawkins, P. and Smith, N. (2010). Transformational coaching. In E. Cox, T. Bachkirova and D. Clutterbuck (eds), *The complete handbook of coaching* (pp. 231–244). London: Sage.

Hayashi, A. (2001). When to trust your gut, *Harvard Business Review*, 79(2): 59–65.

Heidegger, M. (1962). *Being and time*. New York: Harper and Row.

Heidegger, M. (1968). *What is called thinking?* New York: Harper and Row.

Heidegger, M. (2010). *Being and time* (translated by Joan Stambaugh, revised by Dennis J. Schmidt). Albany: State University of New York Press.

Helsdingen, A., van Gog, T. and van Merriënboer, J. (2011). The effects of practice schedule and critical thinking prompts on learning and transfer of a complex judgment task, *Journal of Educational Psychology*, 103(2): 383–398.

Heron, J. (1999). *The complete facilitator's handbook*. London: Kogan Page.

Hiles, D.R. (2005). Contingent narratives: Fears and tremblings. In N. Kelly, C. Horrocks, K. Milnes, B. Roberts and D. Robinson (eds), *Narrative, memory and everyday life*. Huddersfield: University of Huddersfield.

Hodgkinson, G.P., Langan-Fox, J. and Sadler-Smith, E. (2008). Intuition: A fundamental bridging construct in the behavioural sciences, *British Journal of Psychology*, 99: 1–27.

Hodgkinson, G.P., Sadler-Smith, E., Burke, L.A., Claxton, G. and Sparrow, R. (2009). Intuition in organizations: Implications for strategic management, *Long Range Planning*, 42: 277–297.

Hudson, F. and McLean, P. (2000). *Life launch: A passionate guide to the rest of your life*. Santa Barbara, CA: Hudson Institute Press.

Huffington, C. and Hieker, C. (2006). Reflexive questions in a coaching psychology context, *International Coaching Psychology Review*, 1(2): 47–56.

Husserl, E. (1952). *Ideen III: Die Phänomenologie und die Fundamente der Wissenschaften* (translated by T.E. Klein and W.E. Pohl). *Ideas Pertaining to a Pure Phenomenology and to a Phenomenological Philosophy: Third Book: Phenomenology and the Foundation of the Sciences (Husserliana: Edmund Husserl Collected Works) (Bk. 3)*. Springer. November 30, 2001.

Husserl, E. (2001). *Logical investigations I*. London: Routledge.

Hycner, R. and Jacobs, L. (1995). *The healing relationship in Gestalt therapy: A dialogic/self-psychological approach*. Highland, New York: The Gestalt Journal Press.

Hyde, R.B. (1994). Listening authentically: A Heideggerian perspective on interpersonal communication. In K. Carter and M. Presnell (eds), *Interpretive Approaches to Interpersonal Communication* (pp. 179–196). Albany, NY: State University of New York Press.

Hyer, L. and Brandsma, J. (1997). EMDR minus eye movements equals good psychotherapy, *Journal of Traumatic Stress*, 10(3): 515–522.

Hyvärinen, M. (2008). Narrative form and narrative content. In I. Järventie and M. Lähde (eds), *Methodological challenges in childhood and family research* (pp. 43–63). Tampere University Press, Childhood and Family Research Unit Net Series, 4/2008.

Hyvärinen, M., Hydén, L.C., Saarenheimo, M. and Tamboukou, M. (eds) (2010). *Beyond narrative coherence*. Amsterdam: John Benjamins Publishing.

ICF (2011). Core competences. Retrieved 25/1/12 from http://www.coachfederation.org/icfcredentials/core-competencies/

IJsselsteijn, W.A. and Riva, G. (2003). Being there: The experience of presence in mediated environments. In G. Riva, F. Davide and W.A. IJsselsteijn (eds),

Being there – concepts, effects and measurements of user presence in synthetic environments (pp. 3–16). Amsterdam: IOS Press.

Ives, Y. and Cox, E. (2012). *Goal Focused Coaching*. New York: Routledge.

Ivey, A.E., Ivey, M.B. and Zalaquett, C.P. (2009). *Intentional interviewing and counseling: Facilitating client development in a multicultural society*. Pacific Grove, CA: Brooks/Cole.

Ixer, G. (1999). There's no such thing as reflection, *British Journal of Social Work*, 29: 513–527.

Jackson, P. (2008). Does it matter what the coach thinks? A new foundation for professional development. In D. Drake, D. Brennan, D. and K. Gortz (eds), *The philosophy and practice of coaching* (pp. 73–90). San Francisco, CA: Jossey Bass.

Jackson, S. (1992). The listening healer in the history of psychological healing, *The American Journal of Psychiatry*, 149(12): 1623–1632.

Jacobs, L. (1989). Dialogue in gestalt theory and therapy, *The Gestalt Journal*, 12(1): 25–67.

Johns, C. (1994). Guided reflection. In A. Palmer, S. Burns and C. Bulman (eds), *Reflective practice in nursing*. Oxford: Blackwell Scientific.

Johns, C. (2009). *Becoming a reflective practitioner*. London: Wiley.

Johns, C. and Freshwater, D. (1998). *Transforming nursing through reflective practice*. Oxford: Blackwell Science.

Jones, E.E. and Pittman, T.S. (1982). Toward a general theory of strategic self-presentation. In J. Suls (ed.), *Psychological perspectives on the self, Vol. 1* (pp. 231–262). Hillsdale, NJ: Lawrence Erlbaum Associates, Inc.

Jordi, R. (2011). Reframing the concept of reflection: Consciousness, experiential learning, and reflective learning practices, *Adult Education Quarterly*, 62(2): 181–197.

Jowett, B. (1953). *The Dialogues of Plato*, Vol I, Book XVII, Meno. London: Oxford University Press.

Judd, C.H. (1908). The relation of special training to general intelligence, *Educational Review*, 36: 28–42.

Kabat-Zinn, J. (2003). Mindfulness-based interventions in context: Past, present, and future, *Clinical Psychology: Science and Practice*, 10: 144–156.

Kahneman, D. and Klein, G. (2009). Conditions for intuitive expertise, *American Psychologist*, 64(6): 515–526.

Karpman, S.B. (1968). Fairy tales and script drama analysis. *Transactional Analysis Bulletin*, 7(26): 39–43.

Karpman, S.B. (1976). *Transactional analysis: Principles and applications*. London: Allyn and Bacon.

Kee, K.A., Anderson, K.M., Dearing, V.S., Shuster, F. and Harris, E. (2010). *Results coaching: The new essential for school leaders*. London: Sage.

Kegan, R. (1982). *The evolving self*. Cambridge, MA: Harvard University Press.

Kegan, R. (1994). *In Over Our Heads*. Cambridge, MA: Harvard University Press.

Kemp, T. (2006). An adventure-based framework for coaching. In D.R. Stober and A.M. Grant (eds), *Evidence based coaching: Putting best practices to work for your clients*. London: John Wiley.

Kemp, T. (2008). Coach self-management: The foundation of coaching effectiveness. In D.B. Drake, D. Brennan and K. Gørtz (eds), *The philosophy and practice of coaching: Insights and issues for a new era* (pp. 261–275). San Francisco: Jossey-Bass.

Kemp, T. (2011). Building the coaching alliance. In G. Hernez-Broome and L.A. Boyce (eds), *Advancing executive coaching* (pp. 151–176). San Francisco: Jossey-Bass.

Kernfield, B. (1995). *What to Listen for in Jazz*. New Haven, CT: Yale University.

Kline, N. (1998). *Time to think: Listening to ignite the human mind*. London: *Cassell*.

Kolb, D.A. (1984). *Experiential learning: Experience as the source of learning and development*. Englewood Cliffs, NJ: Prentice-Hall.

Kolb, A.Y. and Kolb, D. (2005). Learning styles and learning spaces: Enhancing experiential learning in Higher Education, *Academy of Management Learning & Education*, 4(2) 193–212.

Kondratyuk, N. and Peräkylä, A. (2011). Therapeutic work with the present moment: A conversation analytical study of guidance into immediacy, *Psychotherapy Research*, 21(3): 316–330.

Kraut, R.E., Lewis, S.H. and Swezey, L.W. (1982). Listener responsiveness and the coordination of conversation, *Journal of Personality and Social Psychology*, 43(4): 718–731.

Kray, L., George, L., Liljenquist, K., Galinsky, A., Tetlock, P. and Roese, N. (2010). From what *might h*ave been to what *must* have been: Counterfactual thinking creates meaning, *Journal of Personality and Social Psychology*, 98(1): 106–118.

Kreber, C. and Castleden, H. (2008). Reflection on teaching and epistemological structure: Reflective and critically reflective processes in 'pure/soft' and 'pure/hard' fields, *Higher Education*, 57: 509–531.

Kuhl, J. and Quirin, M. (2011). Seven steps toward freedom and two ways to lose it: Overcoming limitations of intentionality through self confrontational coping with stress, *Social Psychology*, 42(1): 74–84.

Labov, W. and Waletzky, J. (1967). Narrative analysis. In J. Helm (ed.), *Essays on the verbal and visual arts* (pp. 12–44). Seattle: University of Washington Press. (Reprinted in *Journal of Narrative and Life History*, 7: 1–38.)

Ladyshewsky, R. (2010). Peer coaching. In E. Cox, T. Bachkirova and D. Clutterbuck (eds), *The complete handbook of coaching* (pp. 284–296). London: Sage.

Lagaay, A. (2008). Between sound and silence: Voice in the history of psychoanalysis, *Episteme*, 1(1): 53–62.

Lakoff, G. and Johnson, M. (1981). *Metaphors we live by*. Chicago: University of Chicago Press.

Langer, E.J. (1989). *Mindfulness*. Reading, MA: Addison Wesley.

Lave, J. (1988). *Cognition in practice: Mind, mathematics and culture in everyday life*. New York: Cambridge University Press.

Lawton-Smith, C. and Cox, E. (2007). Coaching: Is it just a new name for training? *International Journal of Evidence Based Coaching and Mentoring*, Special Issue, 1: 1–9.

Lee, G. (2003). *Leadership coaching: From personal insight to organizational performance*. London: Chartered Institute of Personnel and Development.

Lee, G. (2010). The psychodynamic approach to coaching. In E. Cox, T. Bachkirova and D. Clutterbuck (eds), *The complete handbook of coaching* (pp. 23–36). London: Sage.

Linley, P.A. and Harrison, S. (2006). Strengths coaching: A potential-guided approach to coaching psychology, *International Coaching Psychology Review*, 1(1): 37–46.

Lobato, J. (2006). Alternative perspectives on the transfer of learning: History, issues, and challenges for future research, *The Journal of the Learning Sciences*, 15(4): 431–449.

Lombard, M. and Ditton, T. (1997). At the heart of it all: The concept of presence, *Journal of Computer-Mediated Communication*, 3 (2). Retrieved from http://onlinelibrary.wiley.com/doi/10.1111/j.1083-6101.1997.tb00072.x/full

Mace, J.H. (2010). *The act of remembering: Toward an understanding of how we recall the past*. London: John Wiley and Sons.

MacIntyre, A. (1985). *After virtue: A study in moral theory*. London: Duckworth.

Malouf, D. (1986). *12 Edmonstone Street*. Ringwood: Penguin.

Maltbia, T.E., Ghosh, R. and Marsick, V.J. (2011). Trust and presence as executive coaching competencies: Reviewing literature to inform practice and future research. Retrieved 29/1/12 from http://devweb.tc.columbia.edu/i/a/document/15966_Final_Trust.pdf

Mann, K., Gordon, J. and MacLeod, A. (2009). Reflection and reflective practice in health professions education: A systematic review, *Advances in Health Science Education*, 14: 595–621

Marcel, G. (1971). *The philosophy of existence*. Philadelphia, MA: University of Pennsylvania Press.

Marianetti, O. and Passmore, J. (2010). Mindfulness at work: Paying attention to enhance well-being and performance. In P.A. Linley, S. Harrington and N. Garcea (eds), *Oxford handbook of positive psychology and work*. Oxford: Oxford University Press.

Marzano, R.J., Zaffron, S., Zraik, L., Robbins, S.L. and Yoon, L. (1995). A new paradigm for educational change, *Education*, 116: 162–173.

Mattingly, C. (1998). *Healing dramas and clinical plots: The narrative structure of experience*. Cambridge: Cambridge University Press.

Mavor, P., Sadler-Smith, E. and Gray, D.E. (2010). Teaching and learning intuition: Some implications for HRD and coaching practice, *Journal of European Industrial Training*, 34(8/9): 822–838.

McAdams, D.P. (1993). *The stories we live by: Personal myths and the making of the self*. New York: The Guilford Press.

McAlpine, L., Weston, C., Berthiaume, D., Fairbank-Roch, G. and Owen, M. (2004). Reflection on teaching: types and goals of reflection, *Educational Research and Evaluation,* 10(4): 337–363.

McClure, J. and Hilton, D. (1998). Are goals or preconditions better explanations? It depends on the question, *European Journal of Social Psychology*, 28: 897–911.

McCown, N.R. (2010). *Developing Intuitive Decision-Making In Modern Military Leadership*. Newport, RI: Naval War College. Retrieved from http://www.dtic.mil/cgi-bin/GetTRDoc?AD=ADA535417

McGuire-Bouwman, K.N. (2010). *Experiential Focusing as a Brief Therapy intervention*. Retrieved from http://www.cefocusing.com/pdf/2F2gExperientialFocusingBrief TherapyIntervention.pdf.

McIntosh, W.D. (1997). East meets west: Parallels between Zen Buddhism and social psychology, *International Journal for the Psychology of Religion*, 7: 37–52.

Merleau-Ponty, M. (1962). *Phenomenology of perception* (English translation by C. Smith). London: Routledge and Kegan Paul.

Mezirow, J. (1991). *Transformative Dimensions of Adult Learning*. San Francisco: Jossey-Bass.

Mezirow, J. (2000). *Learning as transformation: Critical Perspectives on a theory in progress*. San Francisco: Jossey-Bass.

Miller, C.C. and Ireland, R.D. (2005). Intuition in strategic decision making: Friend or foe in the fast paced 21st century, *Academy of Management Executive*, 19: 19–30.

Moghaddam, F. (1999). Reflexive positioning: Culture and private discourse. In R. Harré and L. van Langenhove (eds), *Positioning theory* (pp. 74–86). Oxford: Blackwell Publishers.

Molesworth, B.R.C., Bennett, L. and Kehoe, E.J. (2011). Promoting learning, memory, and transfer in a time-constrained, high hazard environment, *Accident Analysis and Prevention*, 43: 932–938.

Moon, J. (1999). *Reflection in learning and professional development: Theory and practice*. London: Kogan Page.

Muller, B.J. (2008). A phenomenological investigation of the music therapist's experience of being present to clients, *Qualitative Inquiries in Music Therapy*, 4: 69–111.

Munch, J. and Swasy, J. (1983). A conceptual view of questions and questioning in marketing communications. In R. Bagozzi and A. Tybout (eds), *Advances in consumer research, Vol. 10* (pp. 209–214). Ann Arbor, MI: Association for Consumer Research.

Myers, S. (2000). Empathic listening: Reports on the experience of being heard, *Journal of Humanistic Psychology*, 40(2): 148–173.

Neenan, M. (2009). Using Socratic questioning in coaching, *Journal of Rational-Emotive and Cognitive-Behavior Therapy*, 27(4): 249–264.

Newman, (2007). *Maeler's regard: Images of adult learning*. Retrieved 18/11/11 from http://www.michaelnewman.info/docs/maelers_regard.pdf

Nichols, R.G. (1948). Factors in listening comprehension. *Speech Monographs*, 15: 154–163.

Nicholson, P., Bayne, R. and Owen, J. (2006). *Applied psychology for social workers* (3rd edn). Basingstoke: Palgrave.

Ntuen, C.A. and Leedom, D.K. (2007). Sensemaking training requirements for the adaptive battlestaff. Proceedings of 2007 CCRTS Conference. Newport, RI (July). Retrieved 19/2/12 from http://www.dtic.mil/cgi-bin/GetTRDoc?AD=A DA486815andLocation=U2anddoc=GetTRDoc.pdf

Oliver, C. (2010). Reflexive coaching: Linking meaning and action in the leadership system. In S. Palmer and A. McDowall (eds), *The coaching relationship: Putting people first* (pp. 101–120). London: Routledge.

Orange, G., Burke, A. and Cushman, M. (1999). An approach to support reflection and organisation learning within the UK construction industry. Paper presented at BITWorld '99: Business Information Technology Management: The Global Imperative, Cape Town, South Africa, 30 June–2 July.

Overholser, J.C. (1996). The dependent personality and interpersonal problems, *Journal of Nervous and Mental Disease*, 184(1): 8–16.

Owen, I.R. (1991). Using the sixth sense: The place and relevance of language in counselling, *British Journal of Guidance and Counselling*, 19(3): 307–320.

Owen, I.R. (1996). Clean language: A linguistic-experiential phenomenology. In A. Tymieniecka (ed.), *Life: In the glory of its radiating manifestations, Analecta Husserliana, the yearbook of phenomenological research, Vol. XLVIII*. Netherlands: Kluwer Academic Publishers.

Parkin, M. (2001). *Tales for coaching: Using stories and metaphors with individuals and small groups*. London: Kogan Page.

Passmore, J. (2006). *Excellence in coaching: The industry guide*. London: Kogan Page.

Passmore, J. (ed.) (2011). *Supervision in coaching: Supervision, ethics and continuous professional development*. London: Kogan Page.

Passmore, J. and Whybrow, A. *(2007)*. Motivational interviewing: A specific approach for coaching psychologists. In *The handbook of coaching psychology* (pp. 160–173): London: Routledge.

Patterson, E. (2011). Presence in coaching supervision. In J. Passmore (ed.), *Supervision in coaching* (pp. 117–137). London: Kogan Page.

Payne, M. (2006). *Narrative therapy: An introduction for counsellors*. London: Sage.

Pearson, M. and Smith, D. (1985). Debriefing in experience-based learning. In D. Boud, R. Keogh and D. Walker (eds), *Reflection: Turning experience into learning*. London: Kogan Page.

Peavey, F. (1992). *Strategic questioning for personal and social change*. Retrieved 20/8/10 from http://www.health.qld.gov.au/capir/documents/19726.pdf

Pemberton, B. (1976). The presence of the therapist. Unpublished doctoral dissertation, Georgia State University.

Perkins, D.N., and Salomon, G. (1994). Transfer of learning. In T. Husen and T. N. Postelwhite (eds), *International Handbook of Educational Research* (Second Edition, Vol. 11; pp. 6452–6457). Oxford, Pergamon Press.

Perry, C. (2008). Toward a theory of perspective enhancement for mental health. Retrieved 3/3/2011 from http://www4.gu.edu.au:8080/adt-root/uploads/approved/adt-QGU20100730.104701/public/02Whole.pdf

Petitmengin, C. (2009). Editorial introduction, *Journal of Consciousness Studies*, 16(10–12): 7–19.

Pinker, S. (2006). Block that metaphor, *The New Republic*. Retrieved 2/3/12 from http://pinker.wjh.harvard.edu/articles/media/2006_09_30_thenewrepublic.html

Polanyi, M. (1967). *The tacit dimension*, Garden City, NY: Anchor Books.

Polkinghorne, D.E. (1988). *Narrative knowing and the human sciences*. Albany: State University of New York Press.

Pos, A.E., Greenberg, L.S. and Elliott, R. (2008). Experiential therapies. In J. Lebow (ed.), *Twenty-first century psychotherapies: Contemporary approaches to theory and practice* (pp. 80–122). London: John Wiley and Sons.

Pretz, J. (2008). Intuition versus analysis: Strategy and experience in complex everyday problem solving, *Memory and Cognition*, 36(3): 554–566.

Price, A. (2004). Encouraging reflection and critical thinking in practice. *Nursing Standard*, 18(47): 46–52.

Pronin, E. and Kugler, M.B. (2007). Valuing thoughts, ignoring behavior: The introspection illusion as a source of the bias blind spot, *Journal of Experimental Social Psychology*, 43: 565–578.

Quine, W.V.O. (1960). *Word and object*. Cambridge, MA: MIT Press.

Ram, A. (1991). A theory of questions and question asking, *Journal of the Learning Sciences*, 1(3 and 4): 273–318.

Reik, T. (1949). *Listening with the Third Ear: The inner experience of a psychoanalyst*. New York: Grove Press.

Reiter-Palmon, R., Herman, A. and Yammarino, F.J. (2007). Creativity and cognitive processes: Multi-level linkages between individual and team cognition. In M.D. Mumford, S.T. Hunter and K.E. Bedell-Avers (eds), *Multi-level issues in creativity and innovation, Vol. 77* (pp. 203–267). Oxford: Elsevier.

Rettie, R. (2005). Presence and embodiment in mobile phone communication, *PsychNology Journal*, 3(1): 16–34.

Rogers, C.R. (1959). A theory of therapy, personality and interpersonal relationships, as developed in the client-centered framework. In S. Koch (ed.), *Psychology: A study of science, Vol. 3* (pp. 184–256). New York: McGraw Hill.

Rogers, C. (1975). Empathic: An unappreciated way of being. *Counseling Psychologist*, 5: 2–10.

Rogers, C.R. (1980). *A way of being*. New York: Houghton Mifflin Co.

Rodgers, C. (2002). Defining reflection: Another look at John Dewey and reflective thinking, *Teachers College Record*, 4(4): 842–866.

Ross, E. (2006). The expert mind, *Scientific American*, August: 64–71.

Royer, J.M., Mestre, J.P. and Dufresne, R.J. (2005). Introduction: Framing the transfer problem. In J. Mestre (ed.), *Transfer of learning from a multidisciplinary perspective*. Greenwich, CT: Information Age Publishing.

Rupert, R. (2004). Challenges to the hypothesis of extended cognition, *Journal of Philosophy*, 101(8): 389–428.

Ryan, D. and Carr, A. (2001). A study of the differential effects of Tomm's questioning styles on therapeutic alliance, *Family Process*, 40(1): 67–77.

Ryan, R.M. and Deci, E.L. (2000). Self-determination theory and the facilitation of intrinsic motivation, social development, and well-being, *American Psychologist*, 55, 68–78.

Sadler-Smith, E. and Shefy, E. (2004). The intuitive executive: Understanding and applying 'gut feel' in decision making, *Academy of Management Executive*, 18: 76–91.

Identifier

Schank, R.C. (1995). *Tell me a story: Narrative and intelligence*. Evanston, IL: Northwestern University Press.

Scharmer, O. (2008). Uncovering the blind spot of leadership, *Leader to leader*, Winter: 52–59. Retrieved 28/05/12 from http://www.allegrosite.be/artikels/Uncovering_the_blind_spot_of_leadership.pdf

Schlick, M. (1932). Form and content. In H.L. Mulder and B.F.B. van de Velde-Schlick (eds), *Reprinted philosophical papers, Vol. 2* (Vienna Circle Collection, Vol. 11) (pp. 285–369). Dordrecht: Riedel.

Schober, M.F. (1999). Making sense of questions: An interactional approach. In M.G. Sirken, D.J. Hermann, S. Schechter, N. Schwarz, J.M. Tanur and R. Tourangeau (eds), *Cognition and survey research* (pp. 77–93). New York: John Wiley and Sons.

Schön, D. (1983). *The reflective practitioner: How professionals think in action*. London: Temple Smith.

Schön, D. (1995). Knowing-in-action: The new scholarship requires a new epistemology, *Change*, November-December, 27–34.

Schooler, J.W. and Mauss, I.B. (2010). To be happy and to know it: The experience and meta-awareness of pleasure. In K. Berridge and M. Kringlebach (eds), *Pleasures of the brain* (pp. 244–254). Oxford: Oxford University Press.

Schwaber, E. (1981). Empathy: A mode of analytic listening. *Psychoanalytic Inquiry*, 1: 357–392.

Schwartz, S.H. (2009). Basic Human Values. In: *Cross National Comparison Seminar on the Quality and Comparability of Measures for Constructs in Comparative Research*, Bozen, Italy, June 2009. The Hebrew University of Jerusalem.

Senge, P.M. (1990). *The Fifth Discipline: The art and practice of the learning organization*. New York: Doubleday Currency.

Senge, P., Kleiner, A., Roberts, C., Ross, R. and Smith, B. (1994). *The fifth discipline fieldbook*. New York: Currency Doubleday.

Senge, P., Scharmer, O.C., Jaworski, J. and Flowers, B.S. (2004). *Presence, human purpose and the field of the future*. Cambridge, MA: The Society for Organisational Learning.

Shapiro, S.L., Schwartz, G.E. and Santerre, C. (2005). Meditation and positive psychology. In C.R. Snyder and S.J. Lopez (eds), *Handbook of positive psychology* (pp. 632–645). New York: Oxford University Press.

Shapiro, S.L., Oman, D., Thoresen, C.E., Plante, T.G. and Flinders, T. (2008). Cultivating mindfulness: Effects on well-being, *Journal of Clinical Psychology*, 64(7): 840–862.

Shear, J. and Jevning, R. (1999). Pure consciousness, *Journal of Consciousness Studies*, 6(2/3): 189–213.

Shotter, J. (2009). Listening in a way that recognizes/realizes the world of 'the other', *International Journal of Listening*, 23: 21–43.

Sintonen, M. (1999). Why questions, and why just why-questions? *Synthese*, 120(1): 125–135. Proceedings of the Lund Conference on Explanation.

Sintonen, M. (2004). Reasoning to hypotheses: Where do questions come? *Foundations of Science*, 9(3): 249–266.

Skiffington, S. and Zeus, P. (2003). *Behavioral coaching: How to build sustainable personal and organizational strength.* Sydney: McGraw-Hill.

Smith, M.K. (1994). *Local education.* Buckingham: Open University Press.

Sonenshein, S. (2007). The role of construction, intuition, and justification in responding to ethical issues at work: The sensemaking-intuition model, *Academy of Management Review,* 32(4): 1022–1040.

Spence, D. (1982). *Narrative truth and historical truth.* New York: W.W. Norton and Co.

Spence, G.B., Cavanagh, M.J. and Grant, A.M. (2008). The integration of mindfulness training and health coaching: An exploratory study. *Coaching: An International Journal of Theory, Research and Practice,* 1(2): 145–163.

Starr, J. (2007). *The coaching manual: The definitive guide to the process, principles and skills of personal coaching.* London: Pearson Education.

Stein, E.W. (2011). Improvisation as model for real-time decision making. In F. Burstein, P. Brezillon and A. Zaslavsky (eds), *Supporting real time decision-making, Annals of Information Systems,* 13: 13–32.

Stewart, L.J., Palmer, S., Wilkin, H. and Kerrin, M. (2008). The influence of character: Does personality impact coaching success? *International Journal of Evidence Based Coaching and Mentoring,* 6(1): 32–43.

Stewart, J. (1983). Interpretive listening an alternative to empathy, *Communication Education,* 32: 379–391.

Storch, M. (2004). Resource-activating self-management with the Zurich Resource Model (ZRM), *European Psychotherapy,* 5(1): 27–64.

Strawson, G. (2004). Against narrativity, *Ratio,* 17: 428–542.

Stuckey, M. (2001). An heuristic investigation of presence. *Dissertation Abstracts International: Section B: the Sciences and Engineering,* 62 (6-B), 2965.

Súilleabháin, G.Ó. and Sime, J.A. (2010). Games for learning and learning transfer. In R. Donnelly, J. Harvey and K. O'Rourke (eds), *Critical design and effective tools for e-learning in higher education: Theory into practice* (Chapter 7). Hershey, PA: IGI Global.

Taylor, S.S. (2003). Knowing in your gut and in your head: Doing theater and my underlying epistemology of communication, *Management Communication Quarterly,* 17(2): 272–279.

Taylor, S.S. and Ladkin, D. (2009). Understanding arts-based methods in managerial development, *Academy of Management Learning and Education,* 8(1): 55–69.

Throop, C.J. (2003). Articulating experience, *Anthropological Theory,* 3(2): 219–241.

Thwaites, R. and Bennett-Levy, J. (2007). Conceptualizing empathy in cognitive behaviour therapy: Making the implicit explicit, *Behavioural and Cognitive Psychotherapy,* 35: 591–612.

Todres, L. (2007). *Embodied enquiry.* London: Palgrave.

Tolle, E. (2005). *The power of now: A guide to spiritual enlightenment.* London: Hodder and Stoughton.

Tolle, E. (2008). *Oneness with all life.* New York: Dutton.

Tomm, K. (1988). Inventive interviewing: Part III, Intending to ask lineal, circular, strategic or reflective questions, *Family Process*, 27(1): 1–15.

Topp, E.M. (2006). Presence-based coaching: The practice of presence in relation to goal-directed activity. Unpublished doctoral thesis. Palo Alto, CA: Institute of Transpersonal Psychology.

Torbert, W. (1999).The distinctive questions developmental action inquiry asks, *Management Learning*, 30(2): 189–206.

Van Manen, M. (1990). *Researching lived experience: Human science for an action sensitive pedagogy*. London, Ontario: Althouse.

Van Ments, M. (1983). *The Effective Use of Role-Play*. London: Kogan Page.

Vermersch, P. (1999). Introspection as Practice, *Journal of Consciousness Studies*, 6(2–3): 15–42.

Wagner, I., Broll, W., Jacucci, G., Kuutti, K., McCall, R., Morrison, A., Schmalstieg, D. and Terrin, J.J. (2009). On the role of presence in mixed reality, *Presence: Teleoperators and Virtual Environments*, 18(4): 249–276.

Weger, H., Castle, G. and Emmett, M. (2010). Active listening in peer interviews: The influence of message paraphrasing on perceptions of listening skill, *The International Journal of Listening*, 24: 33–49.

Weick, K.E. (1995). *Sensemaking in organizations*. London: Sage.

Weick, K.E. (1998). Improvisation as a mindset for organizational analysis, *Organization Science*, 9(5): 540–545.

Weick, K.E., Sutcliffe, K.M. and Obstfeld, D. (2005). Organizing and the process of sensemaking, *Organization Science*, 16(4): 409–21.

Weinstein, N., Brown, K.W. and Ryan, R.M. (2009). A multi-method examination of the effects of mindfulness on stress attribution, coping, and emotional well-being, *Journal of Research in Personality*, 43: 374–385.

White, K.W. (1994). Hans-Georg Gadamer's philosophy of language: A constitutive-dialogic approach to interpersonal understanding. In K. Carter and M. Presnell (eds), *Interpretive approaches to interpersonal communication* (pp. 83–114). Albany, NY: State University of New York Press.

Whitmore, J. (2009). *Coaching for performance: GROWing human potential and purpose – the principles and practice of coaching and leadership*. London: Nicholas Brealey.

Whitworth, L., Kimsey-House, H. and Sandahl, P. (1998). *Co-active coaching*. Palo Alto: Davies-Black Publishing.

Whitworth, L., Kimsey-House, H. and Sandahl, P. (2007). *Co-active coaching*. Palo Alto: Davies-Black Publishing.

Wilberg, P. (2004). *The therapist as listener: Martin Heidegger and the missing dimension of counselling and psychotherapy training*. New Gnosis Publications: www.newgnosis.co.uk.

Wilson, C. (2007). *Best practice in performance coaching*. London: Kogan Page.

Winograd, T. and Flores, F. (1986). *Understanding computers and cognition: A new foundation for design*. Norwood, NJ: Ablex Publishing.

Yanow, D. and Tsoukas, H. (2009). What is reflection-in-action? A phenomenological account, *Journal of Management Studies*, 46(8): 1339–1364.

Yontef, G. (2007). The power of the immediate moment in gestalt therapy, *Journal of Contemporary Psychotherapy*, 37(1): 17–23.

Zahavi, D. (2011). Varieties of reflection, *Journal of Consciousness Studies*, 18(2): 9–19.

Zahorik, P. and Jenison, R. (1998). Presence as being-in-the-world, *Presence*, 7(1): 78–89.

Index

Page numbers in *italics* refer to figures and tables.